On The Road to DISCOVERY

On The Road to DISCOVERY

OVERLAND FROM BOSTON TO HOUSTON AND
FROM MEXICO CITY TO THE PANAMA CANAL

Bron Sinclair

With love to Sally

from Bonni

October 2016

GSP

On The Road to Discovery
Bron Sinclair

Published by Greyhound Self-Publishing, 2016.
Malvern, Worcestershire, United Kingdom.

Printed and bound by Aspect Design
89 Newtown Road, Malvern, Worcs. WR14 1PD
United Kingdom
Tel: 01684 561567
E-mail: allan@aspect-design.net
Website: www.aspect-design.net

ISBN 978 1 909219-39-7

For my sons Mark and Simon.

*'Always remember that you are absolutely unique,
just like everyone else.'*
Margaret Mead

ACKNOWLEDGEMENTS

It is due to all the people who knew of my strange way of life - fourteen years backpacking through the Americas, Australasia and Asia, and who kept saying, 'Oh, you should write about that', that I did at last sit down to make some sense of what I did a quarter of a century ago.

When I started to write this journal, I knew very little about the placement of commas or semi-colons and other points of grammatical punctuation. I extend, therefore, my heartfelt thanks to all my friends who put me straight.

Thanks to Jenny for all her help and especially for the map of my meanderings through the eastern states of North America; to Diana; to Linda whose keen eyes spotted several errors in the final proof-reading and to Jeanni who added most helpful notes.

Without the time-consuming help and encouragement from my neighbour Margaret, I doubt I'd ever have finished this first part of my saga and to her I give a huge thank you.

Hearty thanks to Ian Cook who painted such a sensitive watercolour of my mountains and lonely road for the front cover and also to Gordon, who took the photo of me for the back cover of this book.

N.B. Anne is a fictitious person, but I did, in fact, send many letters, undeveloped films, pamphlets, photographs and leaflets, all to illuminate my daily happenings, back to England.

A few of the names have been changed.

This is the first book I have ever attempted and I've struggled with it through 2015 and into 2016. After more than twenty-five years most of the photographs were badly discoloured or faded and unusable.

Dear readers please excuse the poor quality of the few photos that I have used.

Bron, (known by many as Bonni, but that's another story.)

CONTENTS

3

PART THREE

PANAMA

Part One
BOSTON to HOUSTON

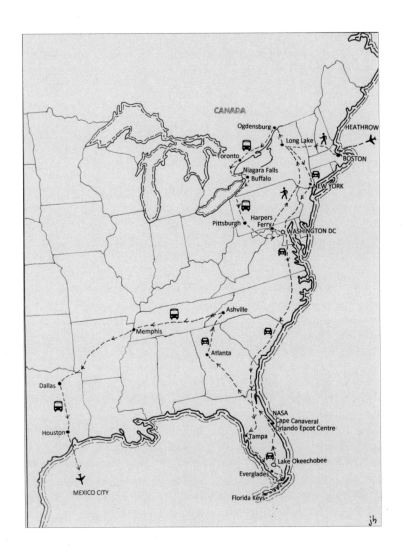

1. THE BEGINNING
Heading into the Unknown

September 12th 1989

Dear Anne,

You said you'd be happy to receive my letters and updates of the news of my travels and would store them all for me. Thank you again and here is the first of my letters.

I sat alone in the winter-dark, on the top-deck of the 6 a.m. bus bound for Heathrow Airport, my stomach knotted, my heart sore. I felt absolutely choked. I couldn't stop the tears. I was glad there was no one to see.

I was heading into the unknown.

Two colleagues from my school had surprised me by being at the High Wycombe bus station to wish me farewell and 'bon voyage'.

No sign of either of my sons.

Even until the evening before they'd not bid me 'au revoir'. They'd shown no interest in what I was about to put myself through. Their absence just compounded my feeling of being unwanted; just a servant, an appendage to their needs.

I was leaving.

Everything.

And I had no idea for how long or when, or indeed if, I'd ever return to England.

I stared at my distorted reflection in the window glass and mulled over my final days at the small, private girls' school where I'd taught Science, primarily Biology, but some Physics and Chemistry to the younger ones. I thought of the staff-room towards the end of the school year when teachers, reaching the ends of their tethers, snapped at each other or burst into tears. 'I'm not staying here another fifteen years to get like that. I'm just not,' I'd vowed to myself. I know you often felt the same but you have more binding responsibilities than I.

Giving in my notice had been so hard – about the hardest thing I've ever done. I had many misgivings and sleepless nights. I'd left it until the very last acceptable day.

I wasn't happy at school.

I was very unhappy at home.

I did what I've always done in unbearable situations – escaped. Some would say 'ran away', although I didn't feel it as such – then.

I turned my mind to my original thoughts of planning an overland trip to Australia to visit my uncle and his family in Perth.

First I'd researched the feasibility of cycling through Europe and the Middle East, but Iran and Iraq were already at war, and then Afghanistan erupted. It didn't seem a sensible option for a middle-aged woman to cycle alone through those territories. I suppose I could have found a way around but I didn't.

Instead, I ruminated over crossing North, Central and South America to Santiago (Chile) and getting a boat from there to New Zealand. The maps in my school atlas scared me – the thousands of miles of the big Andean mountains. I'm 46 years old and not so fit.

After months of research I decided to start in North America. They speak English and I could fairly easily return to the UK should the need arise. The clincher was when my colleague suggested I might start in Boston, where her son and his girlfriend had a flat in Cambridge.

I'd prepared for my epic journey as best I could: taken karate lessons until my sparring partner misjudged his punch distance and broke my rib; been on a survival course in the wilds of Wales, where I'd learned how to avoid hypothermia and dehydration and how to navigate using a watch or the signs of nature; learned how to trap small animals with a wire noose and to fish with hook, string and stick, and how to test for edible plants – a technique that took so long I'd most likely starve first. I'd read books and cut out, to carry with me, the sections I thought I might need – 'knots for all occasions', 'fire-lighting in the wet and dry' and a few other invaluable gems of knowledge.

I'd visited Ms Hilary Bradt who walks alone to research her travel guides.

I'd transferred ownership of my car to my younger son and I'd sorted a home-management agency to take care of the house, my son becoming a tenant.

Ready to go?

No, not really. I felt I was about to dive into a deep, dark and swiftly flowing river without any floats.

And, because I didn't know whither I was bound, I'd been unsure what to pack. So, me being me, I'd packed everything I could squash into my eighty litre backpack and slung my tent from its bottom. Nearly 90lbs all together – I'll grow strong carrying that! thought I.

I also carried a canvas hold-all with my daily needs: book, map, food, water and the other bits and bobs one invariably needs to hand.

To while away the hours to Heathrow airport, I mused on happier thoughts – my 'leaving-do' at school.

We'd all gathered in the wood-panelled conference room next to the Headmistress's study. The Head presented me with a MSR (Mountain Safety Research) multi-fuel, state-of-the-art camping stove complete with gas bottle and spares, and also a light-weight, aluminium cook set. I was emotionally touched.

In return, I entertained the staff by showing what I'd packed into my emergency tins – two tobacco tins, roughly three inches by two inches. I felt like a magician pulling out a never-ending string of scarves from his top hat.

I'd spread a folded sheet from the laundry cupboard on the highly-polished oak table and proceeded to display the following:

Tin 1 had:

fishing tackle

nylon lines of breaking strains 8lbs and 24lbs

2 flies

lead weights of assorted sizes

cork floats, swivels and notes on 'How to fish'

Tin 2 had:

surgical scalpel blades, sterile in their foil packaging

1 single-edged razor blade

a flexible-wire survival saw with snap rings of 1 inch diameter at each end

a piece of plastic drinking straw filled with potassium permanganate crystals and another with iodine crystals (for sterilizing stuff), both bunged with tiny pieces of cork

a durable plastic short straw with a slanted end that would allow me to sup from the surface of a pool without imbibing the gunge beneath

flint block and striker for sparks to start a fire

needles and cotton thread

metal mirror
mini folding tin-opener
mini compass and magnifying glass
pencil stub and very small notebook
the smallest whistle I could find
2 lifeboat matches - guaranteed to light when wet
the foot of a nylon stocking to filter water and a squashed-flat Oxo cube to flavour a distasteful beverage
(In my backpack pockets would go duct-tape, a heavy-duty rubbish bag and water-purification tablets.)

The staff marvelled as I pulled out item after item and explained their uses. I saw envy, awe, disbelief in their faces as they shook my hand and said their final goodbyes.
So that was that.
Now it's up to me.
I'll write to you when and where I can.
May your good thoughts speed me along. *Bron*

2. BOSTON & BEYOND
First steps along my Road of Learning & Adventure

September 14th 1989

Dear Anne,

I spent the next few days in Boston being a tourist.

I'd flown to Logan International in Boston and found the white clap-board and red-brick, colonial-style house in Cambridge, where Brian and his girlfriend rent the third-floor attic flat. They gave me a set of house keys so I could come and go at my pleasure while they were at the University in Cambridge. (Brian is Marion the Chemistry teacher's son and studying law at Boston Uni.)

The next morning I started what was to become my custom on arrival in a new place. Like a mouse in a maze, I first walked round the block to get my bearings and then widened 'the knowledge'.

The streets were wide and tree-lined. I smiled at a woman (very smartly dressed) with seven small dogs of assorted pedigrees attached by their leads to her hands. The dogs wanted to go in different directions. Some were sniffing at the tree trunk and others were forging ahead, or winding around her. At one point the lady stood with arms outstretched wide, pulled in both directions. That's why I smiled. I was unknowing about multi-dog-walkers in cities.

Then I set off to see the famous places for which Boston is well-renowned.

The two-storey, red-brick building of the old MIT (Massachusetts Institute of Technology) is dwarfed by the skyscrapers around. Almost everyone is wearing shades-of-grey suits and carrying briefcases. They look very academic, which they are being some of the best brains around. Many Nobel Laureates have been spawned from MIT: founded in 1861 as a Technical University, it has expanded for a mile along the Charles River during the eight years of its building, which started in 1916.

Next to find out what or who *Old Ironsides* is.

I'd been told to seek out the USS *Constitution* for my answer. So off I went to Boston Harbour (yeah, we all know about the Boston Tea-Party from our History lessons at school) to discover more.

The USS *Constitution* is a three-masted, forty-four-gun (although she is rumoured to have carried up to sixty guns) frigate. She was built in Boston and launched in 1797; being named by George Washington after the newly drafted American Constitution. During the years of the War of Independence (between the United States and Britain) she proved that she could outrun and outgun any other ship sailing the high seas.

There was a battle in progress between HMS *Guerrier* and USS *Constitution* when an astonished sailor observed British eighteen-pound cannon balls bouncing off the twenty-five inch oak hull of her adversary and he cried out, 'Her sides are made of iron!' and so was born the nickname of *Old Ironsides*.

After the fierce battle HMS *Guerrier* was set on fire and sunk, but not before the wounded had been taken off.

Now docked at the quayside, tourists walk around USS *Constitution* admiring the gleaming brass and decks polished so shiny and the pristine white metalwork. The gun deck, one down, is fitted with forty-four enormous cannons poking their muzzles through the netted portholes. I try to imagine the deafening noise as they fired, the shouts of the men, the acrid reek of gunpowder.

Below the gun deck is the berth-deck, a huge empty space the size of a football pitch, it seems, where a crew of five hundred would've slung their hammocks in tiers of three and in rows closely-packed, all swinging from hooks in the metal cross-beams.

During the War of Independence, the USS *Constitution* defeated four British frigates.

I continued my wanderings and chanced across the Old State House.

Of Georgian style and built in 1713. A plaque proudly proclaimed it "The oldest building in Boston". I smiled to myself, 'That's a mere spring-chicken compared to our old buildings!' I said to no one in particular. The Old State House was the centre of political life in colonial Boston and on July 18, 1776 the Declaration of Independence was read from its balcony.

On the road in front of the Old State House is a circle of patterned, coloured cobblestones with the words, "In Commemoration of the Boston Massacre". In fact, when a scuffle broke out between a colonist wig-maker's apprentice and the British sentry, relief soldiers came to the aid of the sentry and five, and only five, colonists were killed. Shall we say a mini, mini massacre?

By now being satiated with history, I walked to Bunker Hill Monument (built on the site of the first major battle of the American Revolution fought on June 17, 1775) for the view. I walked up the steep and gravelled path and was rewarded with a grandstand view across old Boston with its Tea-Party history and across the stilted freeway (motorway) to the jagged line of skyscrapers and beyond into the haze.

September 18th - *Mount Monadnock*

It's now three days since I left Boston and headed north: my next goal being Hastings in Canada.

I used a Greyhound bus to whizz me along. Why on earth did I imagine that I could walk between villages as we do in England? This country is huge! I had no concept of the distances between places.

As the bus carried me north, the rolling, tree-covered hills went on for mile after mile, hour after hour, wave after wave of burning autumn colours just beginning to blaze.

Leaving the bus in the town of Jaffrey, I wandered the two miles to Mount Monadnock Park along the aptly named Forest Road. Scarcely a driveway or road turning off did I see disappearing into the forest on either side. Then, 'Oh, that's funny.' I spied a long, plank, trestle-table with 1, 2, 3 . . . 27 post boxes, all of similar shape but of various colours and adornments, sitting in a line upon it. 'Where are all the houses? I've seen nary a one.'

Each mail box was like an inverted U, maybe six inches high and a foot long. It had a drop-down door at the front and a lift-up metal flag at the side. I was later told that one raised the flag if there was outgoing mail for the postie to collect and the postie (postman) raised the flag if he had delivered mail to one.

Neat system!

An information board at a Mount Monadnock trail-head informed me that: I am in New England, in the state of New Hampshire; that at 3,165 feet Mount Monadnock is the highest peak hereabouts; that I'm sixty-two miles north-west of Boston; that there are many hiking trails criss-crossing the mountain slopes, but it is only four hours straight up to the top and back; there's no poison ivy (I've read about that - nasty stuff! Stings like nettles but much more so and the itching can last for days) and there are no poisonous snakes. Goody! I can wander about with impunity and sleep untroubled.

The evening was drawing towards dark. I made camp and would save tomorrow for the ascent to the summit.

I lay in my two-man tent and listened to the rain pattering and drip, dripping from the branches overhead. The trees on the lower slopes of this mountain are mostly hardwoods but I don't know their names. I think tomorrow I'll camp higher up amongst the redwoods: the bedding is surely softer on needles? This is my first night in the wilds. I've pitched the tent a few yards off the foot-trail; hopefully out of sight of any late walkers, as I don't know if wild-camping is allowed here.

I made it to the top – going the easy way. The peak was very rounded with much bare, smooth, grey rock where small plants had taken hold in the cracks: the early settlers destroyed the top-soil by setting fires to clear the land.

Coming up the foot-trail – quite slidey after the night's rain – I slipped down sideways and fell into the bracken. You'd have laughed at me lying there on my back, legs and arms waving in the air just like an over-turned turtle. I couldn't turn over or even sit up to get up until I'd taken off my backpack.

In spite of the rain last night, I haven't seen a single stream all day so shall have to make do with puddle-water for tonight's camp.

September 23rd - Morgan horses and Joan.

After walking some, hitching some and spending the odd night in the woods or someone's barn, I arrived at Joan's farmstead. She was expecting me – an arrangement made in Boston. (I'd found an isolated phone box and managed to tell her that I was near.)

She's a lovely cuddly lady, just one's idea of a generous farmer's wife. She prepared me a bath and showed me the cosy, comfy guest-bedroom. I was told to come to the kitchen when I was ready for the wholesome meal she'd prepared for me.

The kitchen-wall shelves and the Welsh-dresser were laden with jugs of various sizes all decorated with cows, cows and calves, just calves or bulls; Friesians, Herefords, brown cows, black cows, black and white cows, brown and white cows and foreign-looking cows with long floppy ears that I had to ask the name of. (Joan told me they're Brahmans, bred in the U.S. from cattle imported from India.) My patchwork quilt bedspread was also a landscape of moving herds of cows. I reckon I've come to a dairy farm!

Joan's hobby is quilting. She belongs to a quilting club and has won county prizes for her work. She does a lot of tapestry and embroidery too. I don't know where she finds the time – the lack of a television must contribute to productive output.

But it wasn't just cows on this farm. Near the house was a big wooden barn on which a large, brightly-painted sign proclaimed, "Fresh Apples". Also on display outside the barn-doors were pumpkins and marrows, corn cobs and carrots. Quite a harvest feast – it being that time of year.

The stud farm next door raised Morgan horses rather than cows.

I leant on the coral fence and admired these small and beautiful animals.

A Morgan horse is renowned for its excellent temperament and is so calm that anyone can ride one, anywhere. They are reliable, loyal and tireless and can pull a cart for miles. The breed was founded by Justin Morgan in 1789, from one colt whose offspring have spread far and wide – a bit like Queen Victoria's offspring who took over much of Europe!

(I must get into the habit of talking more to people. It's a good way to find out stuff, but I have to soon write it down or soon I forget.)

I set off again for Canada.

Musing as I walked, I thought of the number of flashbacks I'd had as I passed signs to Hastings, Reading, Manchester, Winchester, Gloucester or Petersfield – small wonder that the Americans qualify their place names: Birmingham-Alabama or Cambridge-Massachusetts.

And then there's the new terminology, or rather, old terminology with new meaning.

I was in a small, rural bus station buying my ticket when the clerk asked, 'C'n I check your baggage?'

I said, 'Of course' and started to open the top.

'Naw, I don't wanna to look inside. I mean, did ya wanna put your pack in the luggage compartment of the bus?'

And the café where I was asked, 'You wan' yer coffee black or light?'

I looked stupidly at the waitress and she said huffily, 'With milk or not?'

Walking the roads I could really admire, close-up, the autumn colours which I'd only seen before in pictures.

The best reds are produced by the sugar maples (*Acer saccharum* to name the most famous one) from which maple syrup is produced. I didn't know that there are about nine different varieties of maples growing here. Their colours range from lemon-yellow, through burnt-orange, to post-box red and all the shades in between.

I was waiting by a small bridge (admiring the swiftly tumbling waters of the Blue Mountain Falls making a white, frothy ribbon through the dark-greens of the conifers and the colours of the deciduous trees) when my outstretched thumb procured a ride to Harris Lake camp-ground near Newcomb.

The camp-ground was totally deserted. I could pick my spot – somewhere away from the road (not that there was much traffic passing by) with a fine view across the lake to forest fringing the other side and with the hills making a lumpy backdrop. Idyllic!

I awoke to a cloudless, pale-blue sky and the lake as still as still. The far mountains were mirrored in the middle of the lake as the edges had frozen out towards the centre. 'Oh, photo-shoot,' I muttered but the camera was dead. Damn! Then I recalled that batteries don't like deep cold, (I'm sure the temperatures last night were well below freezing) so I took the battery out of the camera and nursed it in my armpit while I made breakfast.

Having shaken the frost from the tent, I was soon on the road.

I didn't have much luck with lifts today until mid-afternoon, when a pick-up slowed and its driver asked, 'You goin' far?'

'Up to the junction somewhere ahead,' I replied. 'I'm heading for Canada.'

'I'll take you. It's further than you think. Sling your gear in the back.'

I crossed the road and unfastened my pack. But then no way could I lift my heavy burden up and over the side of the pick-up bed. 'Please, could you tell me how to lower the tailgate or help me lift it in?' I said sheepishly. He gave me a look: a 'Huh! Useless woman!' sort of look and reluctantly got out of his nice warm cab.

We chatted the usual chat: Where do you come from? Where are you going to? Why are you hitching alone? And so on and on for about twenty minutes before we got to the road junction.

Although only about 3.30 p.m., the daylight was already fading fast.

We discussed the idiocy of my trying to hitch in the dark. He suggested that I continue with him – he was going to Lake Placid (where the Winter Olympics were held in 1980) to get a pizza for his tea: he'd get two pizzas. Then I'd return to Long Lake with him, stay the night (he had a spare room) and get on my way in the morning.

Sounded a good plan so I said, 'Yes', having no idea where Lake Placid or Long Lake are in the geography of the area.

I stayed two weeks with Dek, which I shall tell you all about in due course.

Loads of love to you all,
Bron

3. LONG LAKE INTERLUDE
Meeting Dek (& Brandy) in New York State

September 16th 1989

Dear Anne,

I know you're dying to hear about what went on in my envisioned love nest. Actually, not a lot in that department as I shall explain.

Dek's spare room was completely bare.
I laid my sleeping mat on the unpolished floorboards and slept well that night after eating our re-heated pizzas, cooled after the fifty-two mile return journey from Lake Placid – a hundred-mile round trip just to get a pizza! Can you believe it?

The morning dawned brightly and set alight the vibrant, flaming colours of the autumnal leaves, made even more intense by being offset against the dark greens and green-greys of the firs and cypresses.

Dek and his little black Labrador, Brandy, live on the upper floor of a two-storey, chalet-style house owned by an uncle. Made totally of wood-boards and painted white, the house is set in a large clearing where the surrounding forest is slowly reclaiming the land. In fact, Anne, it's just the sort of house I could happily live in.

Dek said, 'Let's walk Brandy'. I didn't need to be asked twice.

Ahh! . . . such pleasure to walk without my cumbersome burden, and the fun of having a dog around. I'm sold on the dog, never mind the man.

It's scarcely a month since I said goodbye to Zan, my much-beloved black Labrador-cross, a rescue dog into whom I'd poured all my love – love unneeded in a loveless marriage. Love not wanted either by my younger son of nineteen years living with me but not needing me (or so he told me) and resenting my intrusions into his life. (My older son had gone to live with his father.)

I'd met a woman in the foyer of that big new Tesco when we both worked there part-time selling double-glazing. I'd asked her if she wanted my dog and explained my situation. She and her partner seemed decent animal-loving folk. He worked as an animal-carer in a zoo and she had found a kitten in a dustbin and paid the vet's fees to get it healthy.

I left Zan with them for a weekend to see how he would accept this new home – a converted, big old house in the woods. When I went to collect him, he really didn't seem to be able to choose whether to sit by me or the man. So that was good.

Much as it wrenched my heart, I think I did the right thing; better than going back into a dog-rescue centre and I would never know if he went to a caring home, or was put down.

Dek knows these woods around Long Lake very well. He goes shooting deer in the season and, of course, walking his dog. We spent that afternoon with him teaching me to fire an arrow from his home-made bow, roughly carved from the branch of a yew tree.

I slept there that night too. In fact, I stayed two weeks with Dek, during which time I moved from my sleeping bag in the spare room into his bed; at my instigation I must confess. When he saw me there he looked very surprised, then concern flitted across his face, to be replaced by a happy grin. I was just so desperate for someone to put their arms around me.

Dek is taller than me – that's novel – with a mop of greying hair and a lean and lanky figure. Snuggling together two naked bodies was such a pleasure after years of sleeping apart from my husband even though we both lived in the same house – most stressful and hurting.

And I fell in love, but we never completed the act of making love – he couldn't/wouldn't. (And he wouldn't/couldn't say why.)

When Dek wasn't doing his dish-washing shift at the Hotel restaurant, two miles down the road in Long Lake, we walked the dog. I was shown around the woods. I admired Millpond, (actually it's what I would call a small lake but here gets designated as a pond) and was introduced to his relatives who live locally. Some days we drove his pick-up to Lake Placid, which has more and bigger shops than Long Lake besides all the touristy stuff: It's only nine years since the Winter Olympics were held there in 1980 and some shops still sold souvenirs from that event.

Once we came back along the Blue Mountain Ridge road (not to be confused with the Blue Ridge Mountains, which are much further south) to admire the splendid views of the lakes spread out below, between the hills of Adirondack Park.

While Dek was working, I busied myself around the flat.

The wide, wood steps of the glass-fronted, covered stairway leading up the outside wall into the flat got three coats of clear varnish; the skirting-boards and other wood-work inside the flat had a fresh, white coat; the bathroom and kitchen got a spring-clean – Anne, I know you've done re-decorating and you'll agree that slapping on the paint is the easy part.

I cleaned and cooked and Dek's comment was that he'd never met anyone who worked so hard. Well, that's me. I work hard because I've always worked hard: my Mum died when I was twelve years old. We then lived in an old terrace-house (with a cellar in which I stored my home-made ginger beer) with a hundred-yard-long garden, so I had that to weed and tend, as well as feed Dad and brother and dog and budgie, clean the house, shop, mend clothes, do the washing and so on and on, all around school hours and at the weekends.

Enough of that.

I'll tell you a bit about Long Lake.

The town is a small scattered township of some six-hundred souls. It sits beside the fourteen-mile-long, Long Lake in what they call Up-state New York. Long Lake is a skinny lake, being only about a mile wide at its widest.

Dek works at the Adirondack Hotel, so named because Long Lake town and Long Lake are actually within Adirondack Park.

Long Lake town has a pub/hotel and a general store that also serves as post office. Here, there is no postie to deliver mail to your house, so everyone rents a post-office box and has to collect their own mail. Much to Dek's consternation, I sometimes walked the two miles to the store, along the road between the fir trees and with no pavement.

My conscience was nagging me.

By about now, I was supposed to be in Hastings, Canada, to visit Diane.

I'd met her a few summers ago on an Explore walking tour on Crete and had promised to spend a few days with her. So I very reluctantly kissed my goodbyes with Dek, gave little Brandy a big hug and set off again. The goodbyes were premature.

Dek caught me up not a mile along the road and said, 'Wan' a ride lady?' Of course I did.

He drove me the hundred or so miles north-west to the border-crossing at Ogdensburg – where one crosses the St. Lawrence River into Canada.

We spent the last night in a big double bed in a motel on the American side – Dek doesn't have a passport. Still no sex! What is it with this guy?

I've crossed the frontier with no fuss and now have to await the Hastings bus, so have time to catch up with my news to you.

My next letter will be from Canada, so wait with bated breath.

Love,
Bron

Dek teaching me to shoot the breeze

4. *THE CANADIAN EXPERIENCE*
Getting very Muddled with Numbers

October 9th - 14th 1989

Dear Anne,
      Meeting Diane and meeting the Niagara Falls couldn't have been greater in contrast.
    At Diane's all was luxury; at the Falls I was a bag-lady, as you'll discover below.

    As I leant on the parapet wall, so close to the rushing swirling, thunderous, pounding tons of water pouring every second over Niagara Falls, I kept feeling overwhelmed by the size of everything in this country.
    When I stayed the few days with Diane in Hastings, Ontario, she thought nothing of driving forty kilometres (about twenty-five miles) to get a loaf of her favourite bread.
    (This switching countries and so switching units, is doing my head in. In Canada they use metric and Canadian dollars. In a day I'll be back in the U.S. and then it's back to miles and greenbacks.)
    After the bread shop we went into the shop next door which sold nothing but ice-creams – nearly forty flavours, some combinations I'd never have imagined, like pistachio and marzipan, or flavours I'd never heard of, like crane-berry. Soooo difficult to decide what to sample; perhaps I should try two, which I did.
    I'd met Diane some years ago on a group walking holiday in Crete. With her corpulent figure and office-work life-style, she'd struggled to keep up, but impressed me with her 'I will get there' attitude.
    We'd kept in touch via Christmas cards. Now here I am in her sea-blue kitchen stuffed with shades-of-blue knick-knacks (mostly bottles and birds) and she in her dress of browns and her bright-bronze mass of curly hair matching the seasonal colours.
    Diane, in her mid-thirties, also talked to me about her desire to find a suitable man to father her child. She didn't want the

complications of a man about the house and if necessary was prepared to go to a sperm-bank. (This is a very daring view for the late eighties, don't you think?)

I'd bused the one-hundred and sixty-seven miles from Hastings to Toronto; although Diane had said, 'To go by bus will take forever and the scenery will be very monotonous. Why don't you fly?'

'No, no, too expensive,' I moaned.

Yesterday, I went to Toronto downtown area to climb the Tower. Disappointed that I wasn't allowed to climb the stairs, and get the changing view at each level, I joined the queue of sightseers at the lifts – sorry, elevators! We got out at the public-viewing platform, a glass-enclosed walkway around the tower. The thermal-glass floor, although two-and-a-half inches thick, didn't seem very safe when looking straight down at the ground 1,122 feet below.

I'm glad I don't get acrophobia like one poor girl who had to be hurried into the lift before she passed out. (When I look down from something really high, I get this urge to step into space – no, not ready to die just yet, but I long for my parachute or hang-glider. Just imagine soaring over the tops of these high-rise skyscrapers!)

From the viewing platform of the CN tower I had my first view of massed sky-scrapers, putting any tall buildings that we have in Britain into the miniature category. Impressive too were the many colours of the window-glass used: bronze, topaz, aquamarine, rosy-pink, and dark chocolate scattered amongst buildings with plain glass windows. The whole effect made me think of the autumnal forests I'd been passing through.

By the way, do you know what the C and N of CN Tower stands for? It'd be a good quiz question.

CN originally referred to "Canadian National" – the railway company that built the tower (1,815 feet high) as a TV and radio communications platform. When completed in 1976 it was the world's tallest free-standing structure.

After a couple of nights in Toronto, the next bus carried me to Niagara Falls, eighty-eight miles further on.

I'm now at Horseshoe Falls, on the Canadian side. It's hard to find a quiet place to water-watch, because coach after coach after coach has disgorged its content of tourists clutching their boxes of hotel-packed lunches and cans of soda (pop to us).

So I take to people-watching instead.

My gosh! These Americans are so wasteful!

I see many lunch-boxes (presumably provided by the hotel) looked into and then discarded into the litter bins (oops – garbage or trash cans) fastened to the lamp-posts. When the coaches had departed, I rescued several of the almost untouched lunch-boxes and cans of unopened soda and dined quite royally on sandwiches and rolls and chocolate biscuits, and still had enough to see me through the rest of the day.

Too soon it was early afternoon. Most of the coaches had gone and I could resume my water-watching: rainbows appeared through the spray; whirlpools whirled where the falling water landed far below; the roar of the falls and the perpetual motion of the cascading waters were quite hypnotising and almost sucked me in. I had to hold firmly onto the railing.

Some hundred yards down-river from where I was standing the America Falls formed another spectacle.

The two falls are formed by the River Niagara dividing around Goat Island – a big island with a few houses on it. The boundary between Canada and the States is an invisible line down the middle of the river; hence, the Horseshoe Falls are in Canada and the America Falls in . . . Guess where.

The waters from the two branches rolled swirling together and the River Niagara flowed on and on.

Moving on. I found a bus to take me the nineteen miles to Buffalo (back in the States) where I must change for the Greyhound bus to Washington D.C. (via Pittsburgh).

Niagra Falls

We crossed from Canada into the U.S.A. using Peace Bridge. There a customs man's cursory glance at my passport and a stamp with a flourish allowed my entry anew into the States.

The four-hundred mile journey from Buffalo to Washington D.C. would take several hours. Luckily I had my salvaged snacks!

From that entire journey I recall some impressions vividly: passing alongside Lake Ontario and seeing many silvery, dead fish on the shoreline (pollution I supposed); how deserted was the city of Buffalo, but in fairness I didn't see much of it. I only had to cross the road to get a connecting tram to the Greyhound bus station. Where were all the people on a weekday afternoon? I was in the centre of the town, I think, and it was almost deserted.

I didn't like the feel of Buffalo and was relieved to get away; and how dreary appeared the industrial city of Pittsburgh as I peered through the rain-streaked bus windows.

I don't remember much else until I awoke in Washington D.C. and sat in the bus station to write to you and to wait for Carol to come and sweep me off to her flat.

Have a nice day (that's what they all say here – 'have a nice day') and remember me to all the busy staff.

Bron

5. WASHINGTON D.C.
On Getting a Good Dose of History

October 16th - 21st 1989

Dear Anne,

Looking at the dates, this must be about half-term time. What are you going to do in your free days? Get right away from school I hope.

I'm being a sight-seeing tourist whilst in the U.S. capital.

I was very happy to see Carol, my contact in Washington D.C. She soon came to the bus station and whisked me along the dark, wet, shining-in-the-lamplight streets to her brownstone house in Uptown Downtown – yes, I was perplexed too; it means still in the centre but in its northern part, in Georgetown. It was late and in the dark I couldn't take on-board much of what Carol was telling me about the area we were driving through.

Chatting at breakfast, Carol casually mentioned that the next day she'd be going away to a four-day conference. I must have looked crestfallen, thinking, No time to see the sights, unless I go to stay in the YHA, but then she asked if I would stay alone in her house and mind the cat. Oh, yes please!

Armed with map, bus and metro timetables and instructions on how to get tickets, I waved her off and then set-off on my city-explore.

First, back to Union Station where Carol had met me.
Opened in 1907, the station was completely refurbished for its re-opening last year. Aha! So that's why everything looks so spanking new.

The main hall floor is grey marble. The many orchestrated skylights set into the domed ceiling don't have the function that their name implies, because of the new roof covering the building. Instead there are soft-yellow lights emitting a sunny glow everywhere.

There is a ledge around the main hall (several feet above the level of the tops of the arches that house small shops and cafés) upon which stand twenty-six centurion sculptures. Through my binoculars I see that they are allegorical sculptures which symbolise and personify abstract ideas. Behind them is a frieze, of pictures of industry and nature, painted in soft colours.

The six giants that stand on perpetual guard on the shelf across the width of the concourse are especially fine, sculpted from white granite and white marble and gilded with gold leaf. Reading the information plaque I see that they represent: 'The Progress of Railroading', 'Prometheus' (fire), 'Thales' (electricity), 'Themis' (freedom and justice), 'Apollo' (imagination and inspiration), 'Ceres' (Agriculture) and 'Archimedes' (mechanics).

Christmas gifts and goodies were spilling from the shops into the concourse. I wandered around looking for something different, but lightweight, to post as Christmas gifts for the people I've stayed with.

In the East Hall, while having coffee below the full-size, real, palm trees, I watched my first bag-lady. She was dressed in an old, stained brown coat, a black cloche hat with its long curling feather, a long rainbow-coloured scarf competing with her make-up and trailing around her neck. She was picking and poking through the garbage cans and occasionally putting something in her carrier bag.

Yes, I know, reminiscent of me at Niagara Falls!

Next, it was off to the National Gallery of Art where I thought I'd look at some of the American painters' paintings. I don't have much understanding of art – more a passing interest because my dad painted in watercolours and oils. (If Dad were still alive, would I be here now? I doubt it.)

Two that caught my imagination and are worthy of recording are: Thomas Cole's *A View of the Mountain Pass called Notch of the White Mountains* – a bit of a mouthful, so better known as *Crawford Notch* – painted c.1839. In fact, I bought a print at the gallery shop and sent it to Aunty Marge, hoping she would enjoy the scene and get some idea of the countryside I am seeing. The picture depicted wonderful forest-clad mountains; a small wood and a thatch-roof house nestled at the base of a ridge; a frothing river and a horseman returning home after his hunt – successful to judge by the rabbits and birds he had slung from the saddle.

The other was a portrait; *Child in a Straw Hat,* painted by Mary Cassatt c.1886. About eight years of age, the little girl's woeful expression looked as if she'd been naughty and sent to stand in a corner. Of rosy cheeks and rosebud mouth, she was dressed in a high-necked, grey, sleeveless smock over a white, short-sleeved blouse. What made me smile was the enormous straw hat perched precariously on her straw-coloured hair, which was short and sticking out every which way. I think she must have been quite a tom-boy

Feeling pretty bloated with information, I left the National Art Gallery on Constitution Avenue and turned my steps towards the Potomac River a few blocks away.

On the way, I passed through the garden of the Hirshhorn Museum, on Independence Avenue, where there was a sculpture exhibition by famous artists. I admired the greater-than-life-size *Walking Man* by Rodin. Cast in bronze, those powerfully muscled legs could forever stride the land, but, being armless and headless, he'd better hold that stance and stay put.

I think you'd have enjoyed, as I did, Picasso's *Pregnant Woman* (also cast in bronze) with her ballooning belly and half-melon breasts. Her head was another melon with hair sculpted on the back and with small, close-set eyes either side of a squidgy but pert nose. Her short, strong legs ended in an idea of feet, as did her arms ending in blobby hands – but that's Picasso.

Henry Moore's *Seated Woman* (sculpted from white granite) was also very weird. The legs below the knees were normal looking, but above the knees great swelling thighs melded into ballooning buttocks and swelling belly. The breasts were cones slapped somewhere in the centre of the chest area. The head was almost not – it was so disproportionally small, with hair on one side, a great beak of a nose and eyes that looked as if a kid had stuck its fingers in the clay.

What is in the heads of these men that they have to portray women thus?

I walked along the Potomac River back to Georgetown and let myself in to feed the cat.

During the next three days, I continued to explore this city of the American President.

To get a rooftop view of the Downtown area, I found the Old Post Office and Clock Tower on the corner of Pennsylvanian Avenue and N12th Street. The Old Post Office and Clock Tower was built in 1899 and was used as the city's main Post Office until 1914. After that it rather fell into disuse and 'they' wanted to pull it down. A "Save our History" group became very vociferous and the building was saved and refurbished with pink marble slabs forming the main concourse floor and complimented by the cream, green, grey and ivory colours of the walls. The Old Post Office was re-opened in 1983. A glass-enclosed elevator (lift) carried me up to the observation deck at about three-hundred feet.

That was a novel experience.

One needs a head for heights. The glass elevator crawls up the outside of the wall and one watches the floor of the concourse below slowly receding.

We were allowed into the bell tower to see the Congress Bells in their permanent home. A full peal (which lasts three and a half hours) is rung at the opening and closing of Congress gatherings, State occasions and all National Holidays.

Interestingly, ten of the bells were cast in England at the Whitechapel Foundry and are a replica of the bells in Westminster Abbey. The set of ten bells were presented as a bicentennial gift, in 1976, to commemorate the friendship between the two nations.

The roof-top view couldn't have been more different from Toronto's. The buildings round about were all about six to ten storeys, flat-topped and built of red-brick and yellow sandstone (or maybe limestone). Not a skyscraper in sight. The eight-lane wide, tree-lined Pennsylvanian Avenue moved the eye to admire the U.S. Capitol at its end. In another direction the pointy needle of the Washington Monument, sitting on its green grass mound, stuck up way above the surrounding red roofs. The shining curve of the Potomac River lay behind the needle, framing it.

So I went to visit the Washington Monument.

The needle obelisk was built in 1848-1884. It took so long because work stopped, and then re-started when more stone was sourced from a different quarry. Thus, above one-hundred and fifty-two feet the stone is of a darker hue. The obelisk was dedicated in 1789 to George Washington: the 1st President of the United States.

This letter is becoming a history lesson, so I'll just add here that I peered through the railings, across immaculate lawns, to the White House; didn't go for a visit because the entry queue curved around the paths for a few hundred yards.

The Capitol Building was more tourist-friendly and I was able to gawp at the four enormous paintings garnishing the stairwell and the ceiling paintings of the east and west corridors. From the steps I looked back along three-hundred yards of grass with pedestrian walkways on each side and flanked by rows of trees, to the Washington obelisk. The view's a bit like the ride up to

Windsor Palace but flat and straight, with a large lake and fountains in it and, of course, much bigger.

I do wonder why the Americans built their cities and towns with the streets in such regimented straight lines. I get turned around very easily and have to walk to the end of a block to get my bearings. I so much prefer our winding roads, the alleyways, the surprise emergence into a green square, but I guess it's what you grow up with.

Carol returned, tired but fulfilled with whatever had been discussed at the conference. She was happy with the clean house and her well-fed cat.

After breakfast the next morning, I loaded myself up and set off north, leaving Georgetown along Canal Road and looking for the tow-path running alongside the Potomac canal.

In my next missive I'll explain why I'm returning north instead of heading south.

So until then, I am your wandering friend,

Bron

Walking Man
Rodin

Pregant Woman
Picasso

Seated Womon
Henry Moore

30

6. WALKING NORTH to LONGLAKE
Building Mind Over Matter

October 23rd to November 5th 1989

Dear Anne,

From the sublime to the 'cor blimey', from the known of the town to the wild of the wilderness: I've gone bush.

Striding at a steady pace along the well-maintained canal tow-path allowed my mind to wander. So often in life one small comment leads to a whole new life-path. Don't you agree?

My plan had been to go south from Washington D.C. I'd read about the section of the Appalachian Trail (AT) that continues south to Georgia and had decided that that seemed my sort of challenge. But . . .

For one of my days in Washington, Carol had arranged for me to meet the walking group she belongs to called 'Wanderbirds'. That's an interesting name, I thought. It turned out they were all women. What might they have named a group that included men?

They took me to the Shenandoah National Park and, of course, talk was about me. Shock, horror, was the reaction when I mentioned the AT plan - 'You can't do that in winter and alone! No! No! No! You'll have to cross the Snowy Mountains – impossible! There'll be ten feet of snow on the trail, bears and big cats, snakes and nasty plants.'

I walked slowly behind the group along the narrow foot-trail through the trees now naked of leaves, my thoughts in turmoil. The views from the Blue Ridge Mountain Road showed wave after wave of tree-covered mountains stretching as far as the eye could see.

I'd have to walk through those and with any fall of snow I'd not be able to see the footpath.

So what to do? A brainwave! I would go back north to Dek's. I've never experienced proper cold and deep snow that lasted for weeks, nor ice thick enough to bear the weight of a train.

31

So that's how I came to be walking alongside the Potomac River on the Chesapeake and Ohio Canal towpath (C&O Canal).

I stood to admire the spectacular Great Falls of the Potomac River Gorge, formed as the river cut down through cracks in the Metagraywacke (grey rock) rocks. I do love these impossible-to-pronounce geological words, don't you? The information board enlightened me: Five-hundred million years ago, muddy sand collected far beneath a sea. A sub-marine avalanche off the Continental shelf had slid the accumulation down into a deep trough and over aeons it was buried eleven miles deep! Heat and pressure changed the sand-mud mix into hard Metagraywacke rock.

I took a dutiful photo of the Seneca aqueduct; opened in 1833, it's still supplying water through a nine inch diameter pipe to Washington D.C. and Maryland. On the canal side (my side of the two-arched red sandstone bridge) the water was mirror-still, but looking through the arches the waters of the river beyond foamed white. It formed a pretty picture.

I've been three days on this tow-path and my purposeful striding has slowed to a mind-over-matter painful limping. My feet are a mess of plasters (Band Aids) on the many blisters. My ankles hurt so much after the incessant pounding that I can hardly stand in the mornings and I just want to arrive at Harper's Ferry.

To ease my journey, I thought about the kingfisher I'd stood watching as it flashed brilliant-blue iridescence in the sun, up and down the canal, patrolling its territory.

I kept an eye open for the next woodland loo – a dark-brown, fibreglass, truncated cone complete with sun roof, vent and all mod cons inside.

I counted my steps.

I hummed songs.

The best I can judge, I'm walking about twenty miles a day. I know that's not a lot, but remember I'm carrying about ninety pounds.

At last! There was the spiral metal staircase to take me from the tow-path up onto the footbridge that crosses the Potomac River to Harper's Ferry.

I'll find a place to rest my body, weary after the sixty-three miles I've walked.

I'm having a couple of rest days to find out what's special about Harper's Ferry.

In 1761, Rob Harper ran a ferry across the Potomac River to connect with the C&O Canal. Named after Rob, the town of Harper's Ferry is sited at the confluence of the Potomac and the Shenandoah (cue for a song?) Rivers and also at the confluence of three states – Maryland, Virginia and West Virginia. There weren't many houses along the river banks or creeping up the hillsides. There were even fewer shops. Thankfully, I did find a B&B and slept well.

These days the roads and train-line bring in tourists (mostly from Washington D.C.) on a day's outing.

What's to see?

Lots.

Do you remember us singing 'John Brown's body lies a moulderin' in the grave and his soul goes marching on'? (It was almost par-for-the-course on school coach trips.) And do you know who John Brown was? Well, here I am, where he was, and I can get all the lowdown. John Brown believed he could free the slaves; Harper's Ferry was his starting point. Because he and his band of some twenty men needed weapons, on October 17th 1859, they tried to seize arms from the one hundred thousand weapons stored in the U.S. government's arsenal and armoury: small fire arms were made at Harper's Ferry. The plan was then to hide in the Blue Ridge Mountains and start a guerilla war.

To cut the story short, someone ratted on him; the Government sent U.S. marines (garnered from the three states and led by Colonel Robert E. Lee) to storm the building where Brown and his men were hiding. He was captured, tried for treason against the State of Virginia and hanged as a traitor on December 2nd 1859.

His action and trial brought attention to the slave situation and ultimately led to the American Civil War.

"and tho' he lost his life in the struggle to free the slaves, his truth is marching on."

At last I was on the Appalachian Trail.

I intend to walk only a tiny part of its length (2,200 miles in total). The trail goes from Springer Mountain, in Georgia, all the way north to Maine. Some (very few) folk walk/run the whole way at once, others take several years. I shall take three days to walk forty-three miles to the next main road where I can start hitching north.

The trail, for the most part, is about a yard wide. All the trees are now bare. Gone are the autumnal fires – the colours of a few weeks ago. Vistas of the hills rolling away, far away, can be seen through the trunks.

The trail was thick with autumn leaves. I couldn't judge where the stones were waiting to make me stumble or stub my toes. My ankles constantly twisted. When the trees are in full leaf it must be like walking through a green tunnel for mile after mile. The trail flowed up and down from four hundred feet to one thousand two hundred feet and I was happy to have the views from this ridge of the Maryland Heights.

I took a break in a shallow cliff-cave in which six sheep could lie. I know it's a pot-hole eroded long, long ago by the swirling waters of the river far below. I tried to imagine the river up here or the rocks down there: Impossible!.

I must've been passing the village of Boonsboro, because there was the very first monument to George Washington. It was built from stones by the local villagers to celebrate their Independence Day, July 4th 1827. It looked like an upside down one-third pint milk bottle – those we used to get in Junior School. I used to drink mine and my friend's, although the milk was often slightly warm because the milk-monitors were tardy bringing in the crates out of the sun.

The Union army used it (the monument, not the milk bottle) as a signal station during the Civil War. Sadly, I wasn't allowed up it – stopped by an iron gate.

I found an out-of-sight flat spot off the trail for the night. I didn't make a fire (not allowed I'm sure) nor do any cooking: I don't want any enticing smells to bring a curious black bear – not that I've seen any signs of one around here.

I heard guns. Turkey shooting I guess – it'll soon be Thanksgiving.

The second night I came across a typical trail shelter. Built from split logs, it had only three sides and a very steeply sloping roof of corrugated iron. Inside, three bare planks served as a sleeping-platform at the back, a benched wooden picnic table was in front and in front of that a three-sided low stone wall to protect the fireplace. I slept badly, shivering in my three-season sleeping bag, although I was fully clothed.

I was sitting in the morning sun, dawdling over breakfast, when three hunters in their camouflage gear and leather hats showed up with guns and dogs. They were very surprised to see me, a woman, alone. They were friendly enough and I shared their pot of coffee. I was told it was the hunting season and I should take special care to stay on the trail, walk loudly (with 'ooohs' and 'sod its', as I twist my ankle yet again!) and try not to get shot.

Yes siree. Will do!

That was a good reason to get off the trail at the next point of civilisation.

If you're reading this letter, I'm still alive, I've found a post box and I've not been attacked by a bear or shot as a turkey.

Love 'n' hugs,

Bron

7. WHITE CHRISTMAS at LONGLAKE
My First Experience of Real Cold

December 27th 1989

Dear Anne,

I think of you, so busy getting ready for the Christmas Fayre at school. I must confess that I'm not the teeniest bit envious. I hope that you'll exceed the £8,000 that was made last year. It still amazes me that the relatives of about five hundred girls can spend so much money in so few hours of organised chaos, selling what is really so much tat.

By a mix of hitching and busing I got myself back to Long Lake village and then walked the mere couple of miles to Dek's place. He wasn't in although I'd phoned to say I was on my way back, but couldn't give an exact arrival time. I thought he must be working or had taken the dog for a walk. I knew where the key should be. Anyway, I had my tent.

The snow was already deep. The roads had been snow-ploughed and made for ease of walking (although rather slippery) if I could keep to the ploughed bits. Not so easy when a car wanted priority. If I stepped out of the tyre tracks I sank up to my knees.

Dek came back, with dog, and we all had a joyous, energetic greeting.

It was the end of December and the start of a new phase.

We were going south. But before we set off, I must just note for you a few of my impressions of winter in Upstate New York State.

I never did know the temperatures exactly.

Dek would say, after peering at the thermometer, 'Today, 32 below', or, 'Only 28 below. It's warmer today.'

I'd say, 'Below what? Are you talking degrees C or degrees F?'

'Below freezing,' he'd reply.

Some people think they're very funny! (We've just changed from Fahrenheit to Centigrade, but I am most familiar with ^{0}F and struggle with ^{0}C.)

When stepping outside, breath soon froze even when one breathed through one's scarf: such a sharp, lung-numbing, nostril-disenabling cold.

I remember: walking back one late afternoon in the early dark and being excitedly thrilled by the air filled with sparkle-dust of all the colours of the rainbow – the frozen moisture in the air glinting and glistening and whirling like fairy-dust in the street lamplight; walking through the snowy woods and the only sounds being the plop of snow sliding from a branch or the chirp of some bird; walking out on the ice, thick enough to support a train engine, of Moon Pond where the sorry-looking ducks were sliding around on their bellies; climbing the fire-lookout tower to scan over the tops of the trees and seeing the rolling hills all blanketed in snow; uncomfortably struggling along using snowshoes (which is a bit like walking on tennis rackets that've lost their handles) strapped to boots whose leather laces kept working loose; trying to cross-country ski – we didn't go far because it was surprisingly sweat-making work trying to slide my feet along the ground. I found it greatly difficult not to lift my feet; co-ordinating sticks with strides was not easy! I obviously need lots of practice to acquire this strange mode of locomotion.

On the social side we visited Dek's Aunt Yoli for a Thanksgiving Dinner and drove miles to go shopping in a Mall – strange word. I say Mall as in hall, they say Mall as in pal!

We went into K-mart (a store like a huge Woolworths and sells everything cheaply). I was looking for more trousers (pants) as the ones I'd worn continuously for months were looking tatty. I only mention this because of Dek's strange reaction.

I'd found a couple of pairs that might've done and wanted to try them on, but nowhere could I spot a fitting-room. Another lady shopper told me, 'Oh, you have to take them home to try on and bring them back for exchange if they don't fit.'

Well that wasn't on, so I did no more than hide behind the clothes-racks at the back of the shop, dropped my trousers and tried on the new ones for size – they have funny sizing in America and the numbers meant nothing to me.

You should have seen Dek's thunderous face, hunched shoulders and bunched fists. If Aunt Yoli hadn't been there, I swear he would have been violent (with whom I'm not sure).

Outside, and when he'd calmed down, I asked why he'd been so mad. He muttered that he couldn't bear me exposing my legs for just anyone to see. I told him not to be so damn silly and marched ahead.

Should I be flattered that he cares so much, or annoyed because I'm not his possession? I didn't argue. Twenty years of holding back what I think still very much inhibits me from saying anything untoward.

To explain: in the very early days of marriage my husband asked me what I thought of his new glasses in their heavy black and fashionable frames. I said, 'I don't think they suit you. I don't like them.' He walked out slamming the door and went into a sulk that lasted for three days of silence. He was never a violent man, but I had many instances of days sulking and not speaking to me. So I learned to withhold my opinions.

Another instance of me having limited communication skills: it was Christmas morning and I thought I would surprise Simon (young son) with a phone call to wish him a happy day. The phone rang and rang and rang. I said to Dek, 'Perhaps he's out with his fiancée, I'll try again later'.

Hours later I phoned again. That time a sleepy voice answered, 'Who is it?'

'It's Mum, to wish you a Happy Christmas. Is your girlfriend settled in with you?'

'She changed her mind and left me.' Pause, then a plaintive voice asked, 'When are you coming home, Mum?'

You remember that one of my reasons for leaving the UK was my feeling so rejected and useless. That sense of being unwanted was still very much in my head, so I thoughtlessly and very insensitively blurted out, 'I don't know. I might never come back.'

Days later, I realised that I had got Simon out of bed because I'd totally forgotten the time difference between the two countries.

We had a tasty and filling Christmas lunch (venison shot by Joe) in the late afternoon, with Dek's nephew Joe and his two kids and dogs.

Joe's house, which he mostly built himself from local wood, was spacious and warm with the open log fire. The nine-foot fir, cut from the woods, was well baubled and tinselled to set the festive scene.

The afternoon was spoilt for me by the swearing of Dek's brother-in-law, the uncouth chap who ran the only hotel in the village. He put so many swear words into a sentence that sometimes I actually had difficulty understanding what he was on about. When I mentioned it to Dek that night he said he didn't notice, but would have a word.

Except for that unforgivable boo-boo with Simon (for which I feel so guiltily sorry), I had a very good Christmas.

I hope that you had loads of goodies and booze and spent time with your sons.

I send you my love and belated good wishes for a Happy New Year.

Bron

8. DRIVING SOUTH
And dining in the Epcot Center

December 30th 1989

Dear Anne,

Are you glad that Christmas is over and you have New Year to look forward to?

We're on our way south; leaving behind this deep-frozen white land.

Dek has had a proper hard-top fitted over the flat-bed of the pick-up, so we can use it for our accommodation as we go where the whim takes us. My objective is to visit the Everglades of Florida.

Asked if I'd like to drive I said, 'I'll give it a go.'

We went south (me driving) on a road long and straight like a two-lane motorway. At first the driving was easy, but soon it got very busy; more and more so the closer we got to New York. Driving on the 'wrong' side of the road, in a vehicle I'd not driven before, of course I had to concentrate – big time.

Dek suddenly asked, 'Do you love me?' (He does so demand immediate answers, being like a dog with a rag toy he has to worry and worry at it.)

'Yes, I think so, maybe,' I muttered.

He posed the question, 'If you love me and we were in the mountains and I had an accident and was very badly injured, would you leave me to fetch help or would you stay with me until I died?'

What a thing to ask me in the middle of a strange motorway! There are so many parameters to such a situation that I refused to give a straight yes or no answer. Dek kept on and on at me.

After several miles of this and me getting more and more agitated and a near miss, I pulled-over on the hard-shoulder and got out. 'Dek, I can't concentrate if you won't shut up. You drive,' I stormed at him.

At last, we arrived in New York and eventually found a B&B, not so very expensive and a short metro ride from the centre.

(Dek wouldn't do an overnight in a parking lot. 'It's illegal,' he said.)

The pond in Central Park was frozen and busy with skaters weaving in and out and round about, reviving their summer-dormant skills.

We walked down Fifth Avenue and into Saks, a five-storey, upmarket, high-price store (like the John Lewis that we have in Birmingham, but which caters more for the middle-range market). Saks has the largest and most expensive toy department in the world. A full-sized beautiful 'Black Beauty' pony an adult could sit on comfortably caught my eye and a pedal car for a toddler with a real battery-powered engine.
Anything you could possibly dream of for your child – if you had the money. I was a bit bemused by it all.

January 2nd1990

More by coincidence than design we spent my birthday (I didn't tell Dek) at the Epcot Centre.

Rather surprised by the cost of entry for a single day to one area, we withdrew to debate which to go into – the Magic Kingdom Park, the Epcot Centre or the Disney-MGM Studios Theme Park? Buying a five-day 'passport', which provided admission to all three plus the transport connecting them, would have been the best value. But we couldn't afford that. So we decided on a one park/one day ticket for fifty-eight dollars (about £29 each!).

In the Epcot Centre was the Future World Pavilion which displayed: innovations in health, energy and communications; life-styles of the future – transportation, the land, the living seas and stuff dreams are made of. (Where did the Americans get 'transportation' from? What's wrong with 'transport' as we say it?)

It's 8 a.m. and although the Park had only just opened, the crowds were already building up.

So much to see.

So much to do.

Impossible in one day!

We thought we would walk around the Central Lake first, to get an overview and to think which country we might like to lunch in. Around the lake we passed the pavilions of Mexico, Norway, China, Germany, Italy, The American Adventure, Japan, Morocco, France, United Kingdom and Canada arranged in that order – why? Why site China between Germany and Norway?

41

Of the themed attractions, we first visited the World of Motion Pavilion and took a ride through the Evolution of Transport. We discovered how mankind's progress has been directly related to worldwide innovations in mobility and how tomorrow's transport will change the face of our cities.

Next, in the Horizons Pavilion, we took an incredible journey through the lifestyles of the twenty-first century: the urban environment of tomorrow, a robotics-staffed desert farm, a working ocean colony.

We marvelled at the imagined marvels of the past – such as Jules Verne's cannonball flight to the moon, all brought to life with micro and macro motion pictures.

We took a break for lunch. No prizes for guessing where. Yep. The English Pub. Dek wanted to sample English beers while we sat at an outside table and looked across the lake. We moved to the Chinese Pavilion to try noodles and prawns in a spicy soup. I had rice wine too, but Dek wasn't up for that – too foreign!

To get a beer (or any alcohol) with lunch we had to show proof of age (over twenty-one years). Dek had his State Photo ID and I just happened to be carrying my passport – would it have been no alcohol for me if I hadn't? Do I look under twenty-one? Really!!

The Living Seas' Pavilion boasted the world's largest man-made, salt-water environment. The tank held nearly six million gallons of sea water with more than eighty species of tropical fish and included sharks, manatees and dolphins.

'Oh, look, look! My first live manatee,' I excitedly exclaimed to Dek, my mind boggling at the weight of water pushing against the thick glass walls of the marine tank.

In Sea Base Alpha we travelled to the bottom of the 'sea' in the hydrolator and talked to divers through the speakers and then went on to see the marine scientists working in their labs up top. By the time we had looked at the static displays and Dek had tried on the atmospheric diving suit, we felt enough's enough.

Before going home, we had just time for another drink in a different country; Mexico.

I enclose the PO Box address in Houston for your letter and so look forward to news from you.

But I shall have to contain my impatience until February 20th when I should be in Houston.

I wish you well and quiet classes. Hugs from *Bron*

9. FLORIDA
Hot stuff one way or the other

January 6th to 19th 1990

Dear Anne,
        I'm thinking of you in England in the cold winter months and now I shall make you envious of me in the Everglades of Florida.

After having emptied our pockets and filled our eyes with the sights of Disneyland, we moved on to Tampa to visit a friend of Dek's.

Wayne's ground-floor flat was quite small and manoeuvring a wheelchair around it not easy, especially now that we were cluttering up the space.

Some years ago, Wayne had had a very bad motorcycle accident and virtually smashed himself to smithereens skidding at speed on a bend. That was in NY State where he and Dek were good mates. Wayne'd moved south to be nearer relatives and in the warm – he said that the cold hurt his broken bones.

Wanting to leave them together to talk shop and re-live memories, I went wandering to look for some Botanical Gardens I'd seen signposted. Americans build their cities on a grid system and as I said before, I get very turned around; the streets look so much the same. The distances are greater too – to reach the next corner is many minutes of pavement-pounding. The heat was bouncing off the pavement (sidewalk). Very hot! And I wasn't carrying water.

Time was running away and although I still hadn't found the Botanical Gardens I knew I should return.

I got back to the flat and was greeted by a worried looking Dek, 'Where the f…. have you been?'

'Trying to find the Botanical Gardens,' I retorted.

'I'd have driven you.'

'No. I thought you and Wayne wanted chat-time.' I didn't say that I needed me-time.

We slept on the floor, on our sleeping bags – too hot and humid to need coverings. Dek wanted to make love; I felt that would be very insensitive with his handicapped mate only inches away in the next room. But we did anyway – quietly.

I should tell you that during the month I'd lived with Dek, he'd overcome his fear of sex. (For whatever reason he was terrified of putting his penis into a dark and slimy hole – a vagina – in case he could never get it out again! Perhaps he'd watched dogs mating and seen how the dog gets tied to the bitch.) Now he wanted sex all the time, anywhere, everywhere – but like all good things, overuse and the fun palls.

We set off south, and kept to the coast roads as much as possible. Driving across Florida was very boring. The land is so table-top flat for hundreds of miles, with big expanses of grasslands. It reminded me of my cycle ride through Holland: I've told you of the time I cycled to Berlin and camped in the woods without a tent, just sleeping on a ground-sheet with the other ground-sheet pitched across a long, horizontally placed stick supported by forked sticks, about eighteen inches high, at each end. (It sorta kept the drizzle off, but not the slugs outa my sleeping bag.) Often, here as there, the horizon is the nearest hedge, so it was good to glimpse the occasional cliff and the Pacific waves.

Dek and I spent the next few weeks exploring the Florida State Parks, where I learned a lot. I found the area fascinating. Alien to anything I'd seen before.

The first stop was at the Collier-Seminole State Park on Route 4 below Naples. It's about a four-and-a-half thousand acre preserve – almost entirely of mangrove forest. We followed the self-guided nature trail along a board-walk through the leather ferns and various palms (Sabal, or cabbage, Palm, Saw-palmetto Palm and Royal Palm; here being the only place in the U.S. where Royal Palm grows wild) to a tropical hammock – no, not a place to sleep in as you might imagine.

A tropical hammock! I certainly wasn't expecting a hardwood forest! But it's not a forest either – just a small patch of woodland that develops on a three foot high limestone ridge of land that rises out of the flat land surrounding. A hammock is dominated by trees that are characteristic of the coastal forests of the West Indies and the Yucatán, Mexico

I never did spot a mangrove fox squirrel or a red-cockaded woodpecker, but was compensated by gumbo-limbo *Bursera simaruba* trees. (I'm sure you'll have read at some time in your young life the "Jungle Stories" by Rudyard Kipling. I'd always thought a gumbo-limbo tree was some imaginary tree of Kipling's, so I was very happy to see the real thing.)

The trail led us on through the buttonwoods and white mangroves.

Back in the Interpretive Centre all was explained, (I think you've realised by now that I'm the sort of person that spends a lot of time reading information boards) and I bought a map which I'll send you.

Mangroves are salt-loving trees that can tolerate a wide range of salinity as the tides go in and out, and during such times the temperatures also fluctuate greatly, as does the degree of drying of the roots. Mangroves are viviparous, that is, the seeds germinate while attached to the tree. The seed root grows out through the fruit and the propagule (baby mangrove) drops and can embed in the mud below the parent, or better, be water-transported great distances to colonise further shores.

There are three varieties of mangrove which I must look out for.

I made notes which might interest you: a) Red mangroves *Rhizophore mangle* have distinctive arching roots which prop the tree out of the water, so allowing air exchange through the root lenticels (pores). Red mangroves grow closest to open water.

b) Black mangroves *Avicennia* sp. lining the creeks have thick, conical, straw-like root projections sticking up a foot or more from the ooze. These roots are called pneumatophores because their lenticels open for air exchange; there were few black mangroves in the Everglades, although they are common elsewhere. Black mangroves grow behind red mangroves

c) White mangroves *Laguncularia racemosa* grow further inland and have no distinctive root structure. They may have prop roots and/or pneumatophores. Salt glands secrete crystals of salt on the leaves. (That information reminded me of the salt glands of seals who, in fact, are not crying but excreting the excess salt from their blood.)

Buttonwood *Conocarpus erectus* prefers brackish water and can also be found growing towards dry land. It has an ultra-filtration system to keep salt out – the information board didn't explain how that works. Buttonwoods have small, button-like heads of tiny greenish flowers and so disperse by seed and not propagules.

We overnighted in a wilderness-camping camp. That first night we'd ignorantly left the back window of the pick-up hardtop wide open while we cooked tea, and when it came to bed-time the inside was thick with mosquitoes. We spent ages trying to eliminate them; flailing tea-cloths and hands and, as often as not, swiping each other instead of the mozzy – you know how effective is the high whine of a mozzy in your ear to stop you from sleeping. The next day's top priority would be to buy mosquito spray.

The next day we thought to go by water would be a good way to explore the mangroves, so we packed a lunch and rented a canoe. Trouble was the tide was out and we had to walk through knee-deep, squoozy mud to reach any water deep enough to float the boat. We were so busy manhandling the canoe and negotiating the mud we didn't notice that a paddle had slipped off – it'd been balanced across the prow. Silly us! We should have put it lengthwise in the canoe. Now it stuck upright in the mud some fifty yards behind us. Dek struggled back to retrieve it.

From water-eye view, I was really able to appreciate the impenetrable tangles of the red mangrove prop roots. I couldn't help thinking of the films of slaves from sugar plantations escaping through the mangroves and wondered how on earth they did it. With our silent, slow mode of transport I spotted a yellow-crowned night heron standing motionless on a prop root.

We paddled down the tidal channel (marked with buoys) towards the sea looking for a somewhere to land for lunch. We spotted a suitable looking place, paddled across to the shore, tied the canoe and disembarked to pick our way between the mangrove roots to a sort of clearing. But, but, but . . . Oh my! Oh my! Hordes of mosquitoes wanted their lunch too! We scrabbled as fast as we could back to the canoe and ate our lunch out at sea.

Dropping into a Gulf Coast Ranger Station to fill up our drinking-water containers – there are only two drinking-water places in the whole area – we were admiring the alligators in their sanctuary when a humungous roaring blasted our ears. What a strange contraption! It was like an oversized rowing boat, with four bench seats for at least twenty people and two airplane-like propellers mounted in the stern behind the passengers. Advertisement boards hanging from the metal tubing framework at the back announced, 'Wooten's Everglades AIR Boat Tours.' Of course, we had to have a go.

The guide pointed out the red mangroves, drawing our attention to the scattered, yellowing leaves on the trees. He said that the tree deposited its absorbed salt in these ageing leaves, turning them yellow. The leaves died and dropped off, thus ridding the tree of salt. Sounded a good theory, but I wondered how much scientific fact there was.

We drove on through Big Cypress National Preserve, pausing to admire the dwarf, bald cypresses – so called because they are only about three feet high, drop their needles in the winter and appear dead.

There are a few remaining giants, maybe six hundred to seven hundred years old, whose girths were greater than the joined hands of four long-armed friends! But most were logged out in the lumber era of the nineteen-thirties and nineteen-forties.

We popped into the Ochopee garage – very basic with just one pump outside a wooden shack – to fill up with gas. (It is still very awkward for me to say 'gas' (gasoline) for 'petrol'. I think of cooking when someone says 'gas' and still do a double-take when people say, 'I must go get gas.' I give them a frowning, puzzled look before the penny drops.)

We continued along Route 41 and, fifty miles on from the Gulf Coast Ranger Station, crossed Shark Valley whose extensive grasslands look like African savannah. It was covered primarily with saw grass (which grows to six feet and whose leaves have serrated edges – impossible to walk through) and dotted with hammocks. Shark Valley Slough is seventy miles wide at its head to about forty miles wide where it drains into Florida Bay. Most of the water comes from the Okeechobee Lake and oozes away at a quarter of a mile a day.

This area is so flat that the average annual rainfall of sixty inches drains ever-so-slowly into the Gulf of Mexico – the land fall is about two inches per mile. As most of the land is under water for most of the year, attempts at farming were a failure; so they started to drain the land, digging drainage channels and altering the landscape. By the nineteen seventies people were beginning to appreciate the importance of wetlands and the area was made into National Parks.

We didn't stop, but pushed on to the main Visitor Centre, another forty-two miles away, where we stocked up with a few food essentials and water and then decided to continue on to the Flamingo Visitor Centre, only thirty-eight miles more, find the camp site there and sit awhile.

(I've given you the distances so that you can get some idea of the size of this place.)

I think I'll stop writing for a while, while we explore the Everglades during the next few days.

I hope you had a good Christmas with your family and didn't put on too much weight with all the mince pies and cake.

I'll continue my story soon.
With love,
Bron

Pneumatophores of Black Mangroves

Red Mangroves
Tangle of Arching Prop-Roots

10. THE EVERGLADES
Anhingas, Gumbo Limbos & Fixed-wheel Bikes

January 1990

Dear Anne,

I'm so glad that you are storing all my letters and the pamphlets I send to you. I would never remember all the bits and bobs of my travels. Perhaps one day I shall be able to put the knowledge to good use.

Before we go south down the Keys, I'll fill you in with more of what I learned about the Everglades National Park.

The whole area, of some one-and-a-half million acres, was dedicated as a National Park in 1947. Over the subsequent years more areas were added and by 1978 most of the park had been declared a Wilderness Area.

The word 'everglade' means a marsh-land covered with scattered, tall grasses; nothing at all to do with the shady glade within a wood that we might envisage.

As we've seen already, the Everglades are more an expanse of savannah with pine trees and cypresses, creeks and ponds and coastal areas and with the tropical life from the Caribbean islands mixed with temperate species.

Summers are wet with occasional, heavy downpours and temperatures into the high twenties. Winters are dry with average temperatures of twelve degrees centigrade. (With the mosquitoes that we've experienced in the dry season, I'm jolly glad not to be here in the wet!)

After a couple of days sitting around in the Flamingo Visitor Centre, I wanted to know more.

We moved on to the Royal Palm Visitor Centre to see the explanatory video, nosed around the shop and then parked the pick-up at Long Pine Key a short distance away. (I'm enclosing the Everglades Trails map with this letter.)

There were lots of trails, all fairly short, of about half a mile. I selected the Anhinga Trail – where we saw alligators, turtles and anhingas. 'What the heck's an anhinga?' I hear you asking. I can now tell you: it's a bird which looks like a cormorant – the males are black and the females brown. They stand in the sun and hold out their wings to dry, just like a cormorant. When swimming in the water you can see only the head and neck of the bird, hence its common name 'snake bird'. Their feathers have less oil than cormorants and so they don't have so much buoyancy to counteract when swimming underwater.

Another question for the quiz – how do you tell the difference between a croc and a gator?

By its nose of course!

The nose of an alligator is a wide U-shape and rounded to give it a lot of power to crack open turtles, on which it prefers to feed. A crocodile's nose is a longer and a more pointy V-shape. It prefers to catch fish.

Also, alligators are less tolerant of salt water as they don't have the salt-excreting glands found on the tongues of crocs; crocs are more a sea creature and fairly rare in the freshwater Everglades. But gators are plentiful and live in the creeks and ponds and infertile wet places filled with sawgrass *Cladium jamaicense* which they use to build their nests.

The Gumbo Limbo Trail wound through a hardwood hammock (you remember a hammock is a small patch of woodland that develops on ground raised three feet or so above the surrounding swamp). It was like entering a jungle or a hot-house in a Botanical Garden. Ferns, orchids and bromeliads sat in the trees.

Most eerie were the trees festooned with the long, grey streamers of Spanish moss dangling like puffs of smoke from the branches. It was like walking into a Sleeping Beauty stage set. Spanish moss *Tillandsia usneoides* is not a moss but a flowering plant growing as an air plant and getting its nutrients and water from the air. In the Everglades it prefers to grow on the Southern Live Oak *Quercus virgina* or bald cypresses.

The moss used to be used as packing or stuffing material and in the early nineteen hundreds it was used for padding car seats.

The Pa-hay-okee Overlook Trail led to an observation tower from which we could see a part of the vast 'river of grass' and not much else; even through the binoculars I saw no rabbit, no bird.

The Mahogany Hammock Trail took us wandering through another different type of hardwood hammock, to see the largest mahogany tree in the U.S.

Streamers of Grey Spanish Moss

Amongst all that walking-the-trails we hired bikes. The bikes were fixed-wheel so that one had to keep right on pedalling – no rest, no freewheeling, not that there were any hills to freewheel down. The handlebars were raised on long stems so that I felt as if I was sitting with back straight, holding the reins of a horse.

The fifteen-minute-trail took us four hours because I kept stopping to use the binoculars, take photos and peer at the flowers. Dek passed on a piece of perceived wisdom – in the States, birders are the top group of people who get bitten by snakes! I trod more warily before stopping to bird-watch.

We did, in fact, see a diamond-back rattler slithering through the grass and a water moccasin in a pond.

With those thoughts and leaving you wiser than you were in matters of the Everglades (hope I haven't bored you too much), I wish you adieu and a belated Happy New Year.

Your sweaty and much-bitten friend, *Bron*

11. THE KEYS & NASA
Lumps of Blue Jelly & Rockets

End of January 1990

Dear Anne,

I hope you had a good Christmas and that your boys were able to stay awhile.

Here I come again with the next chapter.

Leaving the Everglades we got onto Route 1 and started down the length of the Florida Keys. I had hoped to get to the bottom, to Key West: the haunt of Graham Greene. But it wasn't to be, as you will see.

We took a break in the first underwater State Park in the U.S. – the John Pennekamp Coral Reef Park (John was a bounteous, Miami newspaper editor) near Key Largo. This Marine Sanctuary area was chosen for its coral reefs (the only living reef of the continental U.S.), seagrass beds (how I dream of seeing a manatee grazing the seagrass as I snorkel around!) and mangrove swamps.

I was pottering along the drift-line looking for anything (Dek sat on the sand as he didn't fancy venturing into the unknown – him being a through and through woodsman) when I spotted blue-ish, translucent, oval-shaped lumps of jelly, about two inches long and an inch high. You know how when a long balloon has lost most of its air you get a fat, flaccid bit at the tied-off end and a nipple at the other end, well, that's what these things looked like. No movement, even when prodded with a piece of drift-wood. I stared and stared, racking my brains for what they might be. The penny dropped. They were baby man-o'-war jellyfish – dozens of them. I carefully scooped one onto a rubbish plastic lid and took it back to show Dek. He wasn't the least interested. He was very angry. Now what! My crime was that I'd wandered out of sight and he didn't know where I'd gone.

The incident re-opened an old wound.

Years ago, before we'd married, my fiancé (Mike) and I had gone to Sitges, on the Spanish coast below Barcelona, for a pre-marriage holiday in a rented flat. We'd used the bus to get to a local, sandy beach with good swimming; I was told. Mike was sitting on the beach at the foot of the high, yellow cliffs and I was exploring the shore drift-line and swimming lazily, enjoying the tepid waters. As I looked back across the fifty yards of smooth sea at Mike, a male person walked past him; except that he didn't just walk past, he stopped and chatted to my fiancé, who got up and followed him round the curve of the headland. Very strange, thought I.

I swam around keeping an eye on our stuff. No Mike. I left the sea and waited. No Mike. What was going on?

I don't know about you, but I often get a sixth sense about some things. I felt something was wrong, but just couldn't bring myself to walk round that corner – frightened of what I might witness. The stranger walked back past me, ignoring me. A few minutes later Mike re-appeared looking hot and bothered and very sheepish.

He wouldn't talk to me.

We bused back to the flat in virtual silence. That night I wanted to make love. He pushed me away using the excuse that my sun-rash (I'd somehow become allergic to sunshine and an itchy, spotty rash covered my chest and arms) might be infectious. What rubbish! It hadn't bothered him before.

Mike lay curled, with his back to me. After futile attempts to find out what was troubling him, I gave up, deeply upset. At 2 a.m. I was scrubbing the kitchen floor in frustrated, angry tears.

The incident was never mentioned, ever.

Dek and I drove on along Route 1.

Driving down the Keys became very tedious: the same posh houses and holiday homes alongside the road, shopping malls all catering for the rich and sporty, and bridge after bridge after bridge between the many islands of the Keys all strung in a line like the misshaped beads of a necklace.

The views were spoilt by the concrete electricity posts – they must have been over thirty feet high, marching along the sidewalks carrying three cables slung one above the other between them. Below the electricity cables were two tiers of telephone wires, also travelling in threes, and to add insult to injury, yet another electric cable to light the lamps which illuminate the sidewalk (pavement) – that's ten wires slung between lampposts.

After fifty miles or so we'd had enough and decided not to go all the way to Key West; which would be at least another fifty miles of the same, sameness. We overnighted at Bahia Honda and next day turned around and headed north.

18th – 21st January 1990 – Awe inspiring NASA

From miles away we could see the space rockets pointing their cone-noses skywards as we journeyed towards the National Aeronautics and Space Administration Centre on Cape Canaveral.

We'd cut across country, to avoid Miami, heading north on Route 997 and then cutting inland on Route 27 to pass Okeechobee Lake before heading east to Fort Pierce and the Cape.

Lake Okeechobee is often referred to as 'The Big O.' The word means 'big water' in Hitchiti (the name so given by the Hitchiti Indians). It's approximately five hundred square miles – so not a lake as we might think of one, more an inland freshwater sea with an average depth of about seven feet. So shallow, I could almost walk across – but only if my feet didn't sink into the mud at the lake bottom!

I've mentioned that it's the source of most of the water to the Everglades – the lake water coming primarily from the River Kissimmee which enters the north of the lake and with less important contributors. The lake used to sheet-overflow, like an over-filling bath, flooding big expanses of land round about, but controlling man interfered and channelled the water through dredged canals to the coastal-flowing rivers.

Arriving at NASA we bought our entrance tickets at Spaceport Central and mooched off to browse the information area before popping into the Wildlife Exhibit, (of course) and the Educators' Resources Centre (again, of course). I'd had little idea that so many things we use in everyday life are a spin-off, directly or indirectly, from space research: freeze-dried food; space blankets for firefighting; scratch-resistant (plastic coated) eye glasses; cordless things like dust busters; de-icer; temper-foam that 'remembers' an impression and over a thousand more things – the list seemed endless. By the way, Teflon and Velcro - a Swiss invention in 1940, were used in the Apollo missions.

[Please tell Marion (Chemistry teacher) the following: quote from a notice in the Space Lab – "The absence of gravity in orbit allows scientists to conduct experiments the Earth's gravity interferes with on the ground; for example, many elements do not combine uniformly on Earth because gravity causes the heavier molecules to settle to the bottom. In space they mix evenly and so can form pure crystals. Also, weightless lubricants spread evenly and weightless medical substances can be mixed more uniformly."]

Perhaps one day ordinary scientists will travel to the Space Lab!

The outdoor Rocket Garden guided our steps among authentic, life-size replicas of rockets from various stages of America's Space Program and to read their particulars and histories.

Again overdosed with information, we headed for the more familiar – lunch on the white sands of Playalinda Beach (playa = beach, linda = pretty) at Cape Canaveral. The beach stretched cleanly, dazzlingly, for fifty miles. Small Atlantic waves rolled gently in, but I didn't see any swimmers amongst the few people present. The low dunes were covered with marram grass (same stuff covering our dunes) and nasty, spiny, pointy-leaved succulents.

Five miles north of the Kennedy Space Centre is the Merritt Island National Wildlife Refuge. This was our last chance to see interesting nature things.

I tried to take a close-up photo of an armadillo. Every time I got within six feet it moved off. We saw a white and black wood stork poised on one leg eyeing the shallow water, and a black skimmer skimming the surface of a pond with the lower bill of its open beak scooping just below the surface.

A pair of Sandhill cranes (grey-feathered, big birds the size of an emu, with post-box red faces) stabbed their long, strong beaks into the turf. I wished they'd dance for me. Maybe it's not the season.

There were many varieties of heron and egret, gull and duck, but my bird knowledge isn't good enough to pick out more than a few.

So; goodbye brown pelican, cheerio anhinga, *adios* alligator and *au revoir* armadillo.

I've been awed by the clusters of stalagmite-like 'knees' of the bald cedars poking through the swamp waters, the tangles of red mangroves, the pneumatophores of the black mangroves, the sea of sawgrass and the mosquitoes.

I hope that you continue to enjoy my account and that it is proving useful to someone.

Await with bated breath the next epistle!

Hugs from *Bron*

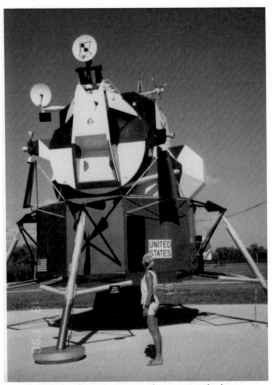

Model of space capsule – actual size

12. *ASHEVILLE*
Georgia & North Carolina

February 13th 1990

Dear Anne,

On the way north from NASA, Dek had said, 'While we're close, let's go visit with my brother.'

We drove for hours from Cape Canaveral to Albany, Georgia, and had a very fine lunch with Dek's brother's family and dog.

We continued our progress north, heading for Asheville – my next stop in the chain of people who know people – following the Blue Ridge Parkway. It was momentarily odd to see the mountains rolling away in choppy ridges into the distance. The hickory nuts and oaks were still leafless, so the views were grand. We paused at Tallulah Gorge (one thousand two hundred feet deep) in Georgia and the Cowee Overlook (elevation three thousand one hundred and ninety-five feet) in North Carolina for me to take photos. I stood to feast my eyes on the mountainous lumps and bumps and the rushing mountain rivers. After the weeks in flat-Florida it was a heart-healing sight.

We drove on through the Great Smokey Mountain National Park in North Carolina – someone told me that the Smokeys are so called because they're so often covered by wind-roiling clouds that they look on fire. (By the bye, should I continue along this road, it's only four hundred and ninety-six miles to the Shenandoah National Park that I visited during my Boston stop four months ago!)

We slept in the pick-up parked in a lay-by with a view, and I washed the dishes in the mountain stream.

Dek in our temporary home

In North Carolina we found the Cherokee HQ of the Northern Band of the Cherokee Indian.

The Cherokee Indian Reservation is a relatively small area when compared to the acreage of the National Parks – that seemed so unfair to me. In the town of Cherokee there was a museum where the Indian workers dressed in the old ways (as expected by tourists), but otherwise the Indians used Western dress.

Handicrafts were in abundance: wood carvings, spiders' webs 'dream-catchers' fashioned from intricately knotted cotton, and there were many other hand-woven objects in bright colours and significant patterns. The tourist nick-knacks filled the shelves and most of the floor.

I bought a postcard of the twenty-foot Indian bust sculpted from a single log. Mounted on two roundels of stones he guarded the museum entrance. His stern face was surmounted by his head-gear, which looked like a turban with a feather as tall as his face was long.

The Cherokee Indians originated in the Great Lakes area and spread south. (They live here, as they've always lived, in log cabins and only use tepees as temporary shelter – it's a bit of a myth that all Indians always live in tepees.) The Indians were very happy, very literate and peaceful agriculturalists, who, in 1828, were the first to publish their own newspaper. In that same year gold was discovered in Cherokee lands and you know what happens when gold is discovered . . .!

In 1830 Federal Government soldiers forced the Cherokee from their home-lands and marched them thousands of miles south to N. Georgia. Of the sixteen thousand who began the march, four thousand died along 'The Trail of Tears'.

The Cherokee rose was adopted as the State flower of Georgia – perhaps in some small compensation, but certainly as a reminder, 'Lest we Forget.'

Arriving in Asheville I bid Dek goodbye – he to return to work in Long Lake, I to find Jayne Ann's house (my next contact in the chain of people who know people) before continuing my adventure of a lifetime.

Did I regret bidding adieu to Dek? Well it wasn't really *adieu*, more *au revoir*. My feelings are very mixed. There is so much to like about him and so much that really annoys or irritates me. His great lack of self-esteem touches the part of me that wants to boost his ego – I feel I need to care for this wounded bird with its broken soul. I still don't know the full story, but I had found out that he'd been refused call-up to Vietnam, he'd spent a short time in prison for stalking and pestering his former lover and he still couldn't decide where to park the truck when I said, 'Anywhere you want'.

As to the au revoir, we'd discussed my onward mission and he'd made it very clear that he'd like to travel with me, but . . . he expected me to fund him – not on! And I'd promised that I would get in touch with a woman friend in England who wanted to join me in Mexico and we'd travel together.

Hence the *au revoir* – I really didn't think that Dek would get his act together to join me in Mexico.

Asheville is a very pleasant college and university town whose claim to fame is that it's the U.S. National Climatic Data Centre.

You're a fan of Charlton Heston. Did you know that the Asheville Amateur Dramatic Society was his teething ground? He even took over the theatre and managed it for a few years.

I wandered the Botanic Gardens and found a *Phallaceae* fungus *Mutinus elegans* with its bright-orange penis look-alike emerging several inches from a white ball base: instant flashback to the time when my ex and I made love in a wood. All the time he was looking around in case someone chanced by. He wasn't 'with' me at all. I just felt used.

I wished I'd been able to attend the 'Scream Session' at Jenny's. (See below.) I moved away from the evocative phallic fungus and found a quiet lake to sit by.

My thoughts turned to pleasanter muses: how very generous were the ladies I'd met, taking me – an unknown stranger – into their homes and treating me so royally.

I didn't stay the whole week with Jayne Ann and her two young children. I spent a couple of nights in Hendersonville with her friend Jenny, whom I'd already met on a trail walk with the Sierra Club. Jenny lived in a two-storey stone and wood house on the edge of her land where she breeds Arab horses.

The afternoon I arrived Jenny said, 'There's a meeting planned for this evening. Please will you stay in your room upstairs and not be worried if you hear a lot of shouting and screaming.'

Intrigued, but not liking to ask questions, I did as I was bid. In the morning I asked what all the noise had been about. Jenny said, 'It was a Regression Therapy Session.' She went on to explain that release therapy is a fairly new idea: groups of women, who had, or had had, man problems, got together and acted out what they would like to do/have done to the man who damaged them, be it an abusive father or controlling husband. (I wished I'd been able to go. I'd have shouted the house down. My ex was never physically abusive, but, my-oh-my, didn't my mind suffer! But, by acting out what I should have done/said, would it have eased the pain?)

Jenny even loaned me her Pontiac Firebird (a 1971 automatic) for the day to drive along the Blue Ridge Highway and see the shining-white rock dome of Looking Glass Rock and later slide down the slide of Sliding Rock waterfall formed by the waters of Looking Glass Creek.

Tomorrow I leave Jayne Ann's blue-grey clap-board bungalow, set in its leafy suburb of Asheville. I've been here for ten days and although I've very much enjoyed the civilisation after weeks of living in the back of the pick-up, it's time to move on.

In the morning Jayne Ann will take me to the Greyhound bus station to catch the bus to Memphis, Tennessee.

So on I go, but often thinking of you all.
Bron

13. A DAY IN MEMPHIS
Woolworth's Dèjà Vu

February 16th 1990

Dear Anne,

I'd survived another overnight bus journey – how I hate them – and arrived in Memphis, Tennessee bus station at 6.40 a.m. Three bus changes during the night had ensured little sleep. I'm at the streaming stage of a cold and after two hours of interrupted sleep, I don't feel like doing the Memphis Rock and Roll – a Blues stroll is more my style.

I've been walking and have got myself back to the bus station and with a three hour wait stretching ahead, I'm trying to write-up my day's doings with the paper balanced uncomfortably on my knee. I'm surrounded by speaker announcements (mostly incomprehensible) and people: some lolling awkwardly, bundled up in their heavy, winter clothes, snoring away the wait-time; others guarding their luggage whilst eating snacks and others making little attempt to control their roisterous children. The aromas of unwashed bodies and the toilets close by soon become deadened as my nose acclimatises. I do hope that tonight's Greyhound bus won't be as full as last night.

On arrival in the bus station I talked to the security guard (carrying a gun) who kindly showed me how to stow my backpack in the largest of lockers and then directed me to Beal Street, where it all happened during the first sixty years of this century. Memphis is the 'Home of the Blues' and Beal Street is the 'Heart of the Blues'.

Reading the first information plaque on Beal Street, I realised that I was within spitting distance of the great Mississippi river. A gusty wind was blowing and dark, scudding clouds threatened rain. Nevertheless, I wandered slowly river-wards and found a sheltered corner on a river-landing where I munched on my breakfast of apple, cheese, yoghurt and nuts before dawdling along the shore road to look at the pleasure paddle-steamers.

Then back to Beal Street which has few remnants from its days of former glory: A. Schwab's, established in 1876, reminded me of our Woolies in the days when everything was sold for under sixpence. The floors were of creaking wooden boards and the goods displayed openly on compartmentalised wooden counters. If you bought something, the money was put in a metal screw-top cylinder and sent whizzing off through pipes to somewhere upstairs. In a few moments the canister came charging noisily back with your change. I remember the Co-op using such a system.

Mr. A. Schwab was a Jewish immigrant from Alsace, France. He came to America to avoid being conscripted into the German army after the Franco-Prussian War.

He started his business as a one-room men's haberdashery. It has expanded into a two-storey, wood-floored building, which has many rooms housing a conglomeration of cheap and tawdry knick-knacks. One can buy: celluloid collars and straight razors, stationery, haberdashery and thermal underwear, Elvis souvenirs, corncob pipes, not to mention love potions, patent medicines and bongo drums.

The store is still managed by the family and has gained a reputation for selling large-size clothes – men's pants size seventy-four hang from the ceiling next to ladies' dresses size sixty.

For some reason the proprietor (he said, but I doubted that)) came trotting up to me and handed me a paper bag of souvenirs for which I, surprised, thanked him as he bustled off.

Over coffee I inspected my booty: a pencil with the slogan: 'If you can't find it at A. Schwab's, it ain't worth havin', a pink pin-badge with the same slogan in black cursive script, three black and white postcards of the shop front in 1939, one coloured post-card of the shop today and an information leaflet.

A little further along the street I came across a Visitor Information Centre which supplied me with a bus timetable and map to get to Graceland. The day was brightening with intermittent gleams of sunshine softening the rather drab and dreary and neglected side of this city.

I strolled along Main Street and found myself in the more prosperous, commercial end of town. Between the empty lots of Main Street were mostly shoe and T-shirt shops. Few people wandered around.

I gazed at a twenty-foot sculpture of piled guitars and allied accoutrements before sauntering off to find my bus shelter. I waited over half-an-hour in the bright sun, at the wrong place! – the Visitor Information person didn't know her information. A passer-by told me where to wait, again, for the number thirteen bus.

McDonalds, Wendy's, Pickin Lickin Chickin, Dairy Queen and other eateries, second-hand car dealers, shopping malls and so on lined the road on both sides all the way to Graceland. I kept my eyes peeled to spot where to get off along Elvis Presley Boulevard. Aha! There it was, his Cadillac of pale-pink and raspberry ice-cream colours. Elvis stood tall nearby, slim-hipped, shirt unbuttoned to his navel and the trademark stand-up collar of his jacket.

It was pretty much as expected – rows of tourist shops filled with Elvis Presley paraphernalia. I wandered around just browsing: to sit in his jet (a Delta) called *Lisa Marie*, see his cars or museum of personal memorabilia or house, all cost money, money, money. I chose the cheapest and saw, "Twenty-five minutes of Elvis's Encapsulated Life History using Original Footage".

As it was only 2.30 in the afternoon, I had lunch and wandered around some more.

I saw that the sky was darkening and thought I'd better get the No.13 bus back into the city. As I stood at the roadside bus stop, the first drops of rain from a rapidly lowering sky portended a downpour of immense vigour. Luckily I had my full-length poncho with me and submerged myself in that. There was no bus-shelter, but I didn't dare cross over the wide and now busy road to the bus-shelter on the far side – that'd be just the time my bus appeared!

The heavens opened. Within seconds the gutter was an eight inch wide torrent. It got so dark and thick with rain that I didn't see my bus until it was only fifteen yards away.

I dripped up the step and put eighty-five cents into the machine by the driver.

There were only coloured folk on the bus, all looking woodenly at me with a sort of, 'Ugh! You're wet! Don' you get sittin' near me,' look: only poor people use the buses.

Back in town with five hours to spare before the Dallas bus left, I pottered slowly around in the now drizzling rain. I sat in a large, empty café run by a family of Chinese and took absolutely ages to drink soup and eat a sandwich while reading my book. I mooched back towards the Greyhound bus station, being wary walking on the wet pavement in wet flip-flops – wouldn't be the first time I've come a cropper.

I was picked-up by an old, black, down-and-out; one eye missing, thick glasses, filthy odiferous clothes, and boots that looked like women's winkle-pickers from the sixties and seemed to hurt his feet as he minced along. He had two inches of a much-sucked cheroot stuck between his lips, he wore an old, black duffle-coat and a pink All-America cap perched on his grizzled Negro curls.

During our two hundred yard walk he wanted to exchange names and addresses, proffered his undying love and persisted in offering to buy me drink/meal/room at an hotel. (I think it should have been the other way around.) I firmly declined all offers and equally firmly thanked him for walking me back and bid him, 'Bye, enjoy your day,' at the Greyhound bus station entrance, thankfully escaping inside.

Two minutes later he'd followed me in, but speedily and noisily got ejected by the burly security guard. He reappeared ten minutes later through the back door, clutching a very dead and dirty piece of honesty which he gallantly presented to me and cried, 'For my valentine.' He plonked himself into the empty seat beside me and pursued his amorous advances – I resisted the urge to put my hand over my nose.

Discovering that I wouldn't mind a cup of tea he shuffled off, to soon reappear with a polystyrene cup of hot water, a tea bag and packets of sugar. At this point the security guard came back and forcibly told him to leave. It was with some reservation that I drank my tea.

You know Anne, one could write a kaleidoscope of cameo sketches describing what people do while waiting for the bus.

There was a young chap, in his early twenties I guess, with dyed dark-brown hair nearly down to his waist. He kept tossing his mane back from his thin face. One arm was intricately tattooed. He wore a black T-shirt and yellow 'n' black, large-check trousers (with the crotch halfway down his thighs) held up by a black, tasselled cord which hung vertically in the mid-line between his legs – you know how men sit. Suddenly he started to continuously open and close his knees and each swing apart caused the tassel to bounce. It looked most suggestive and quite mesmerizing!

Here comes the bus.

Maybe I'll get lucky and find two adjacent seats so that I can doze a while. Take care.

Wistfully. *Bron*

14. DALLAS, HOUSTON & AWAY
Dogs, Horses & Another Tower

February 17th1990

My Dear Anne,

February already! It must be about half-term time at Pipers. Any plans for this holiday? I hope you're still able to ride. I bet you won't be sitting on any long-distance buses.

For me, the trouble with these overnight buses is that one tends to arrive at one's destination very early in the morning, before any shops have opened and people have crawled from their beds to drag themselves off to the office.

I'd sat cramped in the smelly bus, stinky with unwashed humanity, for six and a half hours. As usual the bus was filled with impatient mums and their grizzling kids and half-drunk down-'n'-outs; not a seat to spare, too dark to watch the view, too uncomfortable to sleep.

There *were* stops – unannounced – so one never knew why or for how long before the bus would be off. Would I have time to find the loo? I refuse to use the grotty, pongy bus loos splashed with vomit and shit, so I don't drink and am probably dehydrated.

I'm now in the centre of Dallas.

I studied the street map in the closed booking-office window and noted how to find my way to White Rock Lake. That should do to sit awhile and while away time. (I'm not due at my next hostess's house until the afternoon.)

And that's where I met Karen, a woman in her late twenties, walking her three dogs in White Rock Lake Park.

I was sitting on a lake-side bench feeling a tad lonely and watching the few Mallard ducks and Canada geese cruising around doing what ducks and geese do in the early morning sun, and staring enviously at the wide, grassy field with its dog-walkers and ducks, when a tall, slim chap with long, orange hair, in canary-yellow trousers and a bright-blue shirt and with a scarlet cravat at his neck walked past with his duck (yes, duck) on a lead!

Karen's dogs bounded over to say 'hello' and of course I made a fuss of them, especially the chocolate Labrador. Karen and I chatted for a while and with gentle probing she learned of my circumstances. Then, suddenly, she said, 'Why don't you come and stay at my house for the night?' I looked at her in astonishment. She was quite sure she was sure (one learns to trust one's gut-feelings) so I took her up on her offer. I suppose I wanted 'dog-time' as much as anything.

As I was already on my way to sleep at Sally and Randy's for that night I agreed to visit the next day.

After a fitful sleep on the floor (no mattress, just my sleeping mat) of my host's spare room, I walked two miles along the busy main road to Karen's delightful top-floor flat in a big, old house overlooking the lake. We hit it off very well and spent the days and most of the nights talking.

That afternoon, she took me to her health-club where I tried out all the keep-fit apparatus and saunas and swam in the Olympic-sized pool.

The next morning Karen drove me, in the pouring rain, around Dallas to get money and the various bits and pieces I needed.

The following day – my faith in humanity restored, I set off unencumbered to explore Dallas while Karen was at work.

In a spacious plaza in downtown Dallas there was a pond with fountain and what, for a blink of the eyes, I took to be real horses splashing through the shallows at speed. A small herd of superbly cast-in-bronze mustangs: a proud stallion with nostrils flared and mane flying; several mares – one very hesitant to enter the water at the side of the pool, another paused to sniff at a rock part-submerged; a very young foal bravely jumping in from the low wall.

In 1985 this marvellous bronze sculpture, entitled "Mustangs de las Colinas" (Horses of the Hills) won that year's award for sculpture.

I climbed the many steps of the five hundred and sixty foot high Reunion Tower to the viewing platform which gave an all-round overview of the city. The Tower, opened in 1978, was topped by a geodesic dome which competed for novelty with the dark glass of a trapezoidal tower and the flat-topped sky-scrapers of cubes or rectangles of various shades of pinks or whites. But the view wasn't a patch on Toronto.

February 25th

Anne, thank you so much for all the news of home. I was so happy to find your letter waiting for me in the Poste Restante in Houston. I also got lots of news from step-mother and from my dear aunty. Of course, nothing from my boys; I do so wonder where they are and how they are and what they're doing.

To continue with news of my journey.

By the skin of my teeth I caught the Greyhound bus to Houston International Airport, where I was met by Jack and Judy. I spent my last night in the U.S. of A. in their magnificent mansion on the northern outskirts of Houston. He's a retiring business man and she his elegant lady.

I'll give you some idea of how folk with money live in a different world to the likes of you and me:

The entrance hall of their house has a coloured-glass domed ceiling above curving staircases. Fluted, pretend marble columns support the dome and lots of pinks and pale blues and whites in the décor create a soft illusion of spring.

Showing me into my opulent bedroom, decorated in pastel pinks and apple greens, my hostess said, 'Would you like a hot-tub?'

'Oh, yes, I would please,' was the rapid response – the thought of soaking in a hot bath made me tingle with pleasurable anticipation.

'Fine', said she, 'If you put on your bathing suit and come through to the kitchen, you can have a glass of wine to take with you.' She left me to change.

I felt most puzzled – why on earth would one have a bath in swimmers?

I appeared in their large, light and airy kitchen and Judy led me out into the garden.

Curiouser and curiouser, thought I.

The 'bath' was a warm, sudsy Jacuzzi big enough to seat ten people comfortably. What a welcome indeed!

My last day was spent walking around their leafy suburb (no pavements as usual; the Americans just don't seem to walk anywhere they can drive) admiring how the rich and nearly rich live. Then, to end the day and my stay in the States, I lazed beside their large swimming pool and Jacuzzi.

Jack drove me to Houston airport to catch my flight to Mexico City. The flight's arrival should, more or less, coincide with the flight arrival of the English group: I'd pre-booked a three-week tour with the travel company Exodus. The tour would explore from Mexico City to Meridá on the Yucatán Peninsula.

My idea had been to test the waters, so to speak, and so to decide if I could travel alone in such a foreign country. (Mexico is sure to be very different from France or Spain.)

I've heard so many scary stories about Mexicans; the way they mug and rob with violence, and the way the police are often implicated and turn a blind eye to the robbery of a 'rich' tourist, so that the police themselves can take a share of the profits.

I heard one story of a girl who'd taken a taxi only to be driven into the desert and raped and robbed.

And I don't speak Spanish; nary a word. So all in all, I don't know if I'll feel comfortable travelling on after the tour ends in Meridá, that's assuming that neither Dek nor my English acquaintance want to join me.

I'll keep writing to you and as soon as I can find another Post Restante mail drop I'll let you know, or I'll surprise you and appear on your doorstep. Who knows? I don't.

With love and trepidation (mine) I wish you adieu.
Bron

PART TWO
MEXICO to COSTA RICA

Scale 1:12,500,000

Lambert Conformal Conic Projection,
standard parallels 9°N and 17°N

15. MEXICO
A Joint Journey

End of February 1990

Dear Anne,

I feel decision time is approaching so fast. I try not to think, now, of all the problems I'll have if I go back to UK: no job, house with tenant, no car and not much money, to name but a few. But, on the other hand, shall I really be able to travel on through Central America with Alice? As we don't know each other very well, we may, or not, make tolerable travelling companions. (She's supposed to join me in Mexico at the end of this tour.)

I'll say here that I'm going to Americanise myself a bit more and get into the habit of using kilometres and metres as units of measurement: very roughly, divide the kilometres by two to get miles and multiply metres by three to get height or length in feet. Oh, and I'm slowly remembering that 'gas' is petrol and not gas, if you see what I mean.

Leaving Houston on Continental Airways and disembarking in Mexico City was to arrive in another world: the noise, the smells, the hustle and bustle of swarthy-skinned and black-haired little men who vied with each other to carry my backpack. I declined all help and went to look for the tour guide – holding his piece of cardboard with my name writ large upon it. He will take me to the hotel where I'll meet the rest of the group.

Fifteen intrepid travellers have joined the Explore tour of southern Mexico, briefly entering Belize and Guatemala to finish in Meridá on the Yucatán Peninsula.

The next morning our local guide, Hector, barrel-chested and swarthy of complexion, showed us around the Anthropological Museum. Unfortunately he fancied himself as a narrator-cum-actor and he talked and talked and talked, to the boredom of the group – some of whom quietly slipped away to do their own museum exploring.

In front of the Museum entrance we were in the right place at the right time to watch a fertility ritual going on. Five costumed men, in colourful, wide-sleeved blouses and bright, broadly-striped trousers, climbed a thirty metre pole and stood on a foot-wide circular platform at the top. Four of the men shuffled around the platform thirteen times to 'wind up the pole' (that's 4x13 = 52 for the weeks of the year) and then stooped and tied something to their waists. The fifth sat atop the pole and played some kind of flute. He did much foot-stamping as the four men jumped off the narrow platform and swung down to the ground, head first, suspended by ropes that they'd tied to their waists and to the platform (is it a pre-cursor of Bungee Jumping, which I've heard is the latest fun sport in New Zealand?). The fifth man then slid down his rope, held steady by a man on the ground, thus symbolically joining the sun to the earth.

It was a rite performed for a good crop of Manila hemp; a very important coastal crop. Manila hemp is made from species of wild, seeded banana called *Abacá*. The fibre extracted from the trunk is flexible, durable and resistant to salt water and so was used for fishing nets, ropes and even coarse weavings.

In the afternoon our guide led us around the old part of the city before we had a satisfying meal in a house covered inside and out with blue Dutch tiles called – not surprisingly – the Tile House! The day ended with a walk through the crowds to Garibaldi Square where many groups of mariachi musicians hung around waiting to be hired for an evening's entertainment.

Garibaldi Square, in the centre of the Old City, was re-named in 1910 after Lt. Col. José Garibaldi for his role in the Mexican Revolution.

The following morning we boarded the bus to Teotihuacán.

The San Juan Teotihuacán archaeological ruins lie about sixty kilometres to the north, in the great Valley of Mexico. Called the 'City of the Gods' it was once the largest city in the Americas with about ninety thousand inhabitants. Nobody knows who the first arrivals were; perhaps the Toltec were the first to settle in the valley? The great valley basin of Mexico was very swampy, so channels were cut for canoes. Raised, dense reed beds were thus created as a base for buildings. It's thought that the earliest buildings were built about 200 BC Although early man arrived about 1,500 BC, he mostly farmed the valley and left little trace of his passing.

The two great pyramids of the Moon and Sun were probably started just before the Christian era. The Sun Pyramid was completed in 100 AD and is the larger structure – over two hundred and thirty metres at each side of its base and seventy metres high, of four tiers with a platform on top. The Moon

Pyramid is a similar design to the Sun Pyramid, but much smaller.

The people mysteriously disappeared about 900 AD. The city's influence spread through Middle America; the Maya and later the Aztecs borrowing the decorative motifs and building designs.

Lining the sides of the Avenue of the Dead – which leads to the Moon Pyramid through the length of the city – the sellers of so-called antiquities invited us to buy their wares: woven cloths; crudely carved ivory (?) elephants piled seven high in decreasing size; beads and stone carvings. In the hot sun a seller's wife (?) slept in a wheelbarrow, a cloth over her head. There aren't so many tourists passing by. I hope the sellers make a living. I bought a small obsidian stone, polished shiny black (a good luck piece) for Simon and a small carving of the feathered snake god, Quetzalcoatl, for Mark.

On the way back to Mexico City I stared with horror at the slum-city in the northern suburbs. Tens of hundreds of shacks made clumsily with corrugated iron and bits of wood or cardboard; shacks all squashed together any-old-how. Barefoot beggar children played and fought in the dirt, dogs and cats prowled around sniffing for anything edible. Oh my! I didn't know some people had to live in such squalor.

Our guide hustled us to get the overnight sleeper out of Mexico City. Although the sleeper was comfortable, I was too excited to sleep much. I spent much of the night watching the strange vegetation in the form of giant cacti and scrofulous, unknown plants pass the window as the train crawled along through the arid mountains. I saw a small two-roomed hovel, mud-daubed, about half an hour's train ride from the next sign of habitation, unless there were others up in the hills that I didn't see.

I wonder how people survive in such remote arid locations and why they choose to live there anyway. But even subsistence living in the country must be better than those disease and rat-infested slums outside Mexico City.

Arriving in Oaxaca was like suddenly being transported into Spain – low-level white-washed buildings, streets busy, Indians and Mexicans strolling around. The two predominate Indian groups are the Zapotecas with their beautiful, round, Maya-type faces, and the Mixotecas, who look more like the Red-Indians of North America. I saw some grandmothers with their leathered and very lined faces full of personal history. I would love to have taken a photo, but was too shy to ask and too aware of intrusion into personal privacy to photograph without asking.

The huge indoor market reminded me of the old days in Birmingham Bull Ring. The meat vendors cut the meat into thin slices, or pared it into thin sheets, which they draped over lines like so much washing. These were bought and then cooked on the spot over charcoal burners by the stalls. Add tomatoes, peppers and chillies and lunch is ready.

Some of the cakes and tacos looked good to eat, but they were exposed to the flies, the dust and the dirt of myriads of passers-by, not to mention the traffic outside, and guarded by filthy Indian urchins. We didn't risk buying. We're not used to these bugs.

Indian women carry heavy, cloth bags on their backs, slung by a broad strap from their foreheads, or a basket balanced on top of the head. A child is slung on the back in this manner; the woman puts the child on her back as she bends double, slings a blanket over the child and ties the ends of the blanket in front of her chest and so keeping the kid warm and close and herself hands-free. The women usually also carry bags in the hand and are followed by two or more children in tow. They all walk barefoot through the dirt and muck littering the aisles between the stalls.

Quite a number of the Indians wore their native dress, which is usually a brightly coloured and embroidered tunic-top for the men and a similar blouse for the women. The colour of the women's shawls is also a tribal identification.

Outside the covered market the women sit cross-legged on the hard-packed dirt floor, their goods spread about them, or arranged neatly in piles on a cloth. Their young children sit or sleep near them. Only rarely did I see a male vendor.

Oaxaca has a small zoo exhibiting only animals from Mexico and in particular from the local region. The zoo is sited on a pleasant, tree-covered hillside where birds and agoutis (like a very large hamster) run around freely. I stood many minutes watching a brown, turkey-like bird, whose name was *Penelope* something, dancing in the leaves under some bushes. It bounced each time it put a foot down, as if walking on springs, all the while uttering a soft melodious 'gunk'. Its wings were held out a few inches from its sides and its tail was spread into an umbrella under which ran a single brown chick, peeping as it grabbed any insect disturbed by its parent's feet. When the chick ran out from under its bouncing parent the other identical parent took up the ritual. I can see I'm going to have lots of new names to learn of both fauna and flora.

Back on the bus we crossed the flat isthmus bordered by two mountain ranges on the way from Oaxaca to Tuxla Gutierrez (the capital of Chiapas State). At first, the mountain slopes were covered by those candelabra-shaped cacti, so familiar in any Mexican cowboy film. Some cacti are as big as apple trees and, in places, are the predominant plant. In Tule we stretched our legs to visit the two thousand year old cypress tree guarded within its wire fence.

It seems to me that most places have a spot where people jump to their deaths. The Sumidero Canyon, some one hundred kilometres from Tuxtla, is such a place.

My heart started to pound as I peered over the edge to the tiny strip of river shining two hundred metres below. (Looking down from a great height I still get the urge to step into space – a hang-over from my hang-gliding days.) I visualised the thousand Chiapas Indians pouring over the edge rather than submit to the Spanish rule in the 16th century. Did they flow silently like a stream of lemmings, or, did they shout and grunt like the pouring of the Serengeti Wildebeest into the croc-infested river they had to cross to greener pastures.

As the Indians fell to the River Grijalva rapids, did lovers hold hands all the way down? Did mothers clutch tightly their babies? Did the village priests perform death ceremonies before the leap into the next world? The guide didn't know.

A brief stop at a Mescal factory showed us how the agave cactus (the one that looks like a pineapple top) was grown for eight years before its heart would be cut out, roasted in a conical pit with hot rocks, then removed and crushed in the groove of a big round stone – like our old millstones. A heavy stone wheel rolled along the groove as the eyes-half-closed, head-hanging donkey harnessed to it walked round and round and round. The juice drained into a large vat, then covered with water and left to ferment. Periodically the fibre and foment were separated; the fibre to form fuel for the distillation apparatus, the foment put into another vat to be distilled. From out of the fly-ridden, fusty-looking foment ran clear mescal.

And it tasted sooo gooood.

(Mescal and tequila are the same stuff really, called so in different areas of Mexico, but produced from the same agave cactus.)

The bus climbed up and up and up the Sierra Madres into the clouds spilling from their tops, then down some way to the tiny

Indian town of San Cristobal de Las Casas built at two thousand five hundred metres in the scenic Chiapas range. This town was the antithesis of the clean modern town of Tuxla Gutierrez where we'd stayed last night.

Some of us went on a horse ride along a track into the hills, to see a rather unusual church in the village of Chumla. The horses were skinny ponies. Mine was so narrow at the shoulders I felt that I was sitting on a tilted plank and about to slip off over the horse's head as we went steeply downhill – not so far from the truth as the saddles were carved from a piece of solid wood and only partly covered by a rag of hide. The girth was held in place with bits of string and leather strapping. The stirrup-leathers were about two inches wide and ended in cup-shaped wooden stirrups into which one thrust ones toes. I don't think the saddles had seen any tender-loving-care since the day they left the shop. As for the bridle, that was just a piece of old rope tied around the horse's nose with the other end held by the rider.

We were told that to turn the horse one pulled the rope across its neck and the horse would turn away from the rope.

We all mounted up and set off on the two to three hour ride which passed along main roads, through a village and across the farmed lands of these Indians.

Where a river ran through the valley whole families were gathered, the women in bright blue shawls, to do the wash. The chattering women spread the wet cloth on a flat stone and vigorously scrubbed at it with a bar of soap. The soaped cloth was gathered and rubbed and squeezed and flung against the stone and then rinsed in the river, the suds making foamy islands sailing away. Once suitably clean and rinsed the clothes were spread over nearby bushes or laid out on the grass.

While the women washed, the men lounged around or played with the small children. Quite a picnic air! None of them returned our smiles and greetings and we weren't sure if it was a case of don't stare at us and we won't stare at you, or whether it was genuine hostility at the invasion of the gringos (what the natives call us foreigners) through their place.

Chumla had the strangest little church, no seats or pews inside the simple wooden building. Families gathered in front of their favourite Saint, chosen from the many statues ranged around the walls, and sat cross-legged or knelt on the floor. They lit rows of candles on the floor in front of them, took out a bottle of Sprite or Pepsi which they showed the saint while muttering something and then drank. Someone told me that the bottles were blessed and then drunk to cure illness. One family had even killed a chicken and brought it as an offering. I wondered if they took it away again to eat.

Long pine needles were scattered on some areas of the church floor (I'd seen sackfuls of these needles stacked outside and hadn't imagined what they could be used for). Two men knelt on the floor with small hand-scrapers, scraping off the candle grease and pushing it, together with the needles, into neat rows and didn't at all seem to mind the adults and kids constantly walking through their handiwork.

On pain of death (literally, rumour has it) no photography was allowed inside or outside the church. These Indians still believe that taking photos takes away part of their soul.

Couldn't do much yesterday. I, along with half the group, had the Mexican trots and didn't dare go too far from a loo.

Today we rose at 5 a.m. and breakfasted hurriedly on coffee and toast before our hired bus took us to the public bus station, where we caught the 6 a.m. first-class bus to Palenque.

By the time we'd gone about ten kilometres the bus was crushed full, but still the conductor kept shouting, 'Move back, move back' as he crammed the aisle tighter.

A little girl, whose head just topped my arm-rest, whimpered a bit and then fell asleep, held up by the press of legs around her. Her mother, a buxom Indian in a filthy, apple-green, frilly dress, was clutching her son of about two years old. He was wearing just a grubby yellow T-shirt. She almost sat on my shoulder for most of the way. She dozed, half standing, lolling against the husband, rousing periodically to put breast to child, who removed chewing gum from his mouth before having a suck. And so we were for nearly six hours!

Palenque, discovered in 1952 and liberated from its jungle overgrowth, is a very well-preserved Maya site deep in the tangled forests of Tabasco. Its buildings have beautifully carved stucco ornamentation, delicate bas-reliefs and lengthy hieroglyphic texts. It seemed to me a case of convergent evolution. Many of the carvings were so similar to those I'd seen on Egyptian tombs. The forest clearance had revealed the tomb of the high priest in the Temple of the Inscriptions. On opening his tomb they found his body adorned with an intricately carved jade death mask.

And there was Quetzalcoatl again: the plumed snake god is said to represent joining the heavens (hence the feathers to fly to the sky) to the earth (hence no legs and that's as close as one can get).

The motorised riverboat trip after Palenque made a welcome change to our usual mode of transport, being not so bumpy on suspension or exhaust stinky without and people stinky within.

The four-hour San Pedro river-ride was interrupted by two border-control crossings as we passed from Mexico into Guatemala and then the next day, from Guatemala back into Mexico.

The guards – half the stature of us affluent Americans and English – look so ominous with their dour faces, machine-guns in hands and machetes slung on backs. All a bit of posturing really, like male turkey cocks.

Before they spotted us arriving, we saw them lolling around chatting to their girlfriends, just being ordinary kids. They quickly snapped into action when they saw us, but soon reverted to being human again, once our tour leader had made contact.

The Guatemalan soldiers had built their encampment around a yet-to-be-excavated Maya site and the archaeologist of our group was most dismayed to see their gun emplacement atop a small pyramid. Half a dozen soldiers splashed and fooled in the river, while another dozen or so wielded their machetes to trim the 'lawn' and the flower borders of canna lilies surrounding the stelae. Stelae are upright stone slabs, or columns, standing about one to three metres tall, inscribed with figures and inscriptions from Mayan times.

Our overnight stop at the Jungle Lodge in the Guatemalan town of Flores was a contrast to the civilised hotels that we'd been using. The bunk-beds were made from local branches, a thin straw-stuffed mattress and covered with mosquito netting, hung to make a tent. As Flores is built on an island in Lake Petén Itzá and we had three nights there, some of us got well bitten by mosquitoes.

We found the ruins of Tikal in the tropical rainforest of Guatemala.
Walking through the jungle to the hidden city, there was a sudden tinkle of water from a branch overhead. What on earth!? I looked up, and there was a troop of chattering monkeys grinning down at us with bared teeth and then another trickle of water as a monkey peed on us. So that's what they think of us humans on their patch!

Tikal was a pre-Columbian Maya metropolis discovered in 1848 and can justly be compared with Egyptian and Greek building masterpieces. Its history is written in the hieroglyphs carved onto stelae. Tikal city, located in the fertile uplands, was the capital of a conquest state. It dominated the east-west trade routes across the Yucatán Peninsula and probably traded with Teotihuacán (Mexico) to judge by some artefacts found.

Five great temples and pyramids cover an area of about three square kilometres: initially settled about 600 BC the population grew to an estimated ninety thousand – now that's a lot of people! Even today how many of our towns have a population of over ninety thousand? Think of all the administrative and feeding problems!

Abandoned by its rulers about 890 AD it was totally deserted by a hundred years later and we can only guess why. One of the theories is that the well-water dried up.

All over the Yucatán Peninsula are big holes, called *cenotes* (sink holes caused by the collapse of the roofs of caves to expose the water-table below as rivers or springs).

I was sitting near the top of the tallest pyramid (No 4) looking out over the jungle canopy, when another lady puffed her way up the many steps onto the platform where I sat. I learned that she was travelling alone through South and Central America and hadn't had any problems. She'd come from New Zealand and wound her way to Mexico from Buenos Aires. If she can do it, so can I, I resolved.

I went down to the central mown grass plaza (square) to hug the Giant Kapok (*Ceiba pentandra*), the sacred tree of the Mayas, to ask it what it knew, what I should do? It didn't reply.

From Tikal we'd driven to Belize City, then flown in a small plane the short distance to San Pedro (at the end of the Cays) where we played by the sea, on the sandy beaches and snorkelled in the clear waters, before flying back to Corozal in Belize and crossing again into Mexico.

It took a few days to cross the Yucatán, calling in at Chichén Itzá and Uxmal on our way to Mérida.

The large, well-preserved site of Chichén Itzá shows it developed into a powerful capital and trading centre between the years AD 900-1050. The buildings are of different styles suggesting a diverse population.

Cenotes (sink holes) provided the only source of water in this arid land.

In 1526 along came the Spanish and under the leadership of Francisco Montejo tried to grab what they could. Many battles and retreats later all the natives were gone and the land was converted into a cattle ranch.

In 1588 the Spanish crown issued a land grant.

Then the Americans stepped into the picture and in 1894 the U.S. Consul to the Yucatan, Edward Thompson, bought the now defunct cattle ranch; including Chichén Itzá which he proceeded to explore. During 1904-1910, Edward Thompson dredged the largest cenote, named Cenote Sagrado (Sacred Well) and recovered jade artefacts, pottery and bones and shipped any finds to Harvard Uni.

In 1926 the Mexican government charged him with theft and seized the ranch, but in 1944 the Mexican government changed its mind and declared him not guilty and returned Chichén Itzá to Eddy's heirs who promptly sold the ranch to a tourism pioneer. Such is the complicated inter-weavings of life.

We arrived in Mérida and the end or our trip.

Before we all went our separate ways, Dee (a nurse from San Francisco) and I went to a café on the main boulevard for a last drink. I'd palled up with Dee because we'd often shared a bedroom. We were chatting over the sites and sights of Teotihuacán, Palenque, Tikal, Chichén Itzá, Uxmal, and the lesser known ruins that we'd visited, when there was a screech of car tyres and a loud thump. We looked up just in time to see a man's body fly into the air like a limp rag doll. He went over the car and crashed heavily, on his head, back into the road. Ugh! Someone wasn't looking where they were going!

The police and ambulance soon arrived.

We never knew if he was dead.

Rather spoilt the flavour of the coffee.

My other memory of Mérida is the poor drainage in the hotel – the sink-water takes forever to go down its hole. This is because Mérida is only ten metres above sea level and twelve kilometres from the Gulf of Mexico – not a great gradient. They say that after storms the water takes days to drain away.

We'd been given so much information. I needed to get to a library to read more and consolidate the stories the guides had woven – wishful thinking at the moment.

Parting is so often a sweet sorrow. Addresses have been exchanged with a 'do drop in should you pass by' and 'it's been great to know you'.

The end of the tour is now, (March 16) in Mérida on the Yucatán Peninsula; I shall be sorry to leave the security of the group. It's very easy to let someone else do all the organising.

I don't now find the poverty and squalor as depressing as I did at first, when there was so much contrast with the opulence of my months in the affluent States. It was a wise idea to book myself, when in England, on a tour to explore these countries. It's given me a much clearer idea of what I'm letting myself in for.

It's my last night in a decent hotel. I've spent this morning re-packing my rucksack. It's still way too heavy. I carry the trappings of civilisation and can't bring myself to throw out anything else. I keep telling myself that things like candles, batteries, medicines will get used up eventually. I only have three items of much-washed clothing and I can't jettison my map or book and my sleeping bag is a must.

I'd made tentative plans to travel with Alice through Central America.

I phoned to check that she was still up for it, but she's backed out – that leaves me with the alternatives of travel alone, or go 'home', or travel with Dek.

I phoned him and much to my astonishment he's making plans to join me. Not such a happy thought, and I still don't think he'll show.

Now, my general plan is to go to Isla Mujeres (just off-shore from Cancún).

It's very hot and sweaty here in Mérida. I'll just finish this iced drink before the ice all rapidly melts, then go and check out the trains/buses to Cancún; that will be an exercise in diplomatic relationships as I must decide between 1st or 2nd class seats and whether to book or not to book.

I'll go to Isla Mujeres to mull over whether to continue on or return.

Wishing you well and thanks again for storing all my letters and the information leaflets that I send you.

I hope, one day, to re-read them.

Bron

16. ISLA MUJERES
To Do or Not to Do

March 23rd 1990

Dear Anne,

In my last letter to you I mentioned I hadn't decided whether to get the 1st or 2nd class bus to Cancún. Being the cheap-skate that I am (have to make the money stretch as far as I can) I caught the 2nd class night bus to Cancún and arrived there at 4:15 a.m. Still dark; I hid amongst the bushes on a main road traffic island to sleep – there were too many down 'n' outs sleeping on the floors and wandering around the bus station for me to stay there.

As dawn broke, I rolled up my sleeping bag and hiked a couple of miles north of the town to Puerto Juarez, there to get the ferry across to the Isla Mujeres.

The office selling the ferry tickets was closed when I arrived too early, but only ten minutes to wait. A bearded, skinny lad with a pony tail came up. His sad story was that he'd left his backpack outside the closed office, asking a friendly bobby to keep an eye on it while he went for food. When he returned the pack had gone and so had the copper.

I saw him again, sitting woebegone and full of a cold, in the hostel I where I stayed on the Isla, and heard his story.

He'd spent six months travelling around South America and was on his way back to the States. With his backpack stolen, he'd lost all his memoirs, photos, gifts for family and friends, clothes – everything. He had only the clothes he stood up in, his passport and a plane ticket. He would have to wait until money from the States arrived at the bank in Cancún.

I must take on board what he said and not leave my belongings out of my sight.

The island was named the Island of Women (mujer is the Spanish word for woman) because of the many female fertility figures left there as offerings.

Its shape reminds me of the Protochordate that we studied in sixth form Biology (it's more commonly known as an acorn-worm), whose lineage goes back to the Middle Cambrian: it was

83

on the curriculum as an example of one of those link animals that showed the first characteristics of a neural column along its back.

To my non-biological friends, an unsmoked cigar chewed at one end depicts the shape of the island; about five kilometres long and two kilometres at its widest part, with a small town at the northern end. It's easy enough to hike around, which is how I found this place. The faded, home-made sign on the road pointed to 'Indio's Camping'. Being obedient I turned down the side lane which slid down the cliff and onto the beach.

The sandy beach is only about thirty metres wide and had had restaurants and other now indefinable buildings on it. After the ravages of some hurricane, it looked like a war zone with piles of rocks, gravel and sand haphazardly heaped. A demolished concrete pier jutted out from the broken sea wall. Hurricane Gilbert's handiwork, I was later told.

I poked around in what had once been a restaurant of some twenty-five by ten metres floor area. The square concrete pillars that are still standing in their fractured mortar covering still sport, in places, a faded motif of pineapples and fish. Most of the thick concrete roof has gone and the slabs of the floor are all higgledy-piggledy. Some ten, tiled table tops balance skew-whiff atop their concrete centre-column supports and are surrounded by a plethora of aged, once blue wooden chairs, heaps of nets, ropes, crates, boxes, buoys, floats and other accoutrements of the fisherman's trade.

At one end smoulders a perpetual fire over which the men warm their tortillas and bar-b-q their fish. The tables at that end are covered in a disarray of dirty plates, half eaten food, empty bottles, around which swarm myriads of flies.

Still, the loo sometimes flushed and there was usually water in the taps.

I found myself living with a group of fishermen – David, Gabacho, Wilber, Indio and the two old Peters. Swarthy, moustachioed, and skinny, they all look piratical, except for Indio with his spare tyre hanging over his trouser belt. They seemed to do little in the way of fishing. Granted the weather has been somewhat rough these last few days, with lightning streaking crazily around the skies and the wind pushing the rain into horizontal, penetrating, soaking sheets; weather to encourage one to stay at home.

Yesterday and today have been quite calm, at least here on the leeward side of the island.

I've slung my hammock between two pillars and am making this my home for a week to recuperate from all the group-travel stresses.

David, an American from Alaska, has his tent here. He comes every year and has already been here for two months. The owner, Indio, also speaks English, so I'm not totally surrounded by an incomprehensible lingo. The locals in the group speak their idiomatic Spanish so rapidly that I understand very little, and so it was with some trepidation that I joined three of them to go in their boat to fish or dive – I wasn't quite sure which.

Anne, imagine a heavy wooden boat, about five metres long and powered by an outboard motor, as it slams across the choppy swells to the southern end of the island, where a powerful current from the leeward side pours into the Caribbean Sea and generates piles of waves foaming in every which way. The boat pitches and yaws and slams its prow down so hard that spray soaks us all.

We stopped, thank goodness, and I watched as one man donned flippers, mask and snorkel, grabbed a rope and dropped over the side. With his head under water we slowly towed him along as we quartered the area. Another man sat in the prow and tied a harpoon to a coil of rope. The driver carefully manoeuvred the boat according to the raised hand-signals of the swimmer.

It transpired that we were hunting for a turtle.

After some twenty minutes they gave up.

The swimmer returned his rope to the boat and dived some ten metres to collect a pink, encrusted stone from the ocean bed – which he presented to me – before pouring himself back into the boat. Another fast and exhilarating ride returned us to the fish-restaurant, by which time I was entirely soaked and shivering. The men, kept warm by their activity and consumed rum, laughed good naturedly at me.

(We didn't have turtle soup tonight – barbecued snapper instead.)

Earlier in the day, I'd borrowed David's (not the American) snorkel gear and swum twenty-five metres offshore to try to dive. David is the youngest of the guys (I think), of very dark complexion, bitter-chocolate colour eyes and black, very curly hair. He'd spent time explaining how to use the mask and snorkel, but I hadn't 'got it' as I discovered on my first attempt. I breathed out as I swam down – wrong – and hadn't mastered the technique for blowing water from the mask on surfacing. Perhaps he'll let me borrow his gear again.

Another day: Alaska David (who's down here trying to negotiate fish export deals) and Joe came back from town with air tanks. I joined them for their trip to the coral reef, but I stayed in the boat with the driver while they swam down. We were supposed to watch their bubbles to keep track of their movements, which proved surprisingly difficult in the choppy waters and we lost them. Then the driver spotted David's arm raised amongst the waves, about a hundred meters away. We raced over to pick them up: the idea is for the boat to stay above the divers as there are sharks in these waters!

We got back to shore and there was enough air in one of the tanks for me to have a go. Pottering around beneath three metres of water was a novel experience. I watched orange starfish, about thirty centimetres across, creep amongst the sea grass. I saw a few small silvery fish and a variety of sponges. Now I can't wait to reef dive!

In the evenings we played cards, drank beers and smoked – they their weed and me my ciggies. I became quite friendly with David, the easy-going, curly-black-haired lad who sleeps in his hammock strung across the wasted patio.

Tuesday April 3rd - Left Isla Mujeres

There has been much hustle and bustle these last two days as the nets have been folded and put away, the kitchen has been scoured of its infinite number of cockroaches, new white plastic chairs have appeared and the place no longer looks like 'home'.

Indio grumbles because the electricians and plumbers haven't shown up (same the world over!). I gathered that Indio is having the restaurant restored as the fishing has been so bad for weeks now.

Our last supper was a huge pan of *Pollomote*, a Mexican dish of boiled chicken covered with masses of spicy chocolate sauce and served with rice and the always present tortillas. I contributed a vegetable salad of tomatoes, onions, carrots and a cucumber-like thing with many central seeds and of peppery piquancy. All was washed down with rum-cokes, beers and brandy.

It is with mixed feelings that I bid farewell to my Spanish friends.

Dek hasn't shown up.
Alice has backed out.
So I'm off on my own.

86

From Cancún I caught a bus to Playa del Carmen and stayed at Las Ruinas camp site (quite small and very crowded) on the beach – two nights there, with a day lazing on the sand, then a short bus ride to Akumal, which turned out to be a small, purpose-built holiday resort, quiet but expensive.

I'd headed to Akumal because it is the nearest place I can do a PADI Open Water Dive Course. But, I couldn't afford to stay there and there was no camping anyway; the nearest camp site being five kilometers up the road. OK, I can walk between the two.

I lived for six days at Chemujil, a large and lovely camp site, with shade trees everywhere, a small restaurant and clean toilets.

The five-day diving course was hard work. I had to read and inwardly digest a two hundred and fifty page manual, in the evenings, after days of lectures and practical stuff; like correctly putting on the mask (one has to spit in it first to stop the glass misting up in the cold water) with snorkel, dive tank and regulator while sitting comfortably at the bottom of the resort swimming pool; then, the next day, doing same in the sea – an experience quite different with the waves rocking one to and fro.

We had four dives to do following the leader (dive master) to the coral reefs. I didn't see many fishes, but I was wowed when we went through a narrow cleft between the rocks, filled with a great shoal of tiny silvery fish all glittering and glinting in the sunlight as they whirled about like dry autumn leaves in a breeze.

And how amazing to see all kinds of corals up close.

I managed to get stung by a fire coral and the dive master showed me how to stroke a brain coral and apply whatever I'd stroked off to the stung area. It worked; it must have some sort of neutralising effect.

We were tested at the end of each module and had a final exam.

Now I am the very proud owner of a PADI Open Water Dive Certificate. I can't wait to go under again.

April 10th

Today I moved on to Tulum, further down the east coast of the Yucatán Peninsula.

Tulum is rather special as it was a Maya city (population about one thousand) with a big wall on the landward side and El Castillo (eight metres tall atop a hundred metre high cliff) guarding the seaward approach. They – I've always wondered who, exactly, are 'they'? – think that the castle acted as a light-house marking a break in the barrier reef, opposite a landing cove with a small beach, because Tulum served as a port commanding sea and land trade routes.

By walking, hitching or using a bus when one was around, I got to the site, took my photos and wandered on into the camp site just south of Tulum.

Surprise, surprise, there were Steve and Debbie, the honeymooning couple I'd met at the fish-restaurant on Isla Mujeres. I found them packing up their campervan to go and visit the jungle Maya/Toltec site at Cobá. They kindly invited me along, so I went with them – Cobá is bit difficult to get to without one's own transport. It's a little visited Maya site, inland a few kilometres.

Steve and Debbie are intelligent and well-travelled, so the conversation was about travel experiences and Maya Indians and stele and historical monuments and the cost of food and so on; rather different from my time with the fishermen.

They parked the campervan near the site entrance and I hung Debbie's two-person hammock in a *palapa* – an open-sided wooden structure with a reed-thatched roof.

I slept in Debbie's hammock, a 'proper' one made in Mérida, open weave, tasselled fringes along the sides and a fixed wooden bar at each end and oh sooo comfortable to stretch out in.

In spite of a nearby stagnant pond and a lake across the road, the mosquitoes were conspicuous by their absence.

Rising early the next morning, Debbie persuaded the gate-keeper to let us into the site ahead of opening time – her Spanish is fluent as she was raised for twelve years in Mexico. In the semitropical, dry and thorny jungle I noted: the acacia that had bullhorn thorns in which protective ants live; *Tradescantia* spreading profusely over the ground; begonias with delicate spindly white flowers growing on the forest temple walls. I recognised Maiden-hair fern and something which looked like Hart's Tongue fern in amongst the cacti, palms, scrubby shrubs and trees. A few large *Bromeliads* threw splashes of red against the shining dark-blue of the morning-glories.

We saw various birds flitting, gold or red or yellow or blue, through the trees.

From the top of a small pyramid I spotted a pair of green parakeets and a hawk dashing across the canopy. In the distance, roosting in a treetop was a large bird I can only describe as a huge pink chicken. It had pale pink wings tipped with black and what appeared to be a red cockscomb on its head.

Beautiful butterflies too: iridescent pale-blue, hand-span sized birdwings, smaller ones of black with red or red with black, lime-green with tan stripes, burnt orange and lemon yellow. Ants scurrying along their ant paths patrolled by soldier ants which were twice the size of the workers, and with huge flat-fronted heads and prominent pincer jaws held downwards prodding the ground.

A newly hatched batch of small, black grasshopper nymphs gathered on a leaf and moving in symphony, together then apart, as clouds crossed the sun.

By 11 a.m. it was very hot so we tiredly retraced our steps to find a cool drink in one of the tourist shops.

On the way back from Cobá we stopped at a cenote called the 'Car Wash'! It was an open cave exposing a part of the underground river system that criss-crosses the Yucatán. I don't think people really wash their cars there. Or, perhaps they do?

This cenote looked like an ordinary pond, but the water was so crystal clear that one could see five or seven metres to the bottom. While we were there a group of divers turned up to explore the cavern and caves at the spring end of the pond. I listened to the leader explain what they would do during the dive and wished that I could join in using my newly acquired diving certificate.

Never mind, the swim was very refreshing and a pleasant change after so much sea swimming.

Last night was a very windy night on the beach. I got up early to pack my tent and catch the 7 a.m. bus to Chetumal (a big port town just before the Belize border), where, being Good Friday, the ticket office for the Belize buses was closed. Dam and bother!

I spent a sweaty two hours walking the town to track down the alternative bus service. I eventually got there and found I had to wait four hours for the bus to leave.

What better to do than eat and drink the last of my pesos as I sit writing this letter surrounded by the chatter of the cafeteria customers?

Oh! The Belize bus is getting ready to depart.

Off I go on my next adventure..

Bye for now. *Bron*

17. BELIZE
On Meeting Entrepreneurs

Letter One - April 15th 1990

Dear Anne,

Happy Easter and lots of chocolate bunnies

I hadn't realised it was Easter and so was surprised when I got into Belize and found it shut down for four days; a bad miscalculation. I should've stayed in Mexico longer.

I had hoped to buy maps in Belize City and get more travellers' cheques from the AMEX office. However, I found that nothing, other than a few small back street shops, was open.

No way did I want to hang around Belize City for four nights; too expensive and too much evening time would be spent sitting in my room as I wouldn't dare to walk on my own through the night-streets.

I'd arrived in Belize City late on Friday evening and taken a taxi to an address plucked from my South American Handbook. This old book is proving an invaluable aid, although out-of-date. It's not always correct, hostels have moved or changed use, but it serves to get me in the right direction.

I found a once-nice street of colonial houses, now mostly let, in downtown Belize City. 'Freddy's' was such a place. Run by an elderly couple who had lived there for many years, and, falling on hard times, had had the ground floor converted into bedrooms and a shared bathroom. For thirty-five Belize dollars (BZ$35) I had a clean, quiet room.

(There's about 2 Belize dollars to 1US dollar – I'll leave you to do the conversion to ££s.)

I spent Saturday wandering around the town hunting for gas for my camp stove and other items, all unobtainable because of shops shut.

At the bus station, perusing the bus timetables for buses out of Belize City, I noticed that the nearby Bus Station Hotel had rooms for BZ$26.

It's Easter Sunday and I'm down to my last few bucks until a bank opens on Tuesday. The hotel is not in such a good district (why are bus and train stations always sited in the worst parts of towns?) being in the middle of black shanty town, but I would be on hand to catch an early bus on Tuesday.

To fill up Sunday I found Belize Zoo; a makeshift sort of place with very few animals. (Perhaps they could use an extra pair of hands here?)

In 1983 a film-crew had come to make a documentary about the native animals of the jungle, but what to do with the now half-tame animals when the filming was finished?

A lady helping the film crew kept the seventeen animals and set up the zoo – its aim being to educate the people of Belize with the animals of Belize.

Outside, as I was waiting for a lift down to the main road and hopefully back to Belize City, the most ear-splitting, horrendous noise started up. I can only liken it to a very large and very drunk man being veeery sick in front of a megaphone. I popped back into the zoo and asked, 'What's making that noise?'

'Oh, it's just the black howler monkey declaring its territory.'

'OK, thanks,' said I, having no good idea of what a howler monkey is, and, it seemed, neither did the cage-cleaning lady.

I got a lift back to town in a school bus full of small school kids after their day of animal education. When they learned I was from England the teacher said, 'Children, let's sing a song for our English visitor,' and they sang – you'll never guess – Rudolf the Red-nosed Reindeer!!

Leaving the bus, I walked back across town (holding my nose as I passed by the stinking, black, oily, drainage canals running down the middle of the streets) to Freddy's to collect my gear and relocate to the Bus Station Hotel.

(My meanderings had taken me to the northern fringe of the town where there are posh houses by the sea; thus I leave with a mental picture of Belize City not being composed entirely of Negro's shanty town.)

April 16th

It took three hours for the 'Batty Bus' (yes, that's the name of the bus company!) to get to San Ignacio. I was so happy to get off; relief from usual people-squeeze plus the added fun of a burst tyre and the driver carried no tools on his bus!

I arrived in San Ignacio – near the Guatemala border – in the mid-day heat and found a shady spot on a traffic island, where I sat and leant against a tree trunk, ate ice-cream and drank a large cold cola.

One drinks so much as the sweat is constantly pouring from one's brow and I was glad that I had a head sweat-band. I've developed quite an addiction for colas, not usually Coca-Cola but something pretending to be.

The hotel Maya Lodge was three kilometres down the road. It sounded a pleasant place, but it was full. Pity, it looked good. Well, look on the bright side – I'd saved myself some dollars.

I walked back to town and found a room in the Grand Hotel. Grand!! Ha! Ha! Should've been called the Derelict Hotel! At least the lumpy mattress with springs poking through didn't have any signs of bed-bugs, and the broken window let in a nice breeze, and I'm used to roaches in the bathroom, and smelly toilets, and I get all that for the bargain price of BZ$15! It's a dry place to sleep to the accompaniment of several radios on different stations, creole chatter and traffic noise.

San Ignacio is very sparse on accommodation tonight as there is a small fair down by the riverside packed with happy Belizeans. I went to look. There were two big-wheels and various decrepit roundabouts circling their loads of kids of all ages.

No prizes were awarded on the gun range. Instead, shooting a metal pointer flat made electrical contact and a song blared forth for a few seconds while the gun was re-loaded and the attendant pulled a cord to stand the pointer upright for the next shooter.

Men sat at a betting game. A piece of wooden board was divided into six squares. Each square had a crudely painted symbol: six spots, one large spot, eight crosses, J, or Q, or K. The game owner vigorously shook a cup in which were three die and slammed the cup upside down on the table. The players put money on their favoured square, the cup was lifted and one's money was doubled if the die matched the square's symbol.

Lads strolled around carrying sticks, twice their own height, laden with attached bags of phosphorescently-bright pink or yellow or green candy floss – little puffs of colour in clear plastic bags.

A few stalls were selling second-hand clothes, or jewellery, or odds 'n' sods, and there were the usual stands of food and drinks and that was the fair.

April 17th

Leaving my backpack I set off early, in the morning cool, to walk the sixteen kilometres to Xunantunich – an old Maya ruin partly excavated and almost wholly unrestored. It's sited five kilometres from Benque Viejo del Carmen almost on the Guatemalan border.

I was walking because I'd been told that no buses ran in that direction in the mornings, so I was surprised and somewhat annoyed, but at the same time delighted, when a bus appeared and carried me towards the ruins.

At 9 a.m. I was sitting on a one-car ferry being single-handedly winched across the River Macal by an old weather-worn guy, and then I had to walk the four kilometres along a much rutted and very stony road snaking up and up to the ruins.

The site was on a plateau. The view from the top of El Castillo was superb. This El Castillo – a terraced palace/temple building, height forty metres – is still one of the tallest buildings in Belize. I could see for miles across the jungle to the Guatemala Mountains in the distance.

The clearly depicted moon god, with his rectangle face and bulbous nose, in the astrological frieze was a new character for me to see – a welcome change after seeing so much of Chacmool and Quetzalcoatl in the Yucatán ruins.

Xunantunich-Maya-site-Belize

The rectangular face of the moon god
A bulbous nose close*r*

Xunantunich - Moon God

Having clambered around the ruins and stared enough, I hitched a lift back down the rutted, stony road with a couple of army lads in a pick-up, on weekend leave.

At the main road junction I got off and there downed three bottles of Coke at a kiosk, then, water levels topped up, set off on the trek back to San Ignacio.

After about four kilometres a sign promised, Chaa Creek eight kilometres. I diverted down the side road and was lucky to soon get a lift with a couple of Mexican families heading for the watering hole. Chaa Creek turned out to be an hotel complex of small white, thatched cottages set amongst well-tended gardens in a small part of paradise. I left the Mexicans and headed for the creek. As jungle-covered hills were intersected by sharp valleys, I couldn't see the river until I was almost upon it and then was able to have a cooling swim in the silky, slow-flowing, deep water, to refresh my overheated body – lovely.

I was just getting out when the Mexican families arrived with their ghetto-blaster-radio to shatter my peace. Kids and parents jumped in fully clothed and made much splashing and laughter, while I sat and ate my lunch watched closely by three golden Labradors. They were the nicest looking dogs I've seen to date. Most street dogs are so very skinny and usually have festering sores or ominous bare patches on their skins, with ticks and fleas feeding where they can.

Adjacent to Chaa Creek was the Panti Medicine Trail set up by Dr. Rosita Arvirgo, who, in conjunction with a local, old, Maya medicine man, was cultivating jungle plant species with medicinal properties. She, together with her husband and daughter, had cleared away the jungle and built their home set amidst gardens of herbs and medicinal flowering plants.

Rosita and her husband had graduated in Naturopathy from Chicago University and now she is an important person supplying jungle samples to industry and universities for pharmacological analysis. Their latest project has been to clear a trail for a hundred metres or so through the jungle and label specimen trees.

My knowledge is building. I now know that: gumbo limbo bark is an antidote to poisonwood sap; how to get water from vines; how to flavour my cooking with allspice berries and how to make tea from its leaves. I've collected some leaves but haven't brewed them yet.

If I wasn't on a mission to get to Australia (to see Uncle Reg and Aunty Ev in Perth) this is the sort of place I could live and be useful.

A mix of hiking and hitching got me back to San Ignacio in the late afternoon.

April 18th

Today I moved out of the tatty Grand Hotel to the much more salubrious Maya Mountain Lodge and was invited to join a party setting out for a motorised jaunt around Mountain Pine Ridge. We bumped along miles of logging trails to the Hidden Valley Falls where a spectacular three hundred metre waterfall plunged into the valley far below.

At Hidden Valley Falls, while drinking a ubiquitous coke, I met Dr. Ed Boles and wife. He had almost brought to fruition his life's dream (and what about hers? I thought). They had purchased a piece of land on a mountain spur overlooking the panoramic views of the surrounding valleys and mountains and on which, using local labour, they had built their house and a school room as an environmental field centre. It already had a fair supply of books and equipment.

They called their place Cockscomb Jaguar Reserve and await the first researchers next month – perhaps to work on the very elusive jaguar? (Or, perhaps, I should stay here and help set up the field centre?! I'm sure my biological teaching skills would be welcome.)

We journeyed on to see the Río Frío (Cold River) cave; a huge cavern filled with waterfalls pounding over the rocks. The echoing sound was quite impressive. The water had created a massive stair-cascade of white limestone that poured solidly down a cliff in a sheet-stalactite waterfall – such a pity that it was covered with graffiti.

The pine forest ridge was very different from the jungle only a few hundred metres below. Our last stop was to enjoy a swim in the tumbling pools of the Río On. The rocks were very slippery, so one could easily slide from one level to the next below, and that was fun.

Behind a small waterfall I sat curled up, gazing through the shimmering cascade and wishing that my boys could experience this.

April 19th – A lazy day today

I spent several hours dawdling along the nature trail behind Maya Lodge, watching ants and trying to spot the tagged specimens that some researcher was studying. I got a bit disorientated on the indistinct trail around the Maya ruins and went too far down the wrong side of the hill and had to pant all the way back up and return down the original route.

Back in San Ignacio I came across another entrepreneur, George, in the now dilapidated and almost empty Shangri-La Club. At seventy-six years-old George leases three acres of jungle, upriver, on which he has built his house. He was a highways-engineer in Belize City and has lived here, in San Ignacio, for twenty years.

Over beers, we chatted idly about this and that until it was dark.

Tomorrow I'll be passing through Belmopan, almost in the centre of Belize, so hope to find a post office in this oh-so-young town.
(Belmopan is intended to be the new capital of Belize, but, as yet, has very few scattered buildings.)

My good wishes and fond memories to all.
                    Bron

Dear Anne,

I'm really enjoying travelling alone. One meets such interesting people who're always willing to help a lone woman. I'm also losing track of days and dates, so hope the following isn't too disjointed.

Halfway along the Hummingbird Highway (one of only four main roads from Belize City to the cardinal points of Belize) the bus stopped to let off some passengers at the Blue-Hole National Park entrance. So I got off too.

Only opened in 1986, the Blue-Hole truly lives up to its name. The water is the sort of blue that forms when the dye comes out of new jeans in the wash.

The hole wasn't very big, about ten by fifteen metres across. It was bounded on three sides by steep, approximately ten metre high cliffs trailing their ferns and palms. A zigzag path stepped steeply down the fourth side to a beach. The water welled up from some underground spring, ran along the base of one cliff face and disappeared underground again about twenty metres further along. It was crystal clear and I could easily see the fish that swam over the gravelly bottom shelving down to a depth of some five metres.

According to the information board, it's the light refraction and absorption at this depth that gives the pool its unique blue colour.

Another strange effect, which I'd never seen before, appeared as I was standing in the water: I saw, from the corner of my eye, another person standing near me, armpit deep in the water with his legs lengthened and enlarged, but his chest almost disappeared so that the swimming trunks appeared pulled up to his armpits. (Yeah, go on smile. I had to turn my head away I was grinning so broadly.)

Standing in the water, I put my arms down by my sides and tiddly little arms sprang from my shoulders. Weird! The effects were rather like being in a hall of mirrors at a fun-fair. The water was good to drink too. I rinsed my salt-laden T-shirt and shorts and sat reading in the sun while they dried.

Dressing, I donned pack and picked up bag to hike along the jungle trail to Hangman's cave. The walk took just over an hour and involved some steep step-climbing up and down as the path crossed two ridges. Some steps were hand-hewn into the hillside, the dirt held in place by pegged boards. The steps were very uneven and some of the boards had rotted away, which made climbing quite a challenge. Coming down wasn't much better. Wooden ladders were laid on the ground, often with a tread or two missing and the handrail was not to be trusted either. I heard something large crash away in the jungle – tapir, jaguar?

The jungle here is full of fountaining ferns and wild coconut palms with nuts about the size of ostrich eggs. The nuts are collected for the cottage-industry in the local villages. Small boys are put to work smashing the nuts, the meat of which is then ground up and boiled to extract the oil. The oil has a distinctive flavour and is prized in Belizean cooking. The fibrous shells are very dense and make excellent quality charcoal which, I was told, was used in the gas masks of World War II.

Tonight I've erected my home-made mosquito-netting tent in a big glade so that I can lie and watch and wonder at the myriads of fire-flies unzipping the dark like so many tiny shooting stars, flowering into sparks and dying after a few seconds. Only the males flash and the number and duration of the flashes are species specific so that the correct female is courted.

The cicadas too are deafening at the moment with all the thousands of males trying to outdo each other to attract a female. They look like a squat locust and make a buzz-noise like a grasshopper.

Nearby is a cave, big and deep and spooky with bats and fat stalagmites. I can see the water, but shall have to work out how to get at it tomorrow, when there is light.

The next morning, I got to the cave-water down some slippery, rough-hewn steps. The river flowing through was deliciously warm in the cool of the morning. Great for skinny dipping; which I did!

Packed up, I set off along the road to walk the sweaty twenty kilometres to find the house of Rod and Bambi – names I'd been given *en route*. Because of the heat and my load I had to dawdle along, which gave me time to enjoy the beautiful Maya Mountains and the few villages with their thatched, stilted, wooden houses scattered up the slopes.

(The higher up the hill the house, the more important the person occupying it.)

I stopped at a small shack-shop for three Fantas and was sitting at the roadside downing them with cheese and crackers when the woman came out from her shop/house to fill her bucket, I supposed, from the pump across the road. She suddenly changed course, approached me and asked, 'Would you like a tamale?' (A tamale is made from ground maize flour mixed with water into a dough and wrapped around a meat or sweet filling. A maize leaf or piece of banana leaf is wrapped around the filled roll, tied with vine and the whole steamed.)

I peered into her bucket and there, on a plate, was a freshly steamed, corn-husk wrapped tamale; and I'd thought she was so unsmiling and unfriendly when I was in her shop. The tamale was sweet and stodgy and very filling. (That'll keep me going for a while! I thought.)

Again the bus went sailing past, packed with people, the roof piled high with boxes and baskets and animals. Just as I set off to follow it, Rod approached me on the road. I recognised his blue and white Ford Bronco that I'd been told to look out for. I waved him down and introduced myself. He squeezed me-and-pack into the cab, turned around and took me the last few miles to his house.

A brief visit turned into an overnight stop.
Bambi was pleased to see a new face and took time to show me around and explain her plans to set up a pottery shop using the coloured clays that she'd dug from the surrounding hills. She didn't know much about potting and I wasn't much help, but she was full of ideas for washing the clay and where to build a kiln.

A new day dawned and I hung around with Bambi as the bus wouldn't pass until lunchtime. Finishing my book, and a few heavy rain-showers later, I got fidgety and moved out.

I walked the road winding up and up through the mountains. Another sudden heavy shower found me sheltering under a banana tree.

A young man stopped to let my soaked-self get into the back of his pick-up. He gave me a large piece of plastic to wrap around my shoulders. We bumped for several kilometres along the muddy track until we arrived at his village. He invited me in for coffee and told me about his venture to make money.

He and his parents had bought a thousand acres of valley which he is starting to clear for planting citrus trees. He showed me the nursery at the back of his house and explained how he uses sour-orange stock (which grows wild around here) onto which he grafts sweet-orange buds. He also germinates the pips and had about fifteen hundred young trees in various stages of growth, from a few centimetres to about one meter high, awaiting their transplantation.

He showed me maps of his valley and told me about the caves that they'd found, and that had given him the idea of building a few cave-houses for the tourists.

He hasn't actually bought the land yet. The government rents out land – I've heard quoted 50 cents per acre – then if the tenants show that the land will be worked they are given the option to buy, at a low figure, with the rental deducted.

Although Belize is a backward country (relatively speaking) it has a lot of entrepreneurs.

Walking along the road again, once again an over-loaded bus passed me by and, being Sunday, the next one wouldn't until the afternoon. So . . . thumb out.

My next lift was with a British jeep taking three muscular army lads from Holdfast Camp (near Spanish Lookout) south to a rendezvous along the Southern Highway to meet a supply jeep coming north from Rideau Camp (near Punta Gorda).

(My luck's in! Couldn't be better! Now I can swop jeeps and get a lift all the way to Punta Gorda to get a ferry to Guatemala.)

I was expecting the Southern Highway to be a good and paved road, as are the Northern and Western Highways, so was surprised when we turned off onto a hard-packed dirt road that swathed south through the jungle. I sat in the open back and watched as the ribbon of road changed through all the shades of red, from sand to burnt sienna to deep ochre. With the jungle greens on each side it was very spectacular.

We jolted along at 60kmph (they were late) disregarding water-filled potholes. I was soon covered in fine orange dust and mud splashes as I bounced and banged about on the metal 'seat' – the wheel arch.

They realised that the rendezvous had been passed, so, about turn and back to the shop and two houses by the bridge that is the village of Kendal. The jeep stopped in the orange mud. The soldiers leapt out to buy cakes and find out what was what. There was no sign their mate. They were wondering what to do, when another truck pulled up and its driver told us that the jeep from Punta Gorda had a flat tyre and was stopped at Mile 29.

Our jeep wouldn't start, but somehow, by engaging reverse, the driver got the engine to fire then crashed the gears forward and we were off again on the bucking bronco ride. It was just getting dark when we found the stricken jeep with its woebegone driver, a fresh-faced lad who looked no more than nineteen, but later conversation suggested that he was in his early twenties.

He'd spent the last hour and a half trying to loosen two bolts on the wheel, but couldn't shift them – and his spare was flat too. As Billy sat in the mud jacking up his jeep, my beefy boys banged the spanner and jumped hard on it and worked loose the recalcitrant nuts. Then my soldiers transferred their spare wheel to him and his supplies to their jeep.

(The supplies turned out to be boxes of infra-red and other night-time observation equipment; about £60,000 worth.)

The transfer done, I joined Billy in his cab for the gentler ride to Punta Gorda.

The bridges over the creeks were planked affairs; vertical planks stretching from bank to bank connected by horizontal planks nailed to them. On top of those, were nailed more vertical planks for the driver to drive along – very carefully. These bridges often wash away in the rains but are easily replaced.

Five hours had passed since I was picked up on the Hummingbird Highway until Billy dropped me in Punta Gorda. Being very hungry, I immediately went to a restaurant. By the time I'd eaten, the hotels in town (all three of them) were closed. I went back to the restaurant where a couple of men were still dining to ask them where they were staying.

I went with them to their hotel, which wasn't in my book, but that too was shut.

In the end I dossed down on the back porch amongst the builder's rubble and the gardener's junk. Two young puppies played catch-me and tumble-me with their mother until the wee small hours. One kept curling up in the crook of my knees – a hot water bottle I didn't need.

To fill time, I left Punta Gorda yesterday and hitched a ride to San Pedro, sixty kilometres south. My objective was a Ketchi Indian village where Nancy (a twenty-three year old Peace Corps girl I'd met a while back) was spending two years teaching English at their school. She lived in a mud-floored, thatch-roofed, wooden hut and was already quite proficient in the Indian's language.

I watched her teach a class of six-year-olds how to treat a book: her project was to set up a library. The children learned to recognise the difference between pictures and words and how to turn the pages correctly.

The teaching and books were all in English. I was impressed by the kids' good behaviour and how Nancy coped against the background of noise from the classes on either side, where the children were chanting numbers or words at full volume.

About one thousand people live in this village.

Wells had been sunk by other Peace Corps workers – the water was brought up by hand-pumps and that's the drinking water, washing and laundry are still done in the river.

Did you ever apply to do VSO (Voluntary Service Overseas)? I did.

When I left school, and didn't know what to do next in life, I filled out the pages of forms and got the references from my teachers. I was accepted for interview and had to go to London.

I remember a panel of three quizzed me and things were seemingly good until I was asked, 'Suppose we sent you to Africa and there was an altercation with the next village, how would you react?' Being the most apolitical animal around and really having no view on the matter, I tried to be clever and brightly said, 'Oh. I'd help them to fight or whatever they wanted to do.'

Wrong answer! I could see by their faces I'd put my foot in it, big-time.

Well, maybe I didn't really want to spend two years in a mud hut!

On leaving Nancy's village I took a side trip to the Labatoan Ruins, before continuing my seven kilometre walk down the road to the junction with the Southern Highway, where I waved down another patrolling jeep to take me back to Punta Gorda.

April 25th – _Finally leaving Belize_

To get the 2 p.m. ferry across the Gulf of Honduras to Puerto Barrios in Guatemala, I first had to line up at 8 a.m. to get the ticket from the ferry office.

Next to find the lady who could change Belize Dollars to Quetzals, and then to the police station to get an exit stamp in my passport; that was a very long wait because one man was dealing with about sixty people.

The two and a half hour boat ride whisked us across the calm bay waters and then more fun at another border crossing began.

As we clambered from the ferry everyone handed their passport or papers to a dark-skinned guy in a white shirt and beige trousers. He passed the pile on to the comely black woman dressed in green T-shirt and black slacks standing at his side. She stuffed everything into an old, black leather bag and marched off, speedily disappearing between the shacks of storage sheds and repair shops.

'Help!' I muttered to the fish, '"Never let your passport out of your sight" say all the books.'

The ferry passengers moved down the pier and between the sheds to follow the disappeared woman. I went with them. They seemed to know the ropes.

As we rounded a corner I saw an untidy queue forming at the customs' shed, which was just an open-fronted stall. Two guys stood behind the trestle table, one opening travel bags and the other taking money. After a cursory pat on my backpack and a quick look into my handbag, two quetzals (Q2 about 50p) were demanded and I was through; but where-o-where has my passport gone?

Nothing for it but to join the flow of passengers.

We walked about four hundred metres along a disused railway track running along the sea front and then turning in between two rows of ramshackle houses. At the end, around another corner, the passenger group was spilling out from a very small room – standing-room only. Inside was a door which periodically opened as the woman in green came out to shout a name and that person went into the office.

The crowd lessened, leaving the Americans and Brits until last.

It became apparent that more money was changing hands when the Americans were relieved of Q25 each (about £6).

(I had become familiar with the fact that Americans and Australians, and sometimes New Zealanders, had to go to embassies and buy entrance visas – something to do with tit-for-tat between governments. On a British passport one had immunity from all that – secret smug smile.)

I was getting worried as I seemed to be the only person without a passport. My turn came at last and in I went. There was my passport on the desk, with my tourist visa poking out. Q25 was demanded. I didn't have Q25 – truly.

All my Spanish instantly fled my head and the only words that registered were twenty-five. I said that I didn't need a visa with a British passport. He insisted that I pay Q25 – a lot of rubbish really as I know that tourist cards are free. I waved Q4 at the man and said that I had no more money until I went to a Bank. He shrugged, gave me my documents and waved me away.

Now at last I'm in Guatemala. I've found a small hotel, had a meal in the market, bought my bus ticket to Guatemala City for tomorrow and am all ready for a few weeks in my next country.

I still do not trust the post to wing my letters on their way. So I'm entrusting this letter and a film (not developed) to a guy who's returning to UK and has promised to post them there.

It might be a while before I can write again.
Love to all.
Bron

18. GUATEMALA
Settling into the Old Capital

(Panajachel and Lake Atitlán at 1,562msl (metres above sea level, or, as they say in Spanish: metros sobre el nivel del mar - msnm)

(Q = quetzal. Q4.25 = $1US = 60 pence. The money is named after the Resplendent Quetzal – the national bird)

Letter One - April 27th 1990

Dear Anne,

A new country to find my way around in.

New money to figure out.

A new Spanish accent to fathom out.

I wonder what adventures lie in store for me?

Six hours on the express bus should give you some idea of the distance from coast to capital, except that many roads were badly pot-holed and travel only walking pace. But, all in all, not a bad ride for £2.50 (20Q) and I was in Guatemala City.

It's a long time since I've been in a big city and – phew!! – choking on the clouds of oily black exhausts. It's so busy here, people and buses and every other kind of 4 or 2-wheeled vehicle swarm along the streets.

I found a nice hotel – for a change – and booked in for a couple of nights at Q35 per night. It was recommended by the helpful Tourist Office at the bus station where I also got good maps and bus information.

Thursday was frittered away exploring the city. The Amex Office had no letters for me, perhaps because I'm here too soon.

I spent a quiet hour in the University Botanical Gardens, which were very neat and tidy, and then on to the Zoo – never seen so many cafés and eating stalls in such a small space. The zoo had several species of big cat, one elephant, one hippo, a few deer, half-a-dozen species of bird and three kinds of monkey. It didn't take long to go round.

The Zoo Museum was a joke: a slashed and balding tiger skin; about ten glass-boxes with shrivelled snakes; a few pickled, unidentifiable specimens all of which had badly handwritten labels, including some with the name crossed out and changed, and some boxes of jumbled, broken skulls and skeletons which probably came from animals that had died in the Zoo.

The Museum of Natural History wasn't much better – a new, big, concrete and glass building. Only one room was open and contained some seven, glass display cases containing stuffed birds, which looked as though the cat had played with them for a long time before they died of fright. The two small cases of animals were no improvement – what tatty moth-eaten specimens, some with the stuffing coming out!

Shame on your museum Guatemala City!

However, the Anthropological Museum was as a museum should be, housing the finds from the many Maya sites around the country.

I went to the British Embassy this morning and they strongly advised against doing the volcano climb that I had planned to do when I get to Atitlán. They gave me a list of areas to be avoided, because the guerilla activity has hotted up again, and advised that I stay in the main towns.

The hundred and forty something kilometre bus ride to Panajachel took four hours and cost Q5 (about 65p). It passed through Sololá where a colourful market was in full swing: the native peoples (indígenas) in Guatemala wear distinctive, very colourful dress, different in each village. The cloth is hand woven, sometimes using prehispanic techniques and at others using the foot-operated loom introduced by the Spanish. I hope I shall be able to discretely photograph some of the different styles – I'm very embarrassed to poke my camera in someone's face, and they obviously don't like it; well, would you?

My room in Panajachel (a village a hundred and forty kilometres to the west of Guatemala City and sited on the shore of Lake Atitlán) is very basic – just a wire-sprung bed with a thin mattress, rickety table and unstable chair. The stone, wash sinks and loos are outside – but all is clean.

As I wandered around the village this afternoon, I stopped to chat to an elfin-like lad, perhaps in his late twenties. On his head was a black fedora festooned with tiny bicycles (of one to three centimetres), motorbikes and their ilk, all crafted from a single piece of wire. I watched while he took a long piece of thin wire and, using sharp-nosed pliers, bent the wire around to create a beautifully proportioned facsimile of a bicycle, including a basket on the front and a carrier on the back.

He had taught himself to do this during his four years of travel around South America. He sold his products to pay for his board and lodgings. What a neat idea! He also earned his keep playing the flute, mime-dancing and selling astrological birth-sign charts – he did a good trade with those in Chile and Peru.

He speaks seven languages and is living across the Lake whilst the tendons in his swollen knee heal, 'Too much cycling around Central America,' he said. He pays Q40 (about £5) a *month* for his room! Hmmm; it must be *very* minimal!

April 28th

I awoke late and had to hurry to catch the 8.45 a.m. ferry to cross the lake to the village of Santiago Atitlán.

Lake Atitlán (surface area, a hundred and twenty-five kilometres squared and three hundred and seventy-nine metres deep) is a volcanic caldera or Crater Lake. Plantations of coffee, avocado, maize and onions grow round about. Some say it's the most beautiful lake in the world and I'm sure that it would be if I could see it properly. The volcanoes and mountains are veiled in clouds and heat haze. I can barely see across the lake, but I can imagine that on a sharp, bright day, with the mountains reflected in the still blue water, it would indeed be a magnificent sight.

The ferry is late. I needn't have hurried. Ahh, here it comes. Better gather my stuff. Oh, jeepers creepers!! Where are my walking boots?

Not here!!

Did one of the waiting passengers take them?
Where? Where are they??

Damn! I left them behind the door in the hostel dorm (which I'd had to myself).

Help!!

(I'd put several hundred dollars wrapped in plastic under the insoles in my boots.)

I just had time to rush back, heart in mouth, in full panic mode.

'Hope no-one's been in to 'do' the room. It's OK. There they are. What a relief. Stupid me!'

As the ferry leaves Panajachel, I can just make out the road I came down yesterday. It drops five hundred metres in seven kilometres, no wonder the bus took it so slowly, winding down the mountain sides that plunge steeply into the lake.

The dress worn by the women in Santiago Atitlán is of sombre blue and green hues woven in personalised stripe patterns.

Quite dull compared with the brilliant reds woven and worn by the Indians of Panajachel.

In the market I bought five small tomatoes and paid the woman Q1. She laughed and said something to the other women, all seated cross-legged on the floor, which caused a ripple of giggles. I guessed that I'd given her far too much.

The men wear trousers, cut just below the knee, of white linen with red or purple vertical stripes. A few have carefully embroidered birds – in all the combinations of colours imaginable – in a wide band at the base of the trouser legs. I just couldn't resist buying a piece of this beautiful cloth (one trouser leg in fact) which I shall send to you to go into my storage box. The lady took two to three months to embroider it and after some bargaining sold it to me for Q60. The trousers are held up by a bright, woven sash and the ensemble is topped by a coloured shirt and jacket.

I hiked some way out from the village to fill time before getting the return bus. I passed men and boys coming back from the fields carrying their hoes. They were very friendly bidding me, 'Buenos días', but I could almost hear them thinking, Why is this gringa (foreigner) walking here?

Every scrap of land between the trees and rocks is immaculately hoed into rows of fine sandy soil in which corn (our sweet corn) is planted. The steep hillsides are terraced into terraces of maybe three metres wide and four metres long.

Coffee bushes bear masses of star-shaped white flowers along the stems and the air is filled with their perfume which smells like the winter-flowering jasmine that we buy in pots. (Remember the huge one the Head used to have during the winter months in her study? We could smell it all along the corridors.)

The prickly pear cacti are in bloom.

Growing wild along a stream bank I saw masses of Easter Lilies perfuming the air.

I got off the bus at San Lucas Tomilán, a real village not geared-up at all for tourists. As I sat by the lake shore, a file of some forty soldiers appeared walking along the opposite shore. They came around the lake and stopped just beyond me. They were in full battle camouflage, with black-streaked faces.

I'd better stop writing now and go and find a bed for this night.

April 30th

I found a clean bedroom in the one and only 'posada' (guest house) in San Lucas Tomilán. Even though I tossed and turned on the hard and straw palliasse, I thought it good value at Q10 for the night.

The morning was bright after the thunderstorms rolling around last night. The Sunday market was in full swing. I waded through a breast-high sea of people, feeling like someone from another planet as they stared up at me and my big backpack. I bought my goodies (as usual, bananas, tomatoes, cheese and bread) for the day's repast and set off to enjoy a care-free day.

I got on the first bus that stopped. It was going to a place called Cocales, which I couldn't find on the map, but the bus was going south so that was OK.

From the bus I spotted a sign to the village of Pululi, which gave me a bearing. Not far beyond, the bus terminated at a busy main crossroads. (Cocales turned out to be the name of a big coffee factory there. I haven't seen much coffee, just fields of sugar cane.)

Another bus took me to Santa Lucia, a bustling town with a dirty market around the bus depot where dozens of multi-coloured buses were churning out their dense, black and suffocating exhaust fumes. I wandered around for a while. (The way they stare at me; I don't think these people have ever seen a gringa.)

I caught another bus that took me all the way into Guatemala City, to get yet another bus to Antigua.

Antigua at last!

As I got off the bus I was pounced on by a horde of kids all wanting to lead me to the 'best hotel'. Then the conductor tried to charge me for putting my backpack on the roof and getting it down again. I was most indignant – the locals don't get charged. I gave him a mouthful of swearwords in English and stalked off followed by the kids. I had to be rude to them too before they gave up. (I hope I'll eventually get used to this or learn to deal with the situation in a more delicate way. When I arrive in a new place I like to sit in a café with my trusty South American Handbook, with its maps and 'where to stay' information, and sort out my own lodgings.)

There wasn't much to do here today. The museums were closed. The shops are all much of a muchness: food, tourist stuff, hardware. The market is big and occupied me for an hour.

As the clouds sat low on the mountains there was no point in trying to walk up the volcano today. Volcán Agua (3,760msl) on the edge of the town is still active. It's every child's drawing of a volcano – a typical cone shape, standing alone. It would be quite something to see fumes rising from the earth.

May 1ˢᵗ - Labour Day and a Bank Holiday

I went for a wonderful horse ride this morning. My Q40 bought a two-hour ride and a hearty breakfast in a posh hotel.

Walking through Antigua to the hotel breakfast, about fifty metres of a street had a central carpet of pine-needles on which the locals were busily arranging yellow and white chrysanthemum flower heads in patterns of crosses, candles, doves, JHC, within a border of more yellow and white flowers. It was so pretty, but I didn't have my camera. A lady told me that there would be a procession. By the time we came back from the horse ride it was all over and the street swept clean.

The horses were sprightly, healthy animals wearing Western saddles with lots of leather strapping, two girths and cumbersome stirrups with solid leather toe-capping.

We took a dirt road up and up the mountain through a couple of little villages where coffee and fruit trees seemed to be the main crops; avocado trees, as big as our mature horse chestnut trees, provided shade over the houses.

The cumbersome saddles were surprisingly comfortable; after all cowboys sit in them all day long. My horse responded readily to neck-rein signals and we had a few stretches of steady cantering.

The views back across the town of Antigua were enlightening – the track up the volcano is longer than I'd thought and I was told that there are soldiers guarding the route, and camped on the top, waiting to shoot guerillas on sight.

After the ride I went to the market to buy pasta and veg for a meal tonight and stopped to try a soup at one of the lunch kitchens there; the chicken soup with rice and veg and a side plate of tortillas was excellent value for Q1.50 – I'll have to stop eating in restaurants and do this more often!

I'm writing this letter in my bedroom while dinner cooks. I have to use ordinary petrol in my multi-fuel camping stove. The petrol – sorry 'gas' – burns very dirty and keeps clogging the jet with soot. It's very slow compared to the Coleman fuel – which I can't get here, and no surprise there. I've bought half pound of tomatoes, half pound of French beans, squash, melon, bananas, bread and pasta. I have enough for two dinners and two breakfasts for the grand total of 80p!

May 4th
		Woooo!! My head's buzzing after being talked at, in Spanish, for the last three and a half hours. I've signed on at a Spanish Language School.

Over several weeks the various teachers imparted much information about Antigua. I've gathered up the bits and pieces and summarize it below.

Antigua Guatemala (Ancient Guatemala) the capital of Guatemala has been re-sited three times! The first was founded on the site of a Maya city on July 25, 1524.

After several Indian uprisings, the capital was moved to a more suitable site in the Valley of Alotenango on November 22, 1527. The new city was destroyed on September 11, 1541 by a devastating lahar (a flow of mud and rocks) from the nearby Volcán de Agua.

As a result, the colonial authorities decided to move the capital once more to a site five miles away in the Panchoy Valley, where, on March 10, 1543, the Spanish conquistadors founded present-day Antigua.

For more than two hundred years Antigua served as the seat of the military government of a large region that included almost all of present-day Central America and Chiapas – which today is the southernmost State of Mexico.

In 1566 King Felipe II of Spain gave it the title of 'Muy Noble y Muy Leal' (Very Noble and Very Loyal).

On September 29, 1717, an earthquake (estimated magnitude 7.4) hit Antigua and destroyed over three thousand buildings. Much of the city's architecture was ruined.

The damage the earthquake did to the city made authorities consider moving the capital to another place; but they rebuilt it on the same site. (Can you believe that?)

It wasn't until the Santa Marta earthquake (1773) destroyed much of the town, that the Spanish crown, in 1776, ordered the removal of the capital to a safer location in the Valley of the Shrine, where Guatemala City (the modern capital of Guatemala) now stands. The old badly damaged city was thereafter referred to as La Antigua Guatemala (Old Guatemala.)

I've found a very pleasant room, about the size of a garage for a mini car, which used to be the maid's. It's on the flat-roof at the top of a house in the centre of town. With the door open, I wake up to views across the roofs to the mountains beyond.

The three-storey house is of old colonial architecture style, with the rooms around a dim and dank central courtyard. From the courtyard I climb the outside stairs to get to the flat-roof where there is a mirror image of my room on the other side.

An old bed-ridden man lives there. One day he called me in and, being friendly, I went to see what he wanted. Mistake!! What he wanted, I wasn't going to give. I'd shaken his skinny hand and he wouldn't let go. Shan't go there again!

The owner is a buxom grandmotherly type, who chats away nineteen-to-the-dozen, so at least I can practise my listening skills. I have free use of her kitchen and bathroom; both are downstairs, primitive and dark.

To do laundry is quite a palaver. In the courtyard there is a very large, rectangular stone tub which is filled with cold water. Built onto the side is another tub, within which is fixed a corrugated, stone washboard sloping down. One puts one's garment on the washboard, uses the plastic pot to scoop water from the tub over said garment until it is well wetted. (Plugs don't exist; however, a sock stuffed into the drain hole suffices.) Next, with the bar of soap, soft and blue (one could choose pink or green), one soaps the garment, then rub-a-dub-dub until it is satisfactorily clean. More pots of water are flung onto garment to rinse away the dirt and soap. Wring out garment and hang it up. Start next item. No wonder doing the family wash takes all day!

I have a front door key so that I can come and go as I please. Luxury!

You have probably heard that most language schools place their students with a family, but as this includes three meals a day (which I don't need) and the inevitable gaggle of kids (which make studying difficult), I choose to do my own thing – as ever. If I get a yen for my mother-tongue I only have to walk to a certain café where all the gringos meet.

I do so hope that the piece of bird-embroidered trouser-leg gets to you.

Once again I've asked a bird of passage from the States to post my small parcel from there on her return.

If anyone back home should care to drop me a line I would welcome news.

My latest address: c/o Amex in Guatemala City is enclosed. I keep on hoping for a reply from son/s, but I wait in vain. They've probably moved on and don't get my letters, postcards and small gifts.

Until the next epistle, saludos (cheers)
Bron

GUATEMALA
Into the Dangerous North

Letter Two- May 17th 1990 – Antigua

Dear Anne,

It's quite a challenge, being a student again, being told what to do and having homework.

I've been studying hard for the last two weeks; an arduous effort after so many months of not thinking a lot. After four hours of intense morning concentration (8 a.m. 'til noon), I reel back to my room and collapse, mentally stuffed, for the two-hour respite before my afternoon class at a different school.

My teacher at the 'Escuela de Español Dynámica' (Dynamic Spanish School) is a lad of 24 years, studying engineering at Guatemala University in the afternoons. I like his style. He explains the grammar to me so succinctly and very clearly – all in Spanish – and tells me such interesting facts about life in Guatemala: last week an early morning bus on its way from here to Guatemala City was driven off the road and fell two hundred metres into the valley gorge. Thirty-eight people were killed. (We later learned that the bus driver had been 'celebrating' the previous night and was still very drunk when he reported to drive his bus in the morning.)

These single-decker buses crowd three people onto small bench seats designed for two. It's very uncomfortable with just one bum-cheek perched on the edge of an aisle seat and no knee room for my long legs. One has to cling tight to the back-rail of the seat in front for counterbalance as the bus swerves round hairpin bends. The aisle gets stuffed with people as the conductor shouts, 'Move back, move back' and more and more people are squeezed in at each stop. I counted about seventy to eighty passengers on one such bus meant for thirty-two.

The narrow overhead racks get filled with bags, boxes, baskets and livestock – usually chickens. What won't stuff into the rack goes on the floor between legs. The bigger baggage goes on the roof and is tied down – tough if it's raining.

I've not seen a fat conductor and when I consider what they do, no surprise there: the conductor has to push (hard) to get between the many standing passengers to collect the fares, he gets off the bus each time it stops to shout the destination and solicit yet more passengers. If a bundle from the roof has to be unloaded, it's a quick dash to the rear of the bus and up the ladder to throw down the bundle. How he remembers whose is what I don't know. Off goes the bus whilst the conductor is swinging down the ladder and in through the rear door.

At certain points along the way are traffic-control police.

As we approach such a check point the conductor yells, 'Get down, get down, por favor' and all the standing passengers squat, or bend, or somehow lower themselves to seat height until the bus is safely past.

My teacher said that passing a driving-test is a matter of slipping money to the examiner. He was amazed at our stringent drink and drive laws. They do have a driving licence which, for a car, costs Q8 and lasts for one year. Very, very few people have car insurance.

He showed me his I.D. papers. These papers have to be carried at all times and bear: one's full name; parents' names; place of birth and of residence; colour of hair, eyes, skin; height; thumb print; education; place of work; get stamped every time he votes (compulsory) and any misdemeanour warranting contact with authority is noted.

I'll give you some more facts and figures to throw around the staff coffee-table, but bear in mind it's all come from the opinion of one young man. Just think – you're all millionaires compared to these poor people!

Schooling is supposed to be compulsory: children of seven years go to Junior School until they are twelve, Secondary School is from thirteen to fifteen and sixteen to eighteen is Tertiary education. Then University – if one passes the exams and can afford the fees. All are supposed to stay in school until they are eighteen, but of the nine million people in Guatemala about 60% are illiterate.

In the State schools the teachers earn 225-825 quetzals per month.

The privately run schools pay their teachers about Q525 per month.

(Remember: about Q4 = 60p.)

The average wage is Q40 per month. My room costs Q70 per week. The bus fare from Antigua to Guatemala City is Q1.20.

Inflation has been rampant, at 200% during the last six months, but seems to be slowing. A few months ago tortillas (the staple 'bread' of the people) were 4 for 5 cents, now they cost 5 cents each.

Wages, of course, have stood still – if they get paid at all. Some school teachers haven't been paid for months.

A cleaning maid might earn Q3.50 for an eight-hour day – that's less than $1US!

As you can see, most people are grindingly poor.

May 19th to 21st

A weekend break to Volcán Tajumulco (at 4,219msl it's Guatemala's highest peak and the highest volcano in Central America).

There's a café just off the main square renowned as a 'gringo hangout'. On its large notice board filled with all sorts of notices: rooms to rent; books for exchange; Spanish Schools; car-shares; travelling companions wanted; I spotted a note from one Stuart seeking companion/s to hike volcanoes. He turned out to be a tall, stringy American of some twenty-six years from New Mexico. He was taking a break from his Spanish schooling and his girlfriend. We got along well enough in the café and after a couple of meetings arranged a trip to climb Volcán Tajumulco.

Saturday morning dawned bright and clear as we made our way to the bus terminal. Stuart had booked us tickets on a cross-country Greyhound bus to travel in comfort the five hours west towards the Mexican border (Q10 return). What a change to sit in comfortable reclining seats!

A bus change at Quetzaltenango put us back on a 'chicken bus' to San Marcos. I had an aisle seat and sat young Orlando on my knee. He did his best to converse, but with our limited Spanish we didn't get much further than answers to his, 'Where you come from? How long you here?' and so on. He said he was eleven years old and lived in San Pedro, a village next to San Marcos.

We too got off at San Pedro to find our recommended hotel. Mid-afternoon found us settled into our room in the hotel at the edge of town, with views of the mountains. It was clean and quiet. Clean loo too and hot shower – what more could a body want? (I was a bit dubious about sharing a twin-bed room, but needn't have worried; Stuart was quite the gentleman.)

We set off to explore San Pedro and San Marcos and buy provisions for the next two days. We got stared at a lot, but everyone was very polite and friendly. Not another gringo in sight. The landlord later told us that recently the news had been full of stories of babies and small children being kidnapped for body parts, or adoption, and sold to rich Americans – that's what they thought we had come for, but once they realised we were just tourists they were fine with us.

Our plan was to get a bus very early on the Sunday morning, go up Volcán Tajumulco and return the same day.

Leaving our unnecessary baggage at the hotel, 5.30 a.m. on Sunday morning found us in the market looking for a bus to San Sebastian – a village at the foot of Volcán Tacumulco. But . . . the bus had left at 5 a.m. and there wasn't another until 9.30 or 10 a.m. So we returned to the hotel to get breakfast and then wandered back to the market, which, by then, had filled with people and traffic.

Our bus eventually left at 11.30 a.m. and wound and ground its slow way over the mountain ranges. The views were fantabulous and Stuart was very busy taking photos, much to the amusement of the locals who wanted to know what on earth he was photographing.

We were deep into guerilla country. The rocks along the roadside were daubed with various symbols: a white star on a green square; a white horse in a blue circle; a red cockerel on a white background; various letters of the different political parties. (The symbols are for those who cannot read.)

The village of San Sebastian is at about 3,000msl, so the vegetation had changed significantly; it reminded me of a cultivated Lake District. The village at the foot of the volcano is small: a few dozen houses; the inevitable shack-shop with one of this and two of that on its almost bare shelves; a church; cottage industries selling tortillas, or baskets, or repairing tools.

There were scatterings of houses and terraced cultivation stretching as far as the eye could see.

Determining the track, we set off hoping to find somewhere to stay the night. We followed a man and his little grand-daughter along a narrow winding footpath that led up between the fields to his house. There was always someone around, hoeing in a field or going somewhere, so it was easy to ask for directions; we were seeking somewhere to sleep. One group suggested we tried the school. They said the teacher spoke English and would know of possible bed-space. But the school was locked and teacher gone to San Marcos and wouldn't be back until the next day.

No matter, there was another school two ridges away.

We followed our new guide up and down and up and down; phew, puff-puff, these slopes are steep! It was a good job we had a guide. There were so many footpaths criss-crossing the fields that alone our journey would have been tediously long.

The next school was locked too, but the women at their wash in the raised stone sinks told us the teacher would come at 3 p.m.

The teacher arrived. He was a dynamic young man somewhere in his thirties, with a mouthful of gold-filled and gold-decorated teeth; obviously one up from the silver stars and edgings that we'd seen on the teeth of other locals. It transpired that he comes three afternoons a week (from another village seven kilometres away) to teach adult literacy classes. We watched as six women with their offspring and four men were taught the alphabet and simple pertinent words; like carrot, field, market and money.

These people are the poorest of peasants. They have a small patch of land by their houses on which they grow maize and potatoes for the family. We later learnt that the peasants don't eat the cabbages and carrots growing in the fields we'd passed – all that goes to market.

The babies were suckled and the older children ran in and out of the room.

The desks were crudely made from planks of wood. Not a book, not picture to be seen. Other locals stood around the door and peered in; I think most of the attraction was us – word had spread and the strangers in their midst just had to be seen.

After the class, Stuart asked if he could take a photo of the teacher and the man we had been talking to. The teacher asked Stuart to wait and disappeared to return ten minutes later on horseback, together with his pal also on horseback. They all lined up and were almost in place when the two horses had a fight. I think they were stallions and didn't like being next to one another. Everyone scattered at speed as grey horse screamed and kicked brown horse hard. Order was restored and Stuart took his photos; then he was given addresses and made to promise to send prints.

We returned to the problem of where to sleep.

A discussion was held between the men and then we were told it would be far too cold to sleep in the schoolroom: the walls don't meet the roof; we had no covers and no-one had blankets to spare. In the end it was decided that we should go to Jesus's house as he has a big room.

And so onward and upward following Jesus.

Jesus – our new guide, who didn't speak a word of English – had volunteered a bed in his house: two rooms each about six by three metres; walls of wattle and daub (a woven lattice of strips of wood and sticks, tied to a framework and daubed with a mud-mix of soil and animal dung); roof of sods. There was one small shuttered window and a stable-door. It was very dark inside. On the mud-packed floor were a few crudely made items of furniture. Dogs, kids and chickens wandered in and out.

When we arrived, Jesus's wife was already busy preparing supper on the wood-burning stove.

We, as the honoured guests, were sat at an oilcloth covered table and given a plate, a cup and a fork each. The rest of the family (five children ranging from four to nine years old) sat around the stove on the hard-packed dirt floor watching us closely. The children all had deep brown eyes, uncombed matted black hair and grubby red cheeks. They ran around shoeless.

(I find it difficult to guess ages here. The children look years younger than they are, while people in their twenties look to be nearer forty. On the way up, I was proudly shown a new infant that I'd thought to be a month old, to be told that it was four months.)

Maize (corn) tamales and potatoes were put in front of us, which, together with one scrambled egg between us, was our meal. We were given a cup of sweet flavoured water which I thought was weak herb tea – wrong, it was coffee!

Not knowing the protocol, we weren't sure how much to eat, so we ate about half of the potatoes and tamales and said we were full. I passed the plate back to the mother. She tipped the food onto the warm stove. Many eager young hands grabbed and rapidly consumed the lot. The mother then used a corn husk to wipe off the table and stove.

The only lamp was a flat whisky bottle half filled with diesel and with the rag-wick emerging from a hole in the bottle cap.

Supper finished, lamp lit, we all sat around the stove, not quite knowing what to do once our limited supply of Spanish was exhausted. It was only 8 p.m., but we thought we ought to suggest bed. It was obviously the correct thing to do. At once everyone jumped up and we all trooped into the bedroom where three double beds and a cot were pressed against the walls. We all watched as the mother unlocked a cupboard, took out a pair of clean pillowslips from a plastic bag and exchanged them for the pillowslips on the bed we were to use.

Under the scrutiny of several pairs of eyes, Stuart and I took off our boots and got under the coarse grey blankets – no sheets. Then everyone else got into their beds. (They do literally live in their clothes, the only concession for bed being to take off hat and boots.)

The mattresses were straw-filled and lay on boards; all very hard and scratchy and rustling. I dozed on and off, but kept imagining that I felt things crawling up my trouser legs. Next morning, no bites so no bed bugs.

Arising in the pre-dawn twilight, we set off with Jesus to continue our volcano climb. Jesus left us and we continued alone up the final three hundred metres to the summit. I've never been so high and found breathing in the rarefied air very laborious – I felt my heart would jump out of my throat. Stuart had to keep waiting for me while I stood and puffed and wheezed. About two hundred metres from the top we stashed our packs, not that we were carrying very much, and finished the climb unencumbered.

I thought the struggle up well worth it for the out-of-this-world panoramic views. Luckily the day was dry and skies blue so that we looked down on the surrounding mountains with drifts of smoky clouds in their valleys. A cloud boiled up on the far side of our volcano as the sun-warmed air met cold valley air.

On the lower slopes, the short grass was starred with the white waxy flowers of some alpine adapted plant; somewhat resembling a primrose. One fuchsia clung to its crack in a rock face.

The summit was bleak, with jumbles of boulders, scree and gritty lava. The crater walls had fallen in in several places; we didn't go down.

Descending was relatively easy and I was able to keep up with Stuart. We didn't see any guerillas, which was just as well as we had omitted to obtain the required written permission; which we should have got at San Marcos – not that we knew that then.

I should like to return in the clear winter months, with camera to capture the silver-gold sunset, the kind friendly people and the strange flowers.

Back in Antigua, my school had an afternoon discussion group on the Guatemalan Civil War – which started back in the '60s.

As you know, I have very little interest in politics (I've never voted in my life) but here, seeing the guerillas marching around in full battle dress, I find I do want to know more.

I summarize: Guatemala held democratic elections in '44 and '51; the U.S. of A backed a military coup in '54 and so began a series of conservative military dictatorships.

The fight was between the government and the leftist rebel groups, mainly supported by the Maya and Ladino peasants.

In 1966 the first forced 'disappearances' were begun by the government security forces removing the opposition.

In 1970 the Institutional Democratic Party took office and the repressions increased.

During the '80s the Guatemalan military assumed almost absolute governmental power, infiltrating and eliminating its enemies at all political, social and intellectual levels, implementing a 'scorched earth' policy. Indigenous villages to the north of the country were sometimes totally annihilated.

It took the assassination of Stanley Rother, a missionary from Oklahoma, in 1981 for the world to become aware of happenings in Guatemala. Also in that year Rigoberta Menchú fled into exile in Mexico. (As a member of the guerilla Army of the Poor, Rigoberta's father had campaigned against human rights' violations. When he died, after barbaric torture, in 1980 during the burning of the Spanish Embassy, Rigoberta continued vociferously in the campaign.)

In Mexico in 1982 she dictated a book of her life, which was translated into five other languages and opened the eyes of the world to the atrocities going on in Guatemala.

In '82-'83, during the dictatorship of Efraín Ríos Montt, 1,400 Ixil Mayans 'disappeared'.

By 1990 tens of thousands had 'disappeared'.

And Stuart and I knew very little of all this when we set out to climb the volcano.

May 28th

Last week I successfully extended my tourist card until July 24th, because I now have a job teaching English Conversation in a private English Language School here in Antigua. I've sat in on the classes that I'm to teach. The current teacher is very dynamic; I'll have a hard job to follow her act.

I have six, separate, hourly classes, for which I get paid the princely sum of approximately 50p an hour. The students are mostly young teenagers with a few adults mixed in. My gosh! Was I tired after that first class?!

Also, I now have my first private student for an hour in the evening, but as his English is already very good, I mostly listen while he chats. I charge him the equivalent of £1 per hour, which helps towards paying my board and lodging.

I had to buy some more clothes – one can't keep on appearing in the same pair of trousers and one of two skirts.

In Guatemala City I found the 'Ropa Americana' selling second-hand clothes imported from the States. I rummaged through piles and piles of clothes all dumped into separate bins: bins for skirts, for blouses, for dresses, for handbags, for trousers, for scarves and so on and so on. There was men's stuff as well – in a separate room!

I found and bought an excellent quality skirt, two dresses, a sweater and two tops for the huge sum of Q15 (approx. £2.00).

So what with my Spanish learning classes and my English teaching classes my days are pretty full.

One gets bits of news of Europe from the travellers. I did hear of the winter gales and wondered about the state of my house. I phoned Ian (the chap who's acting as my attorney) at the end of March, but he had heard nothing.

And you tell me that Marion is off to teach in Colombia. If you get her address please forward it to me. Maybe I will get to see her on my way south. Pipers Corner won't be the same without her to stir things up!

By the way, how're things with the new Head now? Has she settled in?

I send again my postal address c/o American Express in Guatemala City.

I trust all is well with you, as it is with me.
Lots of love to my very special friend.
Bron

GUATEMALA
Being A Teacher Again

Letter Three - June 9th 1990

Hola, (hello) my good teacher friend Anne,

¿Cómo estás? (How are you?) – My Spanish is progressing by leaps and bounds – not! (Notice the strange way they have of putting question marks and exclamation marks upside-down at the beginning of questions and exclamations.)

By now you'll be returned from the school trip to Oberammergau. I'm sure you had a good time and kept a tight rein on your forty small charges. Perhaps if you have time you will write to me of some of their escapades.

By the way, I heard that a pile of mail Ian sent to me at the end of April has gone missing, so if you know of anyone who has written to me, my apologies for not replying.

After two months of living on my own, I went to try living with a Guatemalan family at the other end of town.

In late May I left my nice roof-top abode which, in fact, had become almost like solitary confinement. I couldn't talk much to my landlady – not her fault.

My new landlady has two children of two and seven years and two other Spanish language students living here. We all share this single-storey stone dwelling up a dirt road on the edge of town. Meals are included – that too will be a change for me. We call her house-mother. She is a good cook and provides us with masses of pasta, potatoes, bread, tortillas and rice. I think I'm putting on weight with all this sitting around studying Spanish.

I thought you might like to hear about the English exam held in the private school where I teach and just compare it with what we do at Pipers:

After six months at the Modern American English School my class of twelve to thirteen years-old had finished Book 1.They came after regular school to an extra English class of one hour, four days a week. I found it a difficult class. They didn't want to be there – after all, they'd been at school all day!

The oral exam.

In the courtyard of the school (which had been a Spanish colonial house) had been placed a table and two chairs at the front; the parents and invited guests were arranged along one side; three teachers had their desks on another. The giggling and whispering in a corner classroom hushed as Patty (the Head teacher) rose to address the parents. Patty is a well-built lady: dynamic, effervescent, a theatrical sort of person (ideal characteristics for a good teacher) and always immaculately dressed.

A local lady, Patty conceived the idea of an English Conversation School, which, within a few years, has grown to nearly two hundred students.

The exam started: two children emerged from a classroom and strolled around the courtyard talking to each other (in English) – I was told that their conversations were unrehearsed as they didn't know who would be paired with whom.

After a few minutes they stopped in front of the parents, introduced themselves, then turned to the table and two chairs where they sat and fired questions and answers at each other for about five minutes.

Patty then called them to stand in front of the teachers, where they were subjected to another question and answer session between pupil and teacher. The questions were not easy and long answers were expected – 'Tell me all about your home.' 'What did you do last weekend?'

The children were all dressed in their Sunday best: polished shoes; combed hair; all spic 'n' span for the occasion. Some of the little girls were very nervous with pink faces and fidgety hands and shuffling from one foot to the other, but they rarely faltered in their replies, determinedly completing what they had started to say.

The boys, as usual, were more blasé.

The children were expected to correct each other's mistakes during their conversation. Some remembered to do so.

The whole exercise took about ten to fifteen minutes per couple and then each couple was soundly praised by Patty and clapped by the parents.

As a finale, the whole class stood in a line and sang a song while performing simple dance movements, which incorporated each child presenting a single long-stemmed rose to its parents.

It was a most impressive performance, totally in English using present and past verb tenses.

Why don't you have a word with the foreign language teachers and see if they could do something similar?

Happy teaching.
Hugs for you.
Bron

GUATEMALA
A Weekend Trip to San Lucas & it's Volcanoes

Letter Four - June 9th 1990

Dear Anne,

Life's not all grist to the mill of mental enlightenment: we can nourish the soul too. I do that by getting into the country and so was very happy to join a trip being run by a local hiking group.

It was still the dark dead of night at 3.45 a.m. when I left my lodgings to walk through the town, deserted except for a drunk crouched in a doorway crying and loudly bewailing his woes.

I met my two young friends Sven and Andy (from my Spanish School) at the house of Marcus Julio. (MJ is a member of the Guatemala City Andinista Club – a club whose members spend their free hours climbing mountains. He had invited us tourists to join one of their outings.)

Off we set to catch the first bus out of Antigua, collecting MJ's fourteen year old nephew (a chubby lad who always seemed to be eating) on the way. Even at that early hour the bus soon filled; mostly with ladies carrying their over-full, round, woven-cane baskets and armfuls of flowers to take to the City for the Saturday morning market.

We got off the bus at a major intersection on the outskirts of the City, to wait, in the dawning light, amongst the hustle and bustle of early workers, for a hired bus to collect us. After half-an-hour it arrived, nearly filled with other Club members of varying ages and states of fitness. When I saw the other ladies and a child of about ten years, I knew that I wouldn't be the last up the volcano.

To get to our destination village at the foot of the volcano, we went the long way round because the roads were better: ha, ha, the journey still took three hours. We paused for a few minutes at Cocales (I've changed buses there before) to buy breakfast from the roadside vendors. One could get tamales, fruit, coffee and bottles of sodas sold from amongst the sweets and chewing gum. I tried a concoction of boiled French beans fried in an eggy batter and dumped on two tortillas and served on a maize leaf. For Q1 it was very tasty and filling.

At San Lucas we hung around for nearly an hour, while the leaders sorted out the permit, necessary for us to climb the volcano, with the police.

(The locals looked very poor after the relative affluence of Antigua folk. And there was so much litter everywhere, and skeletal dogs scavenging and fighting for rotting scraps.)

At 9.30 a.m., we trooped off through the village and straggled up through the coffee plantations. We met families coming down loaded with fire-wood. The men carried machetes and sometimes wood. The women and children were well loaded with their bundles of neatly stacked sticks and small branches all tied together in bundles and then all the bundles bound as one big one and slung by a band round the forehead. They looked like stick-stacks with legs.

Beyond the coffee (which grows best at 2,000-3,000 msnm) the trail narrowed to a footpath which wound up through woods before emerging into maize fields. Most of the mountain sides have been cleared and planted with maize interspersed with scrubby peach trees bearing small green fruits. The fields are worked on a communal system; 'all hands to the hoe', so to speak.

After four hours of steady walking, we stopped for lunch. I stretched out on a fallen trunk and slept.

The plan had been to leave our gear hidden in the brush-wood, go quickly up and down Volcán Tolimán, camp the night in the wood and then 'do' Volcán Atitlán the next morning. But . . . (and isn't there always a but?), there was no trail up Volcán Tolimán!

The leaders energetically hacked through the head-high undergrowth, while we balanced as best as we could on the almost vertical mountain side waiting for them to clear a trail. After half an hour of strenuous slashing, they decided the task was impossible to complete before dark, so about turn and we slid back down through the scrub and maize.

Retrieving our gear, we continued up Volcán Atitlán (3,573msl) to make camp at the upper edge of the woods. (Without the leaders, my friends and I would never have found the trail into the woods as the start of it had been wiped out by the newly cleared land now planted with maize.)

Most of the group had tents – some very old. Some folk rigged a large plastic sheet and crawled under that, using another piece of plastic as both ground-sheet and cover over themselves.

I had been given a small tent all to myself – a great honour.

Marcus Julio cleared his patch of ground and dug a surrounding irrigation channel using his machete and hands. Amazingly, he managed to get a fire going with the damp wood before the rain started.

By 6.30 p.m. it was quite dark. A superb thunder-storm developed; the thunder crashed immediately overhead and rolled around the volcano tops. The lightning fleetingly illuminated the forest and the rain poured.

Within minutes of crawling into my sleeping bag my hips were soaked – I was lying in a puddle. The tent leaked so much I could actually feel the rain spraying my face through the fabric. I manoeuvred myself onto the lumps between the puddles and managed to doze a little until we were aroused at 3 a.m.

The rain had almost stopped. It took nearly an hour to gather together all the intrepid Andinistas (hikers). Not so easy in the dark. Cries of, 'Where's my torch?', 'Has anyone seen my other boot?' rang around the camp. Most of the intrepid Andinistas were wet to the bone. Sleeping bags were hung, dripping, from trees to await our return.

4 a.m. and off we filed, following torches through the pitch-dark wood. The trail was very narrow, very steep and very peaty. We had to climb on all-fours in some places to cope with the slippery mud slope. No voices, just the sound of laboured breathing. We still hadn't cleared the trees before dawn broke: a very red sun stained the storm clouds amassed in banks of red and gold and glimpsed occasionally through the trees. It would have been a wonderful sunrise to watch, but by the time we emerged above the tree-line the sun was well up and the beauty gone.

Another hour of stepping on and over stones varying in size from ostrich eggs to ball bearings: I patted myself on my back when I reached the top. (I forget my geology but I guess the stones were basalt – lava of some sort, black and dark-reddish and very friable.) The clouds swirled around; one minute we were enveloped in mist and visibility down to fifty metres and the next it was clear with great views across the mountains.

The volcano crater was off to one side of the summit, about two hundred and fifty metres across and fifty metres deep – so said our intrepid leader. It was just a mass of bare stones and rocks, neither very interesting nor spectacular.

Returning down was fun too. Slipping and sliding, often on the bum, through the woods; well, the fit ones did, some of us were more cautious. From the camp site down, the path through the maize was now scarcely recognisable. The rain had carved a channel half a metre deep and a third of a metre wide in some places. It looked like the aftermath of an earthquake.

Back in San Lucas by noon there was plenty of time for a swim in the lake; then lunch of chicken and rice at a café. Our bus was supposed to leave at 3 p.m. but it was 5 p.m. before the last of the straggling intrepid Andinistas arrived.

A very pleasant weekend – even though I scarcely understood the Spanish spoken.

July 22nd

Chiquimula (pronounced Chee-kee-moo-lah) last stop in Guatemala. Phew!! I'd forgotten how it feels to be so sweaty-hot: nights in Antigua are cold enough for three blankets, but just four hours to the North-East, a sheet will be too much tonight.

You'll remember that I'd got my PADI Open Water certificate in the Yucatán and haven't dived since, so I was very excited when I saw on the gringo café notice board a notice about a SCUBA dive tour bus that would be travelling to South America: the first half to Panama and then to continue on through Venezuela, Brazil, Chile, Patagonia and finish at Buenos Aires in Argentina. The whole trip would take four months and most likely the composition of the group would be constantly changing.

As far as Panama, the bus would be stopping at dive sites in Honduras, Nicaragua, Costa Rica and Panama for divers to get certified – the aim being for everyone to get up to Dive Master.

I left the café thinking, What a great opportunity, to travel in company, get certified and see some great beaches.

On asking around I discovered that this venture was an annual happening. Seb and his converted, yellow school bus appeared in Antigua regularly.

Now I have to think – I've just renewed my visa and am happy enough in my job, so perhaps I could join the trip next time around. Not to be. Seb, the leader, had spent the last four years doing the rounds of Central America and had had enough.

This would be the last trip!
Snap decision to be made.
It's now or never.
It's too good, and cheap, an opportunity to be missed.

There was a meeting last Sunday at the café where Seb (an Argentinian, a big man with a shock of black hair and a thick bushy beard, a gentle giant and quietly spoken) introduced himself and explained the plan to those interested.

Money was taken, but I didn't have any with me, and names written on a list; mine, somehow, didn't actually get included. Twenty seven people declared an interest and most of those put 'their money where their mouth is'.

The meeting went on. Seb said twenty-seven were too many for one bus; a new plan was hatched. One group would go on the yellow school bus to the nearest bit of the Caribbean coast. Then they would spend about a week walking south along the coast for about a hundred kilometres. Meanwhile, Seb would return to Guatemala City, buy another bus, get it converted and come back to Antigua by Thursday, or Sunday at the latest, to collect the left-behind people.

After the meeting we were taken to see the yellow school bus from the States. All the seats had been removed and replaced by benches; the floor had been boarded over; trap-doors accessed the storage space below and there were other modifications to accommodate fifteen or so prospective SCUBA divers.

On Monday I went into the City and dashed around obtaining enough money for the first half of the trip. The next few days were spent writing letters to friends and relatives and saying goodbyes to the friends I'd made in Antigua. Patty (the Head of the Conversation School) was not best pleased – at least I'd given her a week's grace to make other arrangements for my classes.

By Thursday there was no sign of any bus or the other remaining travellers. I spent Friday and Saturday wandering round and round Antigua looking for the bus. I'd put notices in all the likely spots – nothing.

What should I do?

Forget it?

But I was all psyched up to travel.

After a sleepless night worrying over events, I decided to at least have a go at trying to catch up with the group that had left.

The trouble was I didn't really know where they'd gone. I had a vague notion: La Ceiba and Roatán (somewhere on the Bay Islands off Honduras) had been mentioned.

And how difficult will it be to spot a distinctive, canary-yellow school bus?

I was apprehensive as I loaded up my backpack. It must be at least forty-five kilograms – again, with all the warm-weather clothes people have given me for the nether regions of South America (I'd sent all my thermal wear on to New Zealand). And I have a bag full of books and all my Spanish notes, reasoning that there'd be plenty of time on the bus to read and weight wouldn't be a problem.

I've also broken my toe again (the one next to the big toe) by being over-vigorous doing kick exercises in my small bedroom and have been limping and walking awkwardly for the last three days; now the muscles in my leg ache.

Then, when I was packing, I noticed that I'd lost my expensive, slim-line, super-light-weight torch, must have left it at that camp. I have another, just ordinary, and they're easy enough to buy.

Of more concern, I don't have my spare reading glasses any more. I can only think that I lost them in the night camp on Volcán Atitlán. Damn and bother! Bother and damn!

So . . . what with being annoyed at my carelessness, limping, over-loaded and sad to leave Antigua for I know not what, I didn't set off in the best of moods this morning.

It feels strange and a little frightening to be setting out, alone, into the unknown again.

Sitting on the bus to Guatemala City I chatted to my fellow passenger, a man of seventy-two years, who had tried to swim the English Channel back in the 50s! One never knows whom one will sit next to!

In the City, I was lucky with the bus connection to Chiquimula and I arrived here (at Chiquimula) at 1.30 p.m. just as my next bus was starting to leave. Wait a mo' though; that bus would put me at Copan (where the border crossing to Honduras is) in the dark and there's nowhere to sleep-over at the frontier. I let it go and found a hotel, dumped my gear and thankfully changed out of my long trousers and hiking boots.

I spent the afternoon wandering around this market town, saying, 'Goodbye', 'Goodbye' and 'Hello', 'Hello', to small groups of little kids who wanted to practice their few words of English. My blond hair – which is nearly all silver-grey now – does mark me out as a gringa. Perhaps I ought to dye it black!

I was sitting in the market square when a pretty little eight-year-old girl came over and shyly chatted.

After she'd wandered off, a dirty and odoriferous old man lurched over and sat down and proclaimed his love and would I marry him? Boring, boring. His teeth, the few that were left, were disgusting: nicotine yellowed; old food between them; and the smell emanating from him (a mixture of urine and beer and nicotine) defies description. I took off rapidly.

I bought a load of veg in the market and boiled them in my room on my trusty stove, which, together with two boiled eggs, I ate sitting on the tiled floor because that's the coolest place.

I'll leave you now to go and experience confined group living – if I ever find the yellow school bus! (I'd had no idea that there'd be yellow school buses all over the place. Apparently, when the school buses come to the end of their useful life in the States, they are sold off to the developing countries.

I've seen so many old American cars too. You'll remember the super-long and fin-tailed cars the bovver-boys looked so cool in, in the films of the 50s, well, most of them are here now; rusty and tatty but still working.)

We should be in Panama in early September, so I'll give you the Amex postal address there and hope to read your news then.

Lots of love from your intrepid, travelling, crazy-lady friend.

Bron

19. HONDURAS
Beaches, Botanics & Coppers

July 24th 1990

Dear Anne,

I didn't hear my watch alarm. I never do unless I'm already awake. It was 5.30 a.m., should I rush to get the 6 a.m. bus or hang around until 9 a.m.?

I rushed.

I'm going to find my way to La Ceiba and get a boat across to the island of Roatán. Wish me a gentle journey.

The bus left Chiquimula (in Guatemala) and snaked up and up over range upon range of dragon's-teeth-mountains clad in green haze. The one-room houses, scattered along the roadside, were roughly built from wood planks, the cracks filled with a reddish mud, under palm-thatched roofs.

The passengers all piled out at El Florido, the frontier which had just a couple of wooden sheds and the inevitable stalls selling food and drinks of tooth-rotting sweetness.

At the border it cost 5Q to get my exit stamp and then walk a hundred metres down the road (trying to avoid the money changers waving their wads of grubby notes at one and crying, 'Change money, change money,' or, 'Dollar, change dollar') to the Honduras border and pay 5 lempira to get my entry stamp. Easy!

(The Lempira is equivalent to the Quetzal so I shan't have to confuse myself with the maths.)

Five of us travellers with rucksacks piled into the open back of a pick-up truck for the twelve kilometre, slow, jolting climb up a dirt track to Copán village and just beyond it to the Copán ruins. I dumped my load – hiding it in the bushes off the track – and spent two hours wandering around.

I took the nature trail through the jungle and was sitting on the wall of a Mayan ball court eating my breakfast of cake and fresh pineapple, when a small foxy animal came out of the jungle and approached to within about two metres and eyed me, a strange object on his patch, then took off to re-appear at the top of a wall on my other side. When he saw that my head had turned and was still watching him, he took fright and dashed off. He was a bit larger than a big cat, and to judge by the reddish brown colour and the long and very bushy tail, he must have been a fox. One so rarely sees animals in the jungle; it's nice to know they do exist.

The stelae were the most elaborately carved that I've seen, and the carvings on all the steps going up the main pyramid were different too.

I was carefully stepping on the broken stones around the top of another edifice when a heady, honeysuckle scent filled my nostrils and there, just below me, was a tree covered in small, white, hydrangea-like flowers shimmering with hundreds of brimstone-yellow butterflies: some white hairstreaks and dark-coloured birdwing types were in the mix too.

Back at the roadside, I was picked up by a ramshackle mini-bus and sat for an uncomfortable two hours on a hard seat. The bus stopped frequently to pick-up and drop-off its passengers.

I had another bus change at La Entrada for the three hour journey to the large, horrible city of San Pedro Sula. With the radio blaring in one ear (all these buses have constant out-of-tune radios blasting out) and a man trying to talk to me in the other and a small boy in front who shouted and talked to himself the entire time (I think he was a bit retarded as his sounds weren't words), I was very glad when we arrived.

I found a cheap doss-house, then went out to eat before falling asleep on the grubby sheet-less bed (I am so glad I carry my sheet sleeping bag) amongst the cockroaches and the strong smell of mice. I slept for ten hours. The hotelier, if I can call him that, had lent me his creaking electric fan to lull me to uneasy slumbers.

Moving along and two buses later, I arrived at Tela late this morning and found my usual doss-house. Three rooms upstairs had been condemned and only the ground floor rooms were used, but the old manager was pleasant enough. I talked with another old, wrinkled-faced guy who's been coming here for thirty years.

I had thought that Honduras would be cheaper than Guatemala; so far, I think things here are about a third more expensive.

Tomorrow I'm going to have a lazy day on the beach before moving on to La Ceiba and then across the water to Roatán where I shall continue to search for the SCUBA dive bus – or at least its occupants.

My beach day dawned brightly with the promise of another hot day as I got up at 6.30 a.m. to walk a few kilometres along this whitish, firm sand beach lined with coconut palms and the occasional glimpse of the wooden, shanty shacks of the Caribbean.

A thin grey horse, pulling a heavy, crudely made wooden cart with big car-tyre wheels and loaded with wife and daughter, suddenly emerged from a dirt track. Driven by his little, skinny-man driver he was turned along the edge of the sea. The horse put his nose into the water and stopped while he tasted the salt. (His reaction reminded me of my dog after he'd licked a lemon.) The horse shook his head, flapped his ears, squinted his eyes, licked his lips and dipped his head for another unbelievable taste. Perhaps he just craved the salt. The performance went on for several minutes; the horse snuffling at the sea and his driver futilely clucking and jiggling the reins while the wheels sank lower and lower into the wet sand. Eventually the man got his trousers wet when he got down to turn the horse.

I walked as far as I could along the beach, passing what had once been a restaurant but now only served the sea. On the way back I swam in the almost waveless, warm, shallow sea. When I walked into my hotel the proprietor said with concern, 'What's happened to your back?' I looked like a cartoon character with measles: dozens of tiny, red pinpricks sitting in the centres of rosy haloes – the breakfast legacy of sand-flies (minuscule little flies about two millimetres long) that had been helping themselves unbeknownst to me. At least their bites aren't too itchy – yet.

Later, I called in to see Brigirt and Gerty (German and Austrian girls I'd met before). The heavens opened as we chatted and the houses disappeared under a deluge. The cloud-burst only lasted about half-an-hour before stopping completely.

It now being too dull for a beach day, we girls decided to walk to Lancetilla, a botanical garden and research centre some five kilometres from Tela. We eventually found our way there along cart-track back roads and spent a slow couple of hours wandering around the grounds. (The bamboo tunnel was most impressive: a hundred metre sandy track, over-arched by bamboos up to twenty metres high with stems the thickness of men's thighs – a truly majestic grass.)

The Lancetilla Experimental Station was founded by the United Fruit Company (UFC) in 1926. The initial purpose of the station was to test the adaptability of selected exotic fruit trees for Central America and thereby diversify the crop plantings throughout the region.

By 1960, over a thousand varieties of plants, from every continent and with varied economic importance, had been established in Lancetilla.

Of particular interest were: the African Keppel Fruit, which acts as an internal body deodorant; the Miracle Fruit, which alters your taste buds and causes all food to taste sweet; the Strychnine and Ackee fruits, which are poisonous when green and edible when red-ripe and the pods split open. The African oil palm (*Elaeis guineensis*) proved highly successful and now there are over twenty-five thousand hectares of this palm planted in Central America; the extracted oil is used as lard.

Numerous timber plantations were established from 1948-52: *Eucaluptus deglupta*, initially tested at Lancetilla, is now widespread throughout Costa Rica. Other promising timber hardwoods, such as Teak and Mahogany, are being tested.

The UFC ceded the station to the Honduran Government in 1974. Later, the experimental station was transferred to the Honduran Forestry Development Corporation and the garden managed as a tourist attraction.

The National Orchid Collection is held here: the original collection being the work of the botanists Dr. Wilson Popenoe et al.

All this colour and flowers and fruits and foliage bring in the birds. Over two hundred species have been identified including trogons, motmots, oropendulas, parrots and toucans, and a few rare ones such as the Central American Curassow. (I'm not going to try to describe these strangely named birds – perhaps a discovery project for your students?)

We hitched a lift back into Tela, but then suffered mental trauma by the too sudden transition from the tranquillity of the jungle greenery to the different jungle of a busy seaside port town.

Thursday 26th

I pressed on with my self-imposed 'hunt-the-yellow-school-bus'. I felt a bit like a private eye but without the resources. (I remember mentioning the American discards I'd seen in Belize, well, they're here too: outcast cars and unwanted yellow school buses.)

I arrived at La Ceiba at 11.30 a.m.

The first thing to do was to find a boat going to Roatán from the loading pier at the other end of town. Off I traipsed through the dusty mid-day heat and after much asking around found a cargo boat that would load me too. I had been expecting a daily ferry – silly me!

Captain Harry Cooper lifted his sweat-stained and very grubby cap, scratched his thatch of sweat-wet red hair and reckoned they'd be finished loading and ready for the off about 3 p.m. In amongst the freckles on his lobster-red skin were patches of dead-white skin. I wondered about skin cancer. His front teeth were missing as were the front teeth of several loaders – legacies of past fights perhaps.

I left my heavy backpack on the boat (I know, I know, 'bit trusting', I hear you say) and set off to find the airport; perchance Seb and group had flown to the islands. A deckhand took me to the bus and I joined the horde of noisy school children crammed into it.

It was a partly successful venture – Seb had been there asking about fares, but that was some weeks ago and he hasn't been seen since.

Back at the loading pier even more cargo had arrived. The departure time had been put back to 5 or 6 p.m. I took off again, to ask in hotels if Seb had been seen. La Ceiba (named so for a gigantic Ceiba tree which grew near the old dock) is quite a small town, founded in 1877 so people tend to know people.

Back at the pier, again, the cargo was still being loaded with: one thousand four hundred creosoted wooden lobster box-traps; a Datsun; hundreds of bags of flour, maize, sand, cement; sacks of potatoes, cabbages and I don't know what; metal pipes, rods of all sizes and rolls of wire. I saw tables, chairs, cookers, fridges – you name it, it went on.

A strange mix these people; from blackest Africans to sun-bronzed, pale-haired whites and all the shades of skin colours and physiognomies in between. Language at the dockside is an incomprehensible mix of Caribe, Spanish and English with spicings of local idioms and sailor-speak thrown in.

Not knowing what else to do, I sat on an upturned bucket and, while waiting, had the usual succession of fellows coming to chat. One young man poured out his heart-story of some broken affair, then took me to one of the eating sheds at the end of the pier where I had fish, rice, avocado and coffee all for the equivalent of forty pence.

It was 2 a.m. before the passengers were allowed aboard!

Nineteen people, including a band and all their equipment, scrambled over the cargo and found somewhere to sit or lie. Fortunately, amazingly, my backpack was still accessible and I was able to pull out my sleeping bag. I found a spot, on top of a pile of mattresses, to get a few hours sleep while the cargo boat ploughed through the flat sea.

6.30 a.m. and there was the island, hazy on the horizon. I had thought that we'd be going into the main town on the middle of Roatán. Wrong again! Everything had to be unloaded at the eastern end first. I gave up, got off and a couple of minibuses later arrived at my destination at the western end. Here was a lazy, spread-out place with a few wooden houses badly in need of paint, a couple of churches, a few restaurants and one small shop, all strewn along the shore. The beach was clean, silver sand edging the beautiful, transparent, aquamarine sea.

I checked into a boarding house this afternoon and was later spotted by Barbara, a German girl who recognised me from the Antigua meeting. She had been in phone contact with Seb and is waiting for his arrival here. What a relief to find someone with some definite news. But it's still all a bit wait-and-see.

Saturday 28th

The boarding house, called *Miss Sareenies*, had an owner with very sticking-out ears, of ninety-six years (His wife was eighty-four). He said, 'Cum along de back. Dey's mangoes out dere.' So I followed him as he walked, very slowly, leaning on his stick. We plodded along a disused cart track, carefully trying to keep to the fairly-clear-of-vegetation wheel-ruts. I was wearing flip-flops and shorts. A black boy, carrying buckets, came along too.

(I find the term 'boy' is applied to any dark-skinned male person of any age and is used in the way that we might say kiddo or mate – in this case the 'boy' must be in his 30s.)

We followed the track for about a hundred metres alongside his now overgrown coconut plantation, until we came to a huge mango tree, its branches heavily laden with bunches of green and yellowing mangoes. The floor was littered with them and the air overpoweringly sweet with the smell of the rotting fruit. We collected two full buckets of mangoes, picking them out of the grass growing around.

The boy was peering at his legs and picking at and brushing his skin. 'Ticks', he kept repeating, 'Deys ticks heya.' I peered too, but couldn't see anything on his black skin amongst the short curly hairs.

We looked at my legs. One foot looked to be covered with ground black pepper, but the specks were moving very rapidly – baby ticks hundreds of them. We squashed as many as we could see. I marched back rapidly and ran straight into the sea for a good scrub with sand. Back at the house the boy was spraying himself with one of those sprays reputed to knock down dead everything that crawls or flies in the insect world. I got a good spraying too, 'Nuttin'll live in dat,' he promised authoritatively.

As the day wore on the burning, prickling sensation developed and intensified, even though I tried to wash off the insect spray. 'Keep pets and children out of sprayed area' the label instructed, as I later discovered.

No. Jungle walks are definitely not for those in shorts and flip-flops.

But the mangoes were good, very good.

Sunday 29th – How a coconut should be eaten

Sunday 29th – How a coconut should be eaten
We have time to kill before Seb and the rest turn up. Babs has had no further contact and he may be days away. Who knows?

When I have time to spare, (and I don't have to give you five guesses as to what I do), I walk of course. I went along the North Coast Road the six or eight kilometres to Sandy Bay; towards the end of the island and towards the end of signs of human habitation.

I was sitting under a coconut palm – choosing a tree without coconuts as they (the nuts) have a habit of suddenly falling – and struggling to open a greenish coconut with my penknife. I've done it before and have got it down to a fine art. One chips away at the pointy end of the nut and after half an hour of hard, hand-wearing digging and cutting at the tough fibrous husk, one at last exposes the brown inner shell.

Next problem; no hard rock to smash the shell and throwing the nut against the palm tree stumps didn't work – the stumps were way too soft. Back to the penknife, but I wasn't making any impression when my saviour turned up.

A local man wandered by and saw my struggles. With his long machete and a few swift blows, he split and prised off the green husk, then expertly chipped off the brown inner shell to hand me the milky whiteness of the denuded nut.

A coconut has three 'eyes' at the pointy end and it is through one of them that one can access the milk. He smilingly watched me as I frustratedly tried to break through one of the 'eyes' with my penknife, then he took the nut back and in a blink of time, with the point of his machete pierced two of the 'eyes'. (Why two holes? Air in one as liquid pours from the other.) A drink at last!

He warned me not to eat white coconut meat when it is really soft because it would be bad for the stomach. I didn't like to tell him that the coconuts we buy in England would be considered unfit for human consumption here and fed to the pigs.

He said to me, 'When you return from the beach, drop by my house and I'll fix you a proper coconut drink'. They call it 'agua de coca'.

I never got to drink much from the one I held. Jessica appeared with her three young cousins in tow. Jessica was a bright-eyed picannini with her curly hair sectioned into squares, each bunch of hair being tightly plaited, curled up and fastened with two grips to her scalp. Nine years old, she stood all of a metre tall on her badly bowed legs. She gravely introduced me to her younger playmates, and then fed them the coconut milk, making sure they had fair shares. I broke open the nut and they gravely chewed on a piece each, spitting out the chewed remnants.

We all walked back along the beach to 'her' dock from which we jumped into the sea and swam around taking turns with my rented snorkel and mask. (The children kept on their raggedy T-shirts and shorts. Maybe they felt self-conscious in front of me.)

The sea bed was covered with tiny, sand volcanoes but I couldn't figure out whether crabs or fish lived within. Something disappeared with a puff of sand every time I drifted close. There were also many of what, at first, I thought were strange sea anemones, but, in fact, were upside down buff-coloured jellyfish pulsating away. One would lift itself, drift slowly a few metres and settle again, upside down on the sand. Strange behaviour!

Jessica could swim a little, but only underwater! I supported her in the water and tried to teach her the breaststroke. She got the idea with her arms, but her legs just trailed.

Leaving the children, I walked back through the sparse grove of coconut palms and was passing the coconut man's house – he was busy cooking at an earthen oven in an outside shed – when he spotted me and called out, 'Your coconut's ready'.

He had cut down a large, fresh, green one. I watched as he deftly sliced off the top and poured out nearly half a litre of the delicious watery milk; it had quite a different, sweeter taste than the more mature nut. When I had drunk the milk, he split the nut in half and gave me a spoon and a hunk of his freshly baked bread. (Young coconut meat is quite soft; it sets like a jelly and is very filling.)

I was given mangoes, to eat and to take away, and brought other strange fruit to sample or not; manchineens (beach apples) and sea grapes. Manchineen is a member of the spurge family, very sweet on first bite but the toxins in the latex-like juice devastate the mouth within minutes. On the other hand, sea grapes, when they ripen to dark-plum purple, are delicious.

Monday 30th

I slept badly last night, tossing and turning to find a cool place in the bed.

This morning I set off along a red, dirt road across the hills to the south side of the island to find Flowers Bay Village. It took me hours to get there as I spent most of that time dozing in a dry river bed away from the road. (Flowers Bay Village is much like West End, the village where Babs and I are waiting for Seb, but even more primitive – the latrines are built on the ends of precarious piers over the sea for instant sewage disposable!)

Of the two wooden churches in the village only the Methodist Church looked functional. The other, of undetermined denomination, was all shuttered and boarded up.

I went into the Methodist Church after finding an unlocked door on the seaward side – the wood was too warped for the door to be closed. Inside was cool and dim, a good place to escape the noonday heat. There were rough plank pews and a simple altar cross (made from fluorescent light tubes) by the side of a large, stained, poster of Jesus. Dilapidated stairs led up to pews in the balcony and there I went, disturbing a bunch of bats that flew around distractedly before disappearing through a partly open hatch into the belfry. (I reckoned they'd come down into the cool of the Church.)

I read and dozed there amongst the dusting of fine sawdust (evidence of beetle busy in the rafters) and the faint smell of bats.

The walk back to West End passed cliffs of jagged pinnacles of weather-eroded limestone, through mangrove swamps, coconut groves, palms with bunches of tiny white berries and open grassland. I ate succulent, yellow fruits fallen from a tall tree with ash-like leaves. The fruit tasted like a cross between peach and lychee. I tried the fruits of a prickly pear cactus, after carefully picking a red ripe fruit with hands wrapped in leaves to avoid the tiny, skin-penetrating hairs of the cactus skin. Inside was bright pink with a mass of shiny, black seeds.

Flavour? Not much.

Shan't bother with them again.

I found more sea grapes and a purple fruit, about the size of a thumb nail, which also tasted vaguely of grape but had a single large seed.

After a swim in a tiny cove, luxuriating in the warm water and wearing just my birthday suit, about three hours of walking found me back at West End Bay and then only half-an-hour along the sandy shore to West End.

Tuesday 31st

I joined the two young American girls who were staying at my hostel, to go to a moonlight bar-b-q at Jimmy's beach shack. We provided the chicken and Jimmy, a local guy, brought potatoes, onions, ketchup, foil, rum and coconuts.

Using a sun-bleached log for seating, we set about preparing the simple feast: Jimmy set a driftwood fire on the sand. The chicken was quartered, lathered with a mix of onion, salt and ketchup, wrapped in foil and put on the grill. There wasn't enough room for the spuds too. They went directly into the hot ashes.

While it all cooked we sat drinking our coconut milk with rum (rum 'n' coke with a difference), listening to Jimmy sing as he played his guitar, watching the moonlight dance on the shushing wavelets and wriggling our toes in the still-warm sand.

Wednesday, 1st August

Seb turned up at 9.30 a.m.!!

After effusive greetings, Babs and I packed our bags, said a hurried goodbye to Jimmy and leapt into a pick-up that had been commandeered by Seb from its job of collecting empty oil drums. We dashed to the tiny, island-airport and rushed aboard the 11 a.m. flight waiting with its engines running to take us to La Ceiba, about 20 minutes flight away. It was the antithesis of my boat crossing to Roatán.

We waited through several tedious hours in La Ceiba while Seb did some business; he is always very cagey about what, exactly, he's doing – he works on a 'need to know' basis.

Another small plane took us to Utila, an island at the western end of the Bay Islands.

The island is very flat and is inhabited by descendants of pirates. Like the Pitcairn islanders, these islanders have evolved for two hundred years without influence from outsiders. The people are mostly whites with a few blacks and much interbreeding. They talk among themselves in almost unintelligible English – a remnant from the 18th century. It would be interesting to compare the evolution of Island English with UK English.

We waited with our bags and baggage and boxes of food on a wooden pier, while a boatman was found to take us out to Diamond Cay, just off Utila.

By now the sun was setting, the wind blew and the wave swells built so that the dory surfed the waves, making a fast surge up and a slow slide down. (A dory is like an overgrown flat-bottomed rowing boat, pointed at the prow, straight across the stern, with an outboard motor.) It was dark as we arrived to see the glow of candles and lanterns lighting the rest of the group eating their evening meal. Now we're all hooked-up and should be here about a week. Let's hope for some good diving days.

The next morning I woke to see bodies everywhere. People had found their own niche to sleep in; hammocks, tents, floor inside and outside the house, beds, chairs, or sofa. Half unpacked bags and backpacks littered all over. Sacks of rice, beans, oranges – enough food for twenty people for a week – lay around. Cooking and eating utensils filled the kitchen and half the dining area.

Water was fetched by bucket from a rain-water storage tank under the house – to be used sparingly as all the diving gear has to be fresh-water rinsed daily.

The one-storey, open-plan house, with walls of plank and roof of corrugated iron, was on a flat coral atoll, of about a hundred and thirty by eighty metres and with a few coconut palms.

Going to the toilet was a new experience. At the end of a small dock was a hut with three sides, the fourth open and facing to the sea. Within was a wooden box-seat, its top with a roundish hole through which the sea was visible below.

(There are lots of fishes in that patch of water and I must take care not to swim too near!)

Monday 6th – Leaving Diamond Cay and Utila

Bodies padded about quietly and purposefully. Muted voices reiterated the questions, 'Have you seen the . . . ?', 'Whose is this?' as, at 5 a.m., we packed up the house on Diamond Cay for a change of venue. Twenty people had to collect all their gear, pack all the cooking utensils, eating implements, food, diving gear, sweep the house and leave it ship-shape for the return of the owners.

Three dories arrived and the mass of luggage was loaded. The smallest dory set off, laden with all our backpacks and personal bags, but after five hundred metres had to come back – out of gas – and so we had to add its load to the large dory.

Gas tanks, beer crates, fuel tanks, spare engines, propane cylinders, cooker, etc. etc. were added and we were off as the moon set and the sun rose.

The dories docked at Utila: we then transferred all our stuff on top of the stacks of wood planks that were the ship's cargo bound for Roatán. There was a dodgy moment when, lifting up one of our heavy fuel tanks, the dory moved away from the ship's side and there was momentary danger of us over-balancing and dropping the tank into the sea.

The inflatable boat was the heaviest item to hoist aboard. It had several leaks and much water had entered, but with many pairs of willing hands and a big heave-ho, it was up.

We boarded and some of us climbed atop the planks to resume interrupted slumbers.

Three hours chugging through calm sea brought us to Coxenhole, Roatán, where we unloaded, waited for a truck, loaded up, drove to Sandy Bay (near where I'd stayed last week), unloaded and looked for the owner of the house we were to rent. He was out sailing, so off went Seb in the inflatable to fetch him.

More load carrying; up a flight of precarious wooden steps – one broke through and Ned gashed his shin.

Eventually the tents were up (only four beds in the house), hammocks slung, fridge filled and coffee on. We all looked very tired and were glad of a rest for the rest of the day

August 22nd – Sandy Bay, Roatán

We've been here for two weeks, but it feels like two months and the group dynamics has altered: the Advanced Diving Course started off well, although with twenty people and only one instructor it's all very slow. Each lesson means three trips out in the Zodiac inflatable and the tanks have to be filled with compressed air in between trips and we have only nine tanks. Most days we get only two dives under way so some of us miss out.

Health problems started accumulating: Oliver had a resurgence of some tropical bug that he'd picked up somewhere and had to fly from Roatán to La Ceiba hospital for tests.

Kay was laid low with possible bronchitis and cannot dive, and Nicky split her eardrums descending too fast after a cold – no more dives for her for a while.

Babs developed a bad fungal infection in her ears, and has probably burst an ear drum too, so she also missed out on dives.

Steve got coral cuts; which take ages and ages to heal even though he douses them with iodine several times a day.

Hubert's skin looked dreadful with little blisters which burst and formed nasty acne-looking spots; it might be an allergic reaction to who knows what or bites from some blood thirsty member of the Insect class.

Yon, the cheerful comic of the gang, left as he'd run out of time and likewise Kate – controller and organiser of how much food we should eat, or, 'Go steady on the loo paper'. They will be much missed.

Rick (hired as the truck driver and only along for the drive) left after he found out about our uncertain future.

Anne, you may well think what a sorry group we are and you'd be quite right.

Last Wednesday we had a group meeting and Seb told us what he'd been up to in his absences: The yellow school bus has been left in La Ceiba to be sold!!

He has used our money to buy a second-hand 1978 Mercedes truck – just the cab and chassis – and ordered that a cabin be built on the bed to make our new mobile home. A week has gone by and no progress has been made but for the ordering of parts.

During the second week, while we were waiting on Roatán, only the main-frame struts had been added to the chassis to form a box.

At the meeting Seb said he wanted three or four of the group lads to go and live at La Ceiba to finish the construction. Then, the plan would be for us all to go to Nicaragua for a ten-day stop so that those who had been unable to dive could catch up on the required number of dives. The rest would take those ten days off to do their own thing around Nicaragua.

What is this mess I've got myself into?

There's worse: Seb, John, Nicky and Hubert went off to La Ceiba, leaving the rest of us here on the island to while away the days until further notice.

Oliver left too; to return to Germany for proper medical treatment.

With seven people gone the cooking is easier and the bed-space improved.

Seb's tents proved worthless in the rain and those four bodies moved back onto the house floor. I've been using my homemade, netting-tent with a tarp over the top on wet nights. Not so good. Hubert had a proper tent and he left it for me to use while he's in La Ceiba.

(There are still too many people in the house with all their various snorings and sleep-gruntings and I like to go to bed early and get up at dawn: Hubert's tent is my little luxury.)

There's not much to do in the evenings by candlelight and it's too far and too costly for me to go to the nearest bars. I do remember one evening when 'grass' and 'magic mushrooms' had been obtained. I didn't ask how. We drank beer and smoked the stuff and everyone became very giggly and silly – bursting into raucous laughter at the weakest joke. Although I joined in, I just sat there feeling nothing and prudishly thinking, How childish – until I stood up and found I'd lost the use of my legs. I staggered to my tent and woke in the morning with a desert-dry throat.

Never again!

And I never have.

But I digress.

Last Friday Babs (Barbara) went into La Ceiba and saw Seb. She returned with the stunning news that the Mercedes truck was also being sold and the trip was off! We were all very subdued that night.

The exodus continued: on Sunday Neville left. He wanted to be off to Ecuador as his holiday time was running out – a shame, because our stalwart Aussie lad was a strong member of the group, always cheerful and a hard worker. But . . . he came back bearing a message from Seb – we were to pack everything and be ready to leave on the following morning's boat. We'd started to do that when Seb re-appeared to oversee the operation, but he lost his money-purse. We had to unpack everything until it was found.

Life can be very frustrating and wearisome at times.

We travelled to La Ceiba on a small cargo boat returning empty from Coxenhole. It left Roatán only an hour-and-a-half late! Not so bad.

It's seventy kilometres across the water; about four hours. The sea swells became lumpy as we got into mid-channel. The boat was sometimes broadside on to the swells, which made for much rolling and yawing of the deck. The sky darkened, the wind increased and the rain pelted as we passed through the edge of one of those tropical downpours – all quite exciting. We arrived safely into the calmer, sunny waters of La Ceiba.

Seb had flown over and was waiting to meet us with a railway flat-car to take the luggage along the dock (the same one that I'd waited on for so many hours, three weeks ago: only three weeks? It seems a lifetime) to our newly built truck-home.

The guys had worked so hard to get the box construction done in time. It was very solidly framed, with chicken wire along the base of three sides, but still needed lots of finishing touches in the way of windows and water-proofing. At the moment just sheets of heavy-duty plastic nailed to the frame sufficed.

At last we were all together again, although us 'islanders' were dismayed by the long faces of the 'truck workers' who were very fed-up with the whole venture.

We had a meeting, without Seb, to decide what best to do.

The problem was that more of us had run out of money or time and wanted out. They decided that Seb hadn't fulfilled his promise of a dive trip to South America and they wanted their money back or at least half of it.

At a later meeting with Seb, he said he hadn't enough money to make refunds and therefore the truck would have to be sold; the bus was still unsold. (There is a lot more involved than only this reason, but it's too complicated to detail here.) The meeting dragged on for four hours and finally, by majority vote, the plan for the next few days seems to be this: we wait here until 4 p.m. today when a supposedly interested buyer is coming to see the truck. If he buys, the trip ends here. If he doesn't we go to the big town of San Pedro Sula and try to sell the truck there. We'll stay there until next Tuesday. If there is still 'No Sale' we move on into Nicaragua and try to sell the truck there.

The whole thing has got so messy with all the 'ifs' and 'maybes', it's no wonder people feel so negative. I did feel sorry for Seb. He'd been buzzing around like a blue-tailed fly trying to hold everything together and keep this very disparate group of independent adults happy. On the other hand he'd brought it on himself.

Perhaps school-kids are better. At least one can tell them what to do.

Now it's 4.30 p.m. so I'd better mosey along and find out the latest twist to the tale.

Monday 27th – Still waiting in La Ceiba

The chap who was supposed to come to see the truck at 4 p.m. last Friday still hadn't turned up by 7 p.m.

Another wasted day on Saturday, during which we found out that the buyer chap had been twice to the truck to find no one there and had gone over to Roatán looking for Seb. Phone contact was eventually established and he will be back on Monday morning.

Armin, Rolf and David – now seriously pissed off – left.

And that leaves eight.

On Sunday, Nicky, Hubert and I thought to go the cool of the mountains, but the bus left too late for us to do a round trip in one day; we went instead on the first bus out of La Ceiba to Sambe Creek – a Caribe village, east along the coast.

Hot and Sunday seemed also to be washday. A creek ran parallel to the sea, separated from it by a low sandbar, and was filled with village women busily laundering the family's clothes. Many children played in the creek and the sea. The beach was very dirty with rubbish until we got past the village.

We walked for a few kilometres along the beach and then cut inland to walk back along the railway line barrelling into the distance, straight as a die between beds of reeds, trees and peoples' back 'gardens'.

Pacing the sleepers, with sweat stinging my eyes, I found my thoughts wandering over the snow-covered pines and frost-sparkling iced waters of winter in the Adirondacks.

About fourteen kilometres and several cool Cokes later we found ourselves back in La Ceiba.

'Oops, the truck's gone!' we yelped.

'Probably to Don's,' (a friend of Seb) we said.

Yes, there it was, being loaded with the rest of Seb's diving gear which Don had stored.

An interesting chap Don: 6ft 2ins, 16 stone and 63 years old; he's spent the last thirty years living, for various lengths of time, in unusual places all around the world. He's the sort of chap who gets off the beaten track to go and live in Indian villages and then write about his experiences. At the moment, he's writing some sort of philosophical book about his ideas on the concept of truth and reality. (Sounds a tricky topic. Is your reality mine? Is my truth yours?) Next week Don's going to take a break and stay in a Caribe island village. Should I ask to go with him?

The chap about the truck has turned up and I'm writing this as the wheeling and dealing goes on. It's taking forever.

N.B. A small robbery and a bit of excitement at 2.30 a.m. last night

I've been sleeping at the front end of the truck. It doesn't have any wire mesh yet, only plastic sheeting (which lets in the rain) pending future improvements.

I was awakened by a crackling-plastic-rustling and raised my head to see a face, mere inches away, peering at me. It rapidly disappeared as its owner jumped down from the cab-step and ran off down the empty, lamp-lit road.

Then I saw the empty place just beyond where my head lies. Empty? Empty? Why empty? Where are my trainers, shorts, T-shirt and a poly-bag with my odds and sods such as glasses, sun glasses, ear drops and ear plugs? (Oh, and I later discovered that now I no longer have my penknife or the boxer shorts that I was wearing as shorts because they're light and cool and easy to wash. All exited through the slash in the polythene!)

I woke up Damien to ask him to walk down the road with me so see if the thief might have dropped anything. We walked around the block and met the night watchman from the hospital who had seen someone running.

Back at the truck 'n' bus, all were out and talking worriedly. A policeman appeared. At least we thought he was a policeman. He was in navy-blue uniform with stars on his cap and carrying a gun, but he started lecturing us on interplanetary travel and beings of superior intelligence on this planet, 'Some do be good, some do be evil and create discord and disturbance,' he extolled. Most very odd!!

My early morning walk this morning took me over a small bridge that carries the road over a wide stream. I looked down to see a procession of blackish-looking fish with white eyebrows, about ten to twenty centimetres long. They were lazily cruising downstream. I started to count them, but gave up at a thousand. The endless stream continued for the half-hour that I stood and watched. I could see no sign of the end of the fishy stream. There were lagoons on either side of the bridge. Perhaps the fish were just changing lakes.

Oh! Nearly forgot to tell you: I watched an osprey fishing. Circling the water with slow wing beats, flying with beak half open, turning its head to look into the water. It flew out of the sun, talons extended. It shuddered, stalled and plummeted into the water. It'd spotted a likely meal. Up it rose with a good-sized fish in one talon. A vigorous shake, to spray glistening water drops and off it flew, out of sight, with its catch.

Here comes a glum face. What's new?

The truck hasn't been sold and we're off of San Pedro Sula!

Seb says that that those who want their money refunded – and that's the majority now – can go and do their own thing for a few days and meet us later in San Pedro Sula.

Hey-ho, what a sorry fiasco.

It's nearly six weeks since I left Antigua and very little to show for it.

Tuesday 28th

The truck was parked in a lay-by in a busy part of town. We'd festooned it with big 'For Sale' signs and now we wait.

We had another group meeting with more circular talking, until Seb interrupted and told us what to do. He'd made a good compromise (I thought). He'd written out a list of points and conditions to be applied to the rest of the first half of this 'Trip of a Life-time to Panama and Beyond' which we all signed – although I was sure its legal value wasn't worth a fig. I've smiled to myself watching this group of young adults, mostly in their early twenties, experience group management and truck-selling.

Wednesday 29th – An incident with the traffic police

There's been no sale of truck or bus, so we have to move on, but who will drive? Only Seb has a Heavy Goods Vehicle Driving Licence.

As Hubert and I were the only ones around at that point in time, we were elected to go and get a HGVDL. Seb talked to a policeman on the street who explained the simple process and said for 160 lempiras (about US$30)) he would complete all the necessary paperwork for us. Seb thought that that was too expensive and sent us off to find out for ourselves.

The police station, three long blocks away, was filled with cops being very busy lounging around, drinking coffee and chatting. Three increasingly important officials later, it transpired that we were in the wrong building!

It was extremely difficult to make them understand that our International Driver's Licence did not included Heavy Goods Vehicles. They kept saying, 'You can drive anything with this'.

Off we trudged, to find Brenda in the Oficina de Transporte.

The girl at reception sent us out and round the corner to another entrance to see Brenda upstairs, but the police guard at the entrance wouldn't let us in . . . because . . . we were wearing shorts!! We burst out laughing. (Last night Neville was refused entry into the cinema because he was wearing shorts!)

Sitting on a bench outside, we explained the problem, yet again, to a different cop, who eventually understood and took us back into the first office.

More confusion over the validity of our green International Driving Licence and what we were asking for. The boss-cop gave us some long explanation, only half of which we understood. However, eventually, understanding was achieved. Forms were filled out, stamped, passport photo attached, photocopied and condensed into one of those little plastic-coated ID cards. The process involved five people and us running to and fro between three rooms.

So now, for 100 lempiras, I hold a Honduran Heavy Goods Vehicle Driver's Licence, valid for two years and able to be used World Wide! Yeah, right! – My new scornful Americanism meaning 'I don't believe a word of it'.

(I've never driven anything bigger than the school minibus. What a system! No tuition. No test – nothing but to fill out a few forms and hand over the money.)

We came out grinning triumphantly and there, hanging around, just happened to be our helpful cop and his mate, just lads really. We said, 'Yes, everything is OK' and 'Thank you very much' and walked on. We hadn't gone far when the cop and his crony cruised by and stopped. We thought, 'Oh goody, a lift into town,' but that, apparently, wasn't intended and after more pleasantries we parted. When the cop had driven around the block and approached us for the third time, it dawned in our thick heads that he was seeking a 'present' for his help. That sorted, he left us.

We met Josh sipping coffee in the café opposite the yellow school bus and told him of our adventure. Benefiting from our experience, he went straight to the right office and got his HGVDL in twenty minutes – using his three-year-out-of-date U.S. car driver's licence! (I think Josh has the audacity to talk his way into, or out of, anything.)

So now we have three instant truck drivers plus Seb.

That afternoon, Seb took me out for my first-driving-of-the-truck. The conditions were ideal: 5.30 p.m. rush-hour and dusk falling along with rain! I drove through the town, and then for about half-an-hour along the highway to the next town, where we stopped for a coffee and for me to recover my nerves. I drove back in total dark and with only one headlight – par for the course.

Well, I reckon I can drive this thing in a straight line. Seb will just have to turn it around.

Friday 31st

Yesterday was not a good day. We were supposed to leave at 8.30 a.m. But that didn't happen (why am I not surprised?) Josh, Babs, Hubert and Helen had been out on the town. Hubert came back to the truck at 3.40 a.m. and when entering woke Nicky and me.

We breakfasted on bad coffee and stale bread in the shed-café at the bus station; the only place open at 8 a.m., then said our goodbyes – again – to Neville and Steve, who've got so fed up with all the procrastinations that they'd bought their tickets to Ecuador.

We couldn't wake up Babs and Josh, who were sleeping in an hotel. They finally surfaced with terrific hangovers. (Those two can be so inconsiderate.)

After four hours of sitting in the increasingly hot truck, now moved to park on a main road, I almost reached the end of my tether and oh-so-nearly dug out my backpack from the storage space under the floor.

I'd had enough of the town.

We finally left at 1.30 p.m.

Seb told me to drive the truck.

I cheered up immediately.

The plan was to stop at the lake about half way between San Pedro Sula and Tegucigalpa: the capital of Honduras. We approached the lake just as the skies opened and so we drove on. Then the bus (being driven by Seb) started misbehaving, going slower and slower up the hills and starting to overheat.

Seb moved everyone into the truck. I was to take them to Tegucigalpa, find a motel for us all and then return to see how the sick bus was fairing.

By this time it was dark and still raining.

There appeared in front of me the lights of a highway road-toll. I slowed. I was whistled at by the traffic police – don't think they've ever seen a woman truck driver – and waved to stop at the roadside and then beckoned to get out of the cab and walk over to them. I had been going to stop anyway, although in the wet-dark I couldn't see anywhere to pay the toll and had driven just beyond.

It was with great surprise that my newly acquired licence was confiscated and I was given a ticket. Evidently I should have stopped at the yellow sign about twenty metres before the toll booths.

I wasn't the only driver to suffer.

Shortly afterwards (after I'd dropped everyone at the motel) I turned round and headed back with John and Helen. We stopped at the yellow stop-sign just in front of the toll. The booth on our side was dark and locked. I got down from the cab and ran through the rain to the other toll booth and there was Seb, talking his way out of the same situation!

When I explained what had happened to us, he laughed because he'd done exactly the same. Anyway, some smooth talking and 10 lempiras later I had my licence back.

It sure helps to speak the lingo.

Tomorrow we move on across Nicaragua.
I hope to drive the truck at least some of the way.

Cheers for now.
Bron

20. NICARAGUA
Quickly Across to San Juan del Sur & a Rocky Walk

September 7th 1990

Dear Anne,

I don't remember much about the drive across Nicaragua, except that it was very long and dusty. The countryside looked extremely poor and the roads very pot-holed: they've had years of civil war with the US-backed, anti-Sandinistas against the Sandinista-led government forces.

Violeta Chamorro has only just been democratically elected. She's the first female president of the Central American countries.

I was, very briefly, a millionaire holding so many grubby Córdoba notes, which had now become pretty valueless.

Let me try to get your head around it this way: in 1988 there was an issue of Córdoba, where one new Córdoba is equivalent to 1,000 old Córdoba.

In 1990 when we passed through there were Córdoba notes with face value of twenty thousand, fifty thousand, five million and 10 million in circulation; new money mixed with old money most of whose zeros had been crossed through. A real head-buster working out how much a Coke cost.

About fifteen Córdoba were equal to one U.S. dollar.

(The Córdoba was named after the founder of Nicaragua, Francisco Hernández de Córdoba.)

About half-way, we stopped for lunch at a roadside café. A board outside offered a selection of fare, but inside it was a different story.

We asked for the chicken, 'Sorry, it's off,' said the man.

'How about a piece of pork?' one of us asked.

'None left,' said the man.

'OK, do you have any eggs?'

'No,' said the man.

'So what do you have?' asked our leader.

'Gallo pinto,' said the man.

We all had gallo pinto, without any of the usual extras on the plate.

(Gallo pinto is a mix of white rice and red beans boiled together and then fried. It's usually served with a bit of meat, a smidgen of salad and fried plantain pieces. A plantain is a hard, green cooking banana; not fit for eating raw.)

As we skirted around the war-shattered capital city of Managua, my eye was caught by a young girl sitting on the pavement at a corner where two main roads crossed. She was surrounded by many, many plastic bottles and containers of all colours and sizes. I guess they get salvaged and sold.

We arrived at San Juan del Sur (on the Pacific coast) mid-evening and parked the truck by a sweep of sandy beach. (The Bus had been abandoned in San Pedro Sula, Honduras.)

We've been here a week now and haven't done much in the way of diving.

Some got their Diver Rescue Certificate – me too: it just meant learning to hold a 'body' in a certain way and lugging it back to shore.

Most still have health problems. Morale is low. The remains of the gang seem more interested in enjoying the booze. They sleep late, making a very slow start to the day.

I get up early and go for walks.

For example: 6 a.m. dawned bright and clear, a perfect morning for a walk over the headland to the next bay and back along the beach rocks. I wanted to look for the cave of the tiger that the others had found yesterday.

I eased out from under my sleeping bag thrown loosely over me against the cool night sea breezes, stepped gingerly over the recumbent sleepers flung about in their various poses of dreamland and slowly climbed down from the truck, being careful not to rock it and intrude into their slumbers.

Ramón, the young fisherman, was already standing outside his hut on the sand, wearing his big toothy grin and a pair of shorts. We waved as I set off along the beach around the bay to the headland: treading the fresh-washed sand as the tide had not long turned and was drawing out.

Ramón is a local lad, somewhere in his thirties I guess, who'd spent the last ten years in Costa Rica, but hadn't found a job he liked and had returned home.

I'd sat chatting and smoking with him last evening. His Spanish is so guttural and with dropped endings that once past the, 'Will you be my wife?' stuff we'd sat in silence for the most part.

The cliffs at the end of the bay are quite crumbly with grey rocks piled at the bottom and washed smooth by the sea. The rocks bear little sign of sea-life: no algae, no exciting rock pools, just patches of tiny barnacles and minuscule mussels.

Rounding the promontory into a tiny cove, I was startled by the sight and sound of falling pebbles rolling down a steep sandy slope to bounce amongst the thousands of pebbles already scattered on the sand. As I stood, puzzled, the pebbles moved and started slip-sliding their way across the sand. They were hermit crabs. Hundreds of them, in all sorts and sizes of shells from very, very tiny winkle shells to quite large whelk shells. When I moved they tucked into their shells and came tumbling down the sandy bank.

Leaving the cove, I climbed the sandy path leading up and over the headland. Once amongst the trees the path became several – the headland was much bigger than I'd first thought. Keeping roughly within sight of the sea (glimpsed from time to time through the trees) and after following several inviting, although false paths I'd thought would lead down to the shore, I eventually arrived at the next bay and saw a long sweep of empty golden sand with just one early morning fisherman bringing in his catch.

I looked at my watch – a precious gift given to me by my younger son. It was still only 8 a.m.; plenty of time to get back to the truck before the others woke.

You know I hate to return the way I've just come, so I chose to return via the shore now that I could access it. I love the scrunching sounds of shingle and the physical joy of hopping, jumping and scrambling over boulders.

Keeping to the foot of the maybe thirty-metre high cliffs, I reached a place where the sea was still crashing against the sheer cliff-face. The only way forward was up and across, perhaps fifty metres, and down on the other side. It looked fairly easy.

I was super-careful picking my way between the prickly-pear cacti and the tough columbine-like plant that kept snagging my legs: I didn't want to take an early morning swim from just here.

I made it proudly down the other side.

The going got harder as rocks turned into huge boulders that had to be climbed over or manoeuvred around and one headland turned into another and yet another, and took me further and further out into the Pacific. You know how it is when you think you're nearly at the top of a mountain, only to see on cresting one ridge that there is, invariably, another beyond.

By then I was on rocks where the sea was deep. The shore looked an awful long way away. But I still wasn't in sight of the bay where the truck was parked.

The rocks were worn into long grey shelves tipped sideways, running perpendicularly from the cliff base and disappearing into the sea: they looked like a slipped stack of toast with gullies between the slices through which the breakers surged in and sucked back out with unnerving force. I thought: OK, the tide is still going out, but I can't hang around here. I don't know what's around the next headland. Perhaps I have far to go. Should I go back to the bay? No. How would I get back across the bit I had to climb up and around? I'll try to continue.

Talking to myself, I muttered, 'I think, if I can cross these gullies, I only have to round this last headland and then I should be on the way home. But . . . Hmm . . . I don't fancy trying to clamber down the almost vertical slope of the rock (about a three-metre drop) across the gulley (about one metre wide) and up the sloping rock-face on the other side. Supposing I slip on these sea-weedy rocks and the strong sea-surge drags me out into the Pacific Ocean, never, ever to be seen again!'

So I decided to jump.

It didn't look so far – about two metres across and downhill. I backed up, then taking small running steps, launched myself into space and landed at my destination. But, the slope of the lower rock was such that the whole force of my landing was absorbed by my heels.

Oh boy, I hurt like hell!! I rolled around a bit and was sick. When the pain subsided, I found I couldn't put any weight at all on my right foot. The left heel hurt mightily also, but the pain was bearable.

It was by then 10.15 a.m. The trouble with big headlands is that there are always lots of little intermediary ones too. Every time I rounded a point into the next little bay or cove, there was another headland on the other side.

I made quite good time to start with; crawling on hands and knees with broken foot in the air, or bottom-shuffling using two palms, one bottom and one foot.

After two hours of this, I started to worry about the tide turning. My hands and knees were getting more and more sore and I moved more and more slowly searching for 'soft' rock and smooth shingle. Some hope!

Crawling was a good position to observe the rocks closely. Tiny, warm pools had what looked like sesame seeds stuck to the bottom (don't know what they were) and a few whelks and winkles. One slightly larger, narrow pool had some two-centimetre long black and white splotchy fish darting around.

Then, I spotted a beautifully camouflaged sea slug creeping over what, at first, looked like an encrusting coral but was a mass of sea anemones each about one centimetre across, grass-green and with a ring of brown tentacles. The slug had tentacles like flattened trumpets. Its eye stalks were set far back and the pnuemostome (breathing hole) was towards its posterior. The anemones pulled in their tentacles in a wave of closure as the slug moved across.

Does a sea slug eat anemones?

Some flattened expanses of rock on the beach seemed made of a fine-grained mud-stone, on which, at some time in geological past, an iron-hard layer had been laid. The softer mud-stone had eroded leaving iron ridges, closely patterned and standing sharply proud – so not nice to crawl on. My palms and knees were getting well bloodied; salt water is antiseptic isn't it?

By 2 p.m. I felt a bit light-headed. Not the slightest trickle of fresh water dripped down those cliffs. The mid-day sun, the hot rocks, the warm, very salty pools; I thought – I'm getting dehydrated, I'm very thirsty, I'm very tired and I'm very despondent. I must press on.

I tore the short sleeves from my thin cotton shirt and tried to bind them with seaweed to my rubbed-raw knees. Not very successful – the weed kept slipping down. Where is all the flotsam and jetsam usually found on beaches?

To give a mite of protection to my now somewhat bloody palms, I pushed the stalks of some big thick leaves, which I'd come across at the base of the cliffs, between my fingers and tried to crawl using them as a pad. Sorta worked – but the leaves quickly wore out.

My thin shorts wore through at the back and I turned them around. OK, my pubes are now exposed, but who's to see?

There was very little shade to rest in – the sun was almost directly overhead.

I worried about the incoming tide. I saw from the high-tide mark that the water would be up the base of the cliffs – I must find somewhere out of reach of the high-tide.

Another headland to negotiate! I heaved a big sigh. The tide must've been coming in for three hours by now.

I looked at the waves and knew it would be a tricky hop to cross the short exposure of sand before that next big wave came rushing in.

By the side of me was shaley scree on the cliff, very loose and forbidding. I saw vegetation about ten metres up. If I could only get that far I might be able to climb over the top. I managed about eight metres, but could see no way to progress. Everything I touched fell away. It was so hard to climb as a tripod. I admitted defeat. I sat on my bum and, using my good leg, did controlled slides back to the bottom.

I would have to brave the waves.

I expect you know that every seventh wave is bigger than the rest (my daddy told me so). In the lull between big waves, I managed several metres before the returning biggie hit. Luckily, the water was only knee-high and there were plenty of rock projections to cling to as the wave receded, sucking at my feet.

I crossed another inlet by the same performance, rounded another point, and bliss, oh bliss, I'd made it. I recognised the path leading over the headland to 'our' bay. It'd taken me about nine hours to get here and I suppose I've travelled only a couple of kilometres or so along the shore. I dragged myself up above the splash-zone and lay, curled up, exhausted, against a rock, in a foot of shadow.

I'd just got settled when Ramón appeared, followed closely by David, Hubert and John. They gave me most welcome and much needed water. I drank a litre straight off. They'd brought bananas, bread and dry clothes. Between them they pushed and pulled me up the steep, sandy cliff path and chair-lifted me (two blokes grabbing opposite wrists to form a seat) back through the woods. I slid on my bum down the other side of the headland. Then they chair-lifted me through the now above knee-deep sea and stumbled across the water-covered rocks over which I'd walked and watched the hermit crabs so many endless hours ago.

The truck was fetched around the bay: the whole gang was agog with excitement and relief

Later, when the others had gone for dinner, Nicky sat with me and calmed me and cooled me with wet flannels as the effects of shock (probably exacerbated by the pain killers I'd taken and the unknown drugs from Babs, but suspected morphine base) washed through me. I was alternately shivering and sweating and hyper-ventilating. It's such a good job Nicky's a trained nurse.

We'll leave Nicaragua today and cross into Costa Rica to get me to a hospital to get my heels looked at.

Then we move on to the next practice beach, to practise our skills in the Atlantic waters on the other side of Costa Rica.

So there you have it, my friend. I can't moan that life doesn't have its exciting moments!

I'll imagine the staff reading the above – you say you pass my letters around – and some will think me barmy and some might think me adventurous and brave.

I'll close this section here and add it to the growing pile of letters waiting to be posted.

Cheerio for now.
Bron

21. COST RICA
Stormy Clouds with Brighter Interludes

Letter One - September 26th *1990*
Coping with Colons

[Costa Rica money was named after Christopher Columbus (Cristóbal Colón).
One U.S.D. is worth about 500 colons]

Hello my Dear Friend.

I expect you're well settled into the new term at Pipers Corner. I do hope you've had a very good summer and enjoyed your trip to New York.

I should like to know how my 'A' Level Biology girls fared. All passed with high-flying grades I hope.

As for me, the last ten weeks have been pretty awful on the whole; stormy clouds with bright interludes. This diving group trip was one of my not-so-good ideas, although it seemed a good idea at the time. But that's life.

As I recounted in my last letter, we've had one setback after another, mostly centred around money, or rather the lack of it, as Seb tried to keep the trip on the road. By ones and twos, members of the group took off. Only eight of us stuck it out until the bitter end.

The group had more males than females (but it was the most asexual set of people I've ever come across) and some excellent platonic relationships developed.

They were all donkey's years younger than me, except Seb and he wasn't interested in any dalliance.

It was with frustration and sadness that I watched the happy faces of the last few departing. Now everyone has gone and I am left alone in Cahuita with Seb.

Who knows which way the wind will blow me next. I like to think that nothing happens to us without some purpose; I'm interested to see the outcome of a whim which propelled me to jump across those rocks, smashing my heels in the process.

I'd befriended nurse Nicki: Kiwi, twenty-six-years-old, who had been working in London and is on her way back to New Zealand. I told you how superbly she looked after me when I went into clinical shock after my accident. She's now left to continue her journey into South America. I'm sure I'd have gone with her had I been able.

After crossing from Nicaragua into Costa Rica, the first hospital we came across was in the small town of Liberia. Being Sunday, there was no-one in sight. Seb wandered around knocking on doors and managed to raise someone to x-ray my foot and then my compaction-fracture was swathed in a short-boot cast. Seb reappeared with an old pair of wooden crutches. Goodness knows where he'd found those. He wouldn't say – perhaps he half-inched, (Cockney rhyming slang = pinched) them.

The medical attention, x-ray and cast cost less than the excess on my insurance; I never claimed.

I persisted in hopping around on the other damaged foot and surprise, surprise it wouldn't improve. So I admitted defeat and have spent the last two weeks flattening my bum. At last the pain and swelling are subsiding; but I still keep my perambulations very short.

The chaps have been excellent carrying me around pick-a-back and lifting me into and out of the truck, although the novelty soon wore off and I felt very sorry for myself when they took off on their exploratory walks or went swimming.

Crossing Costa Rica we've arrived at the Atlantic beach village of Cahuita, to the south east of San José: we've come to finish the Advanced Diver's Course using the sea and hotel pool. (Babs's bleached hair turned bright green with the pool chemicals!) The sea in the bay is too murky for decent diving (blame the so-called wet season) so we do most of the swimming-exercises in the pool.

They say that years ago they used to be able to set their watches by the rain starting at 4 p.m. and finishing at 6.30 p.m. Now, with global climate change, Costa Rica's wet season is no longer so wet nor its dry season so dry. I've been here for two weeks and it's rained only four times in Cahuita, usually during the night. There're no sea breezes: it's very humid and hot. The sun's too strong to sit out in, so my tan has faded.

Why am I moaning!! I bet you'd give your eye-teeth to be sitting supping cool beers and smoking cigarettes in the shade of coconut palms on an idyllic Caribbean beach. Let's get things in perspective! Who'd want to be in England with winter approaching and the increased incidence of the SAD syndrome? How's Jill by the way?

Some of us finished the course – some didn't because they've still got health problems; two have gone off to look for Dive Master Jobs. I've done all the theory up to Assistant Instructor level, but still have to finish the water requirements for Rescue Diver and Dive Master and shan't be able to do that for another three weeks, when my cast should come off; hence my dependency on Seb and his truck, not that I could cope with a backpack and crutches anyway.

So I sit alone in this one-storey, clap-board hotel with the bedrooms arranged around two sides of the pool, gloomy showers and toilets on the third side and wait.

Last Sunday I was cleaning my teeth when the front crown fell out and bounced down the plug hole. No problem – I undid the s-bend with those oh-so-useful tools on my penknife and retrieved it, washed it, and pushed it back in. The crown felt secure enough.

The next morning when I said 'Buenos días,' it fell out again and into the shelly sand of the path passing in front of the bedrooms. I spent hours on my hands and knees raking back and forth with a comb, but couldn't find it.

The following day, killing two birds with one stone, Seb took me into Limón; he needed to go there to get the brakes on the truck fixed. He'd sold two sets of fins and masks and now has enough money to do that – yes, he's that penniless. So it seems that we're off to Puerto Limón (ninety kilometres up the coast) tomorrow to sort out the brakes.

Unfortunately the dentist in Limón didn't have the resources to match my quality English crown and referred me to his colleague in San José, who specialises in bridge and crown work. Seb said, 'Wait until Thursday when I have to go into the city.'

I managed, front toothless, not smiling much and speaking with a whistle.

Thursday arrived and Seb dropped me in the city and I took a taxi to the recommended dentist who worked in the suburbs. I got out of the taxi, bag and crutches in one hand, half-balanced on one leg, slammed the door shut and left my finger inside. 'Stop, stop.' I yelled to the taxi driver, 'Please open the door.'

The dentist greeted me dripping blood onto his doorstep and kindly dressed the wound. It wasn't so bad, missed the nail and I think it'll heal OK without stitches. That's the second medical-attention-needing-accident within a month.

So that's that! Now, I should be alright for the next ten years! Ha! Ha!

Back in Cahuita, Seb gave me the Certificates for Rescue Diver, Dive Master and Assistant Instructor (even though I didn't complete all the practical water-work). I could go and teach in a Dive School as Dive Master, but I'd need to build up my number of dives and improve my dive skills before applying for the Diving Instructor exam: held in Miami and very expensive to take.

With this idea in mind, I've bought a full set of dive gear from Seb: he's decided to sell all his stuff and not do any more SCUBA expeditions after all the horrendous hassles of this trip.

So my bag grows heavier and heavier: I'll have to do a Dervla Murphy and get a donkey to carry it all.

Seb took me back into San José and left me at Youth Hostel Toruma.

Bye, bye Seb.

And so here is my dilemma; do I stay in San José and teach English for a few months to get funds or do I teach diving – which would most likely mean going back up to the Yucatán Peninsula in Mexico? Either way, I don't see me getting into South America this year, but there's always next year or the one after. And anything might, or might not, happen in the next two or three weeks while I'm still hopping around.

Hey-ho, it's a funny ole life.

It's now one year and fifteen days since I left England.

I've felt no homesickness, just, at times, an overwhelming desire to chat with my mates and see my boys.

I wonder so very often (as in almost daily) what my boys are doing. I don't even know if they're still living where they were living last spring.

Fondest love.

Your mad-as-ever-mate.
Bron

COSTA RICA

My Dearest Friend,
        Absolutely thrilled to get your so welcome letters. Read them while eating my lunch – mistake, made it too salty!

I've not had any news from anybody for about five months and the enforced inactivity has given me too much time to miss home and real friends. I've had fourteen letters and two postcards, gathered here from Guatemala via Panama to Costa Rica. Well done American Express postal service.

It was like Christmas to hear from teachers at Pipers Corner and aunty and step-mother. I was so excited to hear all the news, even though some of it was nine months old. The letters are particularly poignant at this time when I'm feeling a bit lost and struggling inside with misty indecision.

        Sadly, heart-breakingly, nothing from my boys.

Very many thanks for the news of son Simon. Perhaps if I write to him at D&B via you, (I don't know their address) you might forward it please. I've no idea if he's been receiving the letters and post cards that I've sent, because I don't know if his home address has changed.

Thanks too for the good news of the 'A' Level girls. I'm so pleased that Choi (from China) has got to University. She worked so hard and to think when she arrived as a fifteen-year-old she hardly spoke a word of English.

I've just taken my plastic-wrapped bread and half a tin of sardines out of the drawer in my minimally furnished room (to eat as my breakfast while I scribble to you), only to notice that the plastic bag has tiny holes in it which weren't there last night. Something has been having a mid-night snack, cockroaches I think; the holes are too small for a mouse.

I've moved into a cheap dump ($2.5 dollars a night) in the City centre. There's no hot water, sheet or blanket. It's a good job I carry my own sheet-sleeping-bag. On the plus side, there are cockroaches in the loo (more pets!!) and everything is rather grubby; how would I now cope with clean?

Why did I move from the hostel, I hear you ask? Well, the Youth Hostel had put up their rates to $5 per night; horrendously expensive, I think. Oh, I know the hostel was reasonably clean and spacious in an echoing sort of way, with hot showers – sometimes.

During the three weeks that I'd been there, I'd twice had to move out from my multi-bunk bed dorm to make way for large groups of foreigners coming in for an overnight. So this time when I was asked to shift, yet again, I thought, Enough! and have moved out for good. At least here I have my own room; plus roaches in the drawer – perhaps I can catch one and keep it tied to a piece of cotton as a pet.

By the bye, those large groups – a hundred and twenty-five people came one time – are Nicaraguans, mostly labouring types, being repatriated. They sneak into Costa Rica looking for work and periodically the police round them up from all over the country and bus them back to Nicaragua. They are given money and food to help them resettle (by the USA, I think). I was put in the men's dorm one night (not to be recommended), but still endured the noise of babies crying and small children squealing throughout the night; and the mess they leave behind has to be seen to be believed; showers left on all night and filthy loos: don't they know how to flush a toilet? Perhaps not.

They'd all left by 5 a.m.

I've been in Costa Rica eight weeks (four in Cahuita and four in San José) and I've done very little. Now that my foot is improving I'm getting the itch to move on again.

I took the cast off after four weeks. I found the hardest thing to bear was going to bed with my 'boot' on, usually with a wet sole as I was walking sort-of-crab-wise, on occasion, without crutches. The bottom of the 'boot' was getting worn away so I decided to 'off-the-whole-thing'.

I stuck my leg in the sink, poured water over it to soften the cast then hacked away with a large pair of borrowed scissors. I eventually got it all off, after much huffin' and puffin' and cussin'.

Oh! What a horrible sight! There's still so much multi-colour bruising, especially under the instep; the whole foot must have been so black. And the calf muscle, how wasted it is after only four weeks of non-use!

It's amazing how quickly muscle tissue disappears when it's not being used.

And flaky dead skin.

And ankle still very swollen and so stiff.

For the next two weeks I continued to hop around on crutches: my hands were blistered from the rough wood, not to mention the blisters in my armpits. For a while I used one crutch and then last week did without either. By the end of any day my foot and lower leg look like a mild case of elephantiasis, but the swelling mostly goes down overnight, except for the ankle which stays very 'thick'. Well-meaning souls tell me that it'll take months to get back to complete normality; and then I'll probably always have trouble with it.

Great! Just what I want to know!

I'd been told of a place in San José that sells orthopaedic stuff and been assured that they have a second-hand department.

One afternoon I trudged through the pouring rain (it wasn't raining when I set off) right across town to the shop. Everything looked new. When I presented my repaired, old-fashioned, home-made wooden crutches, the nose of the shop assistant visibly wrinkled. 'Oh no, we wouldn't want those,' said she snootily. Upon my protestations that I'd been told they would buy them, she took one between finger and thumb, and holding it like something nasty from the gutter, took it to a man protected by the plasterboard and glass of his office.

Returning with a grin of triumph she pushed the crutch back at me, 'So sorry. We couldn't use it,' she sneered.

So I hobbled on and chanced across a Red Cross Hospital. They were only too pleased to accept my tatty, rain-sodden, wooden offering. So there, Mrs Snooty!

Now that I'm a bit more able, I've been sitting on buses to get away from the noise, bustle and smells of the city.

I sat on a bus for five hours to get to Playa de Coco; another not very inspiring place. Setting off on my usual exploratory walk along the dirt road between the scattered houses, I cut across the back of the headland to get to Ocotal, with its posh hotel complex, in the next bay. My purpose was to seek out a guy called Mario Vargos, who runs the dive shop there, to ask if he could employ me as Dive Master. The shop was closed. A local fisherman told me that Mario lived in Playa de Coco. About-turn, to hitch a ride back, especially as the rain had started. I did find his house. He didn't want a Dive Master (especially a female I suspect).

So, back to my 'hotel' for a beer and a lonely read.

It rained and rained and was still pouring in the morning.

Last weekend, I took the bus to Puntarenas, but arrived too late to catch the first ferry across to Nicoya Peninsula; however, I was on the next at 9 a.m.

The port of Cóbano on the other side was no more than a wooden jetty, a café or two in sheds, and buses and taxis waiting to grab a fare off the ferry passengers. Being one of the last to leave the ferry the bus was packed full, so I shared a taxi for the three hour bumpy drive to Montezuma.

The countryside reminded me of the Welsh Marches, only tropical of course.

Montezuma is a small, quiet village, mostly of cabins; but it does have the luxury of a couple of small, two-storey hotels within which one finds the only bars.

A pretty, white sand beach – the complete opposite of Playa de Coco where the sand is all sparkly black and makes the whole beach rather dirty-looking and impossibly hot to walk on – is washed by the Pacific breakers which are only about one metre high at the moment, but with a surprisingly strong undertow that swept me off my feet.

I lazed on the beach that day and the next morning hiked up a dirt road up into the hills. I passed some waterfalls and dared a swim in the pool. Mindful of the time and the hike back to Cóbano, I was pleased to accept a lift with an American couple who took me all the way back, in time to catch the 3 p.m. ferry.

Back at Puntarenas I couldn't believe my eyes, such a huge queue for the bus to San José. As it was, they provided six, sixty-seater buses to cram full of weekend trippers.

Tomorrow I'll finish at my Spanish Language school. I've been going there for the last four weeks, attending about three hours of classes each morning. Now I have all the theory; but how does one get to talk? I think it has something to do with having been a teacher and not wanting to make mistakes plus my innate reluctance to talk to strangers.

My foot has been hurting a lot and the swelling won't go down so I went to the hospital and had it re-x-rayed. The fracture had healed cleanly and nothing much else seems to be wrong. 'It'll just take time for the squashed blood and lymph vessels to re-establish themselves,' the Doc helpfully said.

I forked out $38 for that visit and then (just my luck) two of my front teeth fell to pieces and that was $80 for two fillings.

You asked about my wardrobe and am I still wearing the clothes I took from England? Well, not quite.

My wardrobe:

1 pair of long coarse-cotton pants – dark purple with vertical black stripes and outside leg pockets, bought in Antigua market;

1 pair of reversible shorts necessarily purchased after I literally wore out my others on the Nicaraguan beach crawl;

1 long-sleeved shirt now stained purple from contact with said wet trousers;

1 once nice white cotton shirt with small blue flowers – remember I used the sleeves as knee wraps on the beach crawl, so the arm-holes are embarrassingly large;

1 denim, wrap around skirt and 1 coffee coloured roll-neck, long-sleeved thin jumper, both given to me;

1 bikini.

I look into the posh shops and dream of elegant clothes, not to mention shoes – I have canvas pumps, flip-flops and hiking boots.

So who needs clothes?? The 'natives' live in T-shirt and shorts. In these hot countries we only wear clothes because that's what we've been brought up to do.

It's now 12.22 a.m. I've been sitting on my bed for hours writing to you.

Hope you can read all my scribble.

My ankle/foot is a-throbbing, so I'd best get horizontal.

I wish you an uneventful end of term.

With lots of love.
Bron

COSTA RICA

Letter Three - November 26th 1990
Re-direction

My Dear Anne,

Now here's an unexpected re-direction for my life.

One day, for want of entertainment, I'd got on a bus and found my way to the scientific lectures on tropical biology being held at the National University of Heredia in the suburbs of San José. It was the annual Convention of Entomologists and, although all in Spanish, I was able to follow most of the lectures.

The woman I sat next to at lunch works for the Smithsonian Tropical Research Institute (STRI) (of wide renown in the States but unheard of by me) and happened to be based at the research centre in Panama City.

During the course of our chatting, she learned that I was job hunting in Costa Rica, but not with much luck, most likely due to my poor Spanish.

'Why not,' she suggested, 'go to Panama and ask amongst the researchers if anyone could use a pair of hands?' She gave me a few names of current researchers and the departments in which they worked.

Why not indeed, I thought.

During a coffee break, I met another woman who has spent half a life-time studying wasps. (That seems incredible to me: how does one spend 30 years studying wasps?) She works for STRI in San José and has many contacts and connections in the research world. As we chatted and she discovered that I was looking for a job, she too gave me several names to contact at the Smithsonian in Panama. (I'll have to leave Costa Rica soon as my visa runs out in early December.)

At lunch on the second day I sat next to Dr. Philip J DeVries; he was one of the few people speaking English amongst the buzz of Spanish. He's a naturalist extraordinaire and author of "The Butterflies of Costa Rica." He'd spent eleven years compiling his book. He is an unconventional Lepidopterist: he calls himself a naturalist – interested in *all* things natural.

We talked about his work at some remote outpost in the Fila Cotón Mountains which stride through the southernmost part of Puntarenas province of Costa Rica and into Panama. He said that I could visit any time.

Phil was the one at the meeting who couldn't sit still; straddling his chair, standing up, wandering in and out and roundabout. About one metre and sixty centimetres tall, (sixteen centimetres shorter than me) slim-build, slim-moustache, dark hair in a ponytail, he admitted to hating meetings and longed to get back to his forests and mountains.

On finding out that he had driven to San José, I cadged a lift back with him – it's on the way to Panama after all.

It wasn't until we were in his Toyota Land Cruiser and cruising away from San José, and I watched the visible metamorphosis of his character (like a chrysalis hatching), that I realised how uptight he'd been during the three-day meeting.

He chatted avidly to Clare (a butterfly-biologist who had flown down from the States to spend a few days with him) about people they both knew. I sat in the back and greatly enjoyed the stimulating thought flows. Phil graphically illustrated his points with fluttering fingers and hand movements that I came to recognise as butterfly flight patterns.

He periodically punched the car roof and often exclaimed, 'Oh yeah!' in his pleasure at escape.

Clare is a dark-haired, quietly spoken young lady of Italian extraction. She'd spent a few years in Developmental Biology before joining a Conservation group that allows her time-off to spend a few months studying butterflies in Madagascar.

Time (since I first passed along the Pan American Highway with the dive group some ten weeks ago) has wrought changes. Many more flowers are in bloom, but we drove along too rapidly to identify the masses of pink or yellow or white, now mixing with splodges of green to paint the roadside verges. Some looked like bushes of small sunflowers or shrubs of pink or white hollyhock amongst the proliferation of Busy Lizzy that grows wild here.

Seven hours of driving took us south through the changing landscape of Costa Rica, until we turned east off the Pan Am Highway, snaking up a new-made dirt road into the mountains of San Vito. We called in at the Botanical Gardens for Phil to pick up his mail and then lunched in the town.

Another hour through coffee-country and land cleared for pasture, but leaving standing palm trees like so many scattered sentinels: the Indians crop several years' worth of seeds before cutting the palms to extract 'heart of palm' – a vegetable delicacy which is really the tender growing point of the palm tree.

Several miles of dirt-track meandering through fincas (farms) of coffee and cows brought us to the valley containing Alturas; a village of some hundred houses, whose workers live a subsistence life on the wages from coffee and lumber sales.

My goodness, I can't get more Costa Rica rural than this: Alturas has no TV, no radio, no newspaper, and electricity only from 4 p.m. until 8 p.m. I see extended family groupings and young teenagers with babies, maybe theirs, maybe their mum's. I wonder about inbreeding and the genetic consequences.

The park where Phil works extends for several days' march (in any direction) through virgin rainforest. He has cut fourteen kilometres of trail up a mountain, following the lines of old Indian hunting trails and is in the process of marking it, at one hundred and fifty metre intervals, with numbered poles recording the elevation.

Situated some seven kilometres from Alturas, the start of the trail is a flat site which was an Indian village long ago. Now it is cleared for pasture and building a field-station. Phil moans that he has become an administrator as his job at the moment is to sort out contractual contingencies.

We went up to the field-station yesterday for Phil to see what work had been done during his absence in San José.

To my eyes the first building looks very flimsy: crudely-jointed beams of wood and corrugated-iron sheets form the nearly completed workshop. I hope the main building will be more substantial.

Phil periodically went into fits of rapture at the burgeoning of the new plant growth that had sprung up since he left a week ago and was delighted that the deep mud puddles had all dried up: no rain for eight days heralds the start of the dry season and a flush of butterfly activity. He and Clare spit biological names back and forth, but that doesn't matter, I'm picking up all sorts of interesting facts about where butterflies live in forests and good places to catch them.

As in bird recognition, flight patterns are important. Phil's hand swoops or glides, fingers fluttering or still, in various patterns and combinations as he described species to Clare. He recognises the differences between the insects as they flutter past; they all look all brown to me.

Newly emerged adults were pointed out as they jerked clumsily from plant to plant, like young fledglings newly left the nest. Thus, I was later able to say, 'Oh, that's a newly hatched dragonfly,' as I watched the four wings slowly gyrate, like helicopter blades, as the insect wobbled to a new place in the sun. You know how fast dragonflies dart – so fast their wings are just a blur. The slender body of this one was about six centimetres long with wings all transparent, until a wing caught the sunlight and the reflected light turned the wing a metallic-blue iridescence but for a blotch of dark chocolate near the tips of the front wings.   Beautiful and exotic.

I saw my first wild Chestnut-billed Toucan sitting high in a tree, tossing its extraordinary banana-shaped, brown and yellow coloured bill into the air each time it threw its call in argument or duologue with another toucan hidden behind the foliage. It was so animated in comparison with the subdued creatures that one sees in zoo cages.

One night Phil and Clare had been out caterpillar spotting by torchlight. They brought back a small hawk-like bird (about the size of a thrush) that had had an unfortunate encounter with a car. The tiny hooked beak was open in the enlarged gape that one sees in films of nestlings being fed by their parents.

On its middle claw was a comb device. Did you ever imagine a bird combing its feathers?

A too-badly damaged bird, it died.

The weather seems to be holding fair; so I elected to go up the trail to lay out some more markers. (Gotta work for my keep.)

I was given lengths of grey plastic tubing, about one metre long and of two-centimetre bore, sprayed with yellow paint at the top. My job was to write the number in red and altitude in blue on the poles spaced at one hundred and fifty metres.

Sounded simple enough.

I re-packed my backpack with the minimum necessary for two nights out in the forest. Gathering my tubing-poles, the paints, compass, altimeter, notebooks and the fifty-metre length of cord the thickness of your little finger, I set out for time alone to the amazed consternation of the villagers. ('But, thar be jagwars in them thar hills!' they exclaimed. Oh, that I should be lucky enough to see, or even hear one, methinks.)

I knew that about seven kilometres of trail had already been marked (by Phil), but hadn't reckoned that it would take me over six hours to get to the place where he'd left off.

The deep leaf mould and innumerable littering branches and sticks and fallen trunks (partly from natural decay and partly from the slashing activities of a prior work-party that had been through to clear the first part of the two metre wide trail) all made walking slippery-slow.

The trail wound up and down the mountain spurs, crossing mountain streams and creeping inexorably upward. I plodded along the floor of this seemingly endless ocean of green, pausing often to listen to the all-pervading, dense silence broken only by the deafening, pulsing and bellowing bellows of my beleaguered heart and lungs labouring to maintain equilibrium in the rarefied atmosphere.

So again, there was time to notice the little things: an occasional unidentified sound; a lemon-yellow or snow-white toadstool; a splash of pale lilac fungus on a rotting log; the red-fruiting cupules bordering the edge of a bright-green lichen; a cat's paw print in the mud at a stream edge; the crash of a middle-sized something high-tailing off through the undergrowth; twigs or leaves falling from on high draws one's gaze upward, maybe to see a white-faced monkey or squirrel or bird.

I saw a large, dark-chocolate butterfly with bright yellow wing-edging at 1,590msl; an iridescent pale blue butterfly at 2,210msl; heard the brrrrum of a humming bird at 2,770msl. I picked up two-centimetre sized frogs in various pale shades of dress, from soft yellow-green with powder-blue feet to an all over hue of misty blue.

Atop one ridge, I emerged from the forest to cross a few hundred metres of sunlight. My! The views! Range after range of tree-clad peaks. At some time in ages past, a wind has roared across this ridge felling huge-trunked trees, which now lie mouldering beneath their coverings of bracken, leaving others standing as silvered sentinel trunks denuded of branches.

My most exciting find was a mass of feathers; testimonial to a battle between a hunting bird and a quetzal. The quetzal feathers were scarlet or shimmering sax-blue or green. That's probably the closest I'll ever get to seeing wild the national bird of Guatemala. The tail feathers, nearly as long as your forearm, were of glistening metallic-green or blue, depending on how the light caught the colour. They are too long to post to you – I donated them to Phil and Clare – and enclose smaller samples for you to wow over.

At another place I nearly stepped on a low heap of black, furred bits of skin whose short and long, white and black-tipped quills gave clues to the deceased. No blood or skeletal remains; so what skins its prey? I don't know.

Dozens of shiny, blue-black scarab beetles, about one centimetre long, were busily engaged in their undertaker work of balling up the remains and rolling it off for burial (it becomes food for their larvae).

As I climbed higher and higher, I passed through three distinctly different vegetation zones. At about 2,500m came gnarled and twisted shrubby trees, their branches dripping feathered icicles of whitish moss giving the trees a ghostly shroud. About one hundred metres higher up these gave way to tall stately trees festooned with a yellowish brown moss – I wanted to take photos, but by that time I'd dumped my load, including camera: anyway, it was cloud-mist going up and pouring rain when I came down.

I reached the crest of a mountain ridge (not my ultimate goal) when the trail started going down again. Time called a halt. No more exploration just now. I'd promised Phil I'd be back the next day and I knew I had at least four more hours of walking up to get to my goal – the end of the cut trail.

I stopped at 2,770msl amongst huge trees with trunks at least two metres diameter, their tops lost in the mist. Dense patches of flowering bamboo; whose canes leaned any which-way formed impenetrable tangles.

While I sat in a gap among the bamboo eating my peanut butter sandwich and sweet hard-tack biscuits, I heard a humming bird. It was probably zipping around checking me out; the stranger in its territory

Going down ought to have been easier than coming up because I didn't have to keep stopping to pant, but the rain had made the decaying vegetation very slippery underfoot and I glissaded on my bum as often as not.

The stepping stones of a stream, that I'd crossed almost dry-shod a few hours earlier, had disappeared under swirling brown water. A few yards upstream, boulders a metre apart looked a likely crossing point. I crawled across; tricky with pack on back as one had to get the balance just right.

The rain made my trousers so heavy, they kept falling down (Guatemalan rubbish, huh!). The rain soaked down my socks so that I sploshed along in my personal puddles. The rain, the rain – but without the rain this forest wouldn't be the lush green, green that it is.

Late in the afternoon the rain eased off enough for me to set up my sleeping-system in the comparative dry. It consists of a groundsheet, upon which I lay my sleeping mat, over which I erect my home-made net-curtain-tent-contraption and that is covered with my opened poncho. Then I stuff my sleeping bag inside, wriggle in me and there I am, snug as a bug in a rug (as my grandmother would say).

All was snug and warm until the thunderstorm and I awoke lying in a stream as the water found the path of least resistance – the trail upon which I lay, it being the only clear space!

And the night had started so glorious with moon and stars garlanding the trees.

I sit here today, (November 30) in Phil's rented, spacious but sparsely furnished, three-bedroomed wooden bungalow in the village of Alturas, recounting to you my tales of the last few days. This morning was glorious sunshine, but now the fleecy little clouds have amassed to unload their burden again this afternoon. So much for the end of the rainy season!

In between writing, I've been popping in and out drying my clothes, cleaning my boots and reviewing my sleeping system. Yes, I want to go up again, for a longer period, so that I can get to the end of the trail. Part of the exercise will be to devise a new way of keeping some things, and me, dry at night. Next time, I'll try my hammock with the tarp over that and sleeping bag wrapped in poncho. And being up in the air should keep me out of the reach of chiggers – those little mites that will find a way into my hair follicles and live there whilst they develop and cause me furious itching.

Other nuisances to be outwitted: mosquitoes at the lower elevations – easy enough with repellent; pesky persistent little sweat flies that live higher up – they buzz around my face and dive-bomb into my eyes to get the precious minerals that we exude in tears. Insect repellent deterred them not a jot. Swishing with hand or leaf just made them more determined to beat the swipe and hit the eye before the swish. Pieces of fern stuck into my hair and dangling in front of my face were pretty effective, although somewhat blinkering to the vision. I'll try just plain old sunglasses.

All this has digressed from telling you about my job of marking the trail.

Having reached pole No. 47, I must measure one hundred and fifty metres from it with my fifty metre length of cord and insert at that point post No. 48, marking on it the altitude. Sounds easy, doesn't it?

Wrong!

I anchored one end of the cord at pole 47, scrambled and stumbled fifty metres along the narrow, little used trail and anchored the far end to a handy stout twig.

I returned to the start, picked up the first end and walked another fifty metres beyond the anchored end to make now one hundred metres from pole 47. Repeat again to get to position No. 48; one hundred and fifty metres away from No. 47.

Decision, should I trudge backwards and forwards with my backpack or dump it and have to return for it?

After a few false starts I devised my system as follows: tie one end to some suitable plant that will withstand some gentle tugging, then with cord wound round hand and elbow, pack and poles on back, walk fifty metres gently laying out the cord. Having reached the end of the cord, give an almighty heave, the cord tears free and can be wound in: much simpler and relatively snag-free.

And repeat – twice.

A helper would be handy!

You asked about the local food in Costa Rica. That's an easy one – rice and beans, or rice, or beans, or refried rice and beans. The beans are small and dark red and need to be soaked for hours and then take hours of boiling, unless they're fairly young – which they're usually not. The dish may be served with an egg, if the hens have been laying, or a small lump of some meat (goat?), shredded white cabbage and a couple of thin slices of tomato. And/or I can have bean soup, noodle soup or potato soup.

At feeding time Phil, Clare and I go down to the only 'café' in the village to eat our rice and beans. Actually we eat in a family's kitchen, which is dominated by the largest wood-burning Aga cooker that I've ever seen.

We eat surrounded by three generations of the family. All very friendly. They've known Phil for years and are very inquisitive about my presence. 'Um, just passing through,' says Phil. 'She's giving me a hand with marking the trail.'

And so I shall.

I'll write again with my mountain news when I return, as I intend to go up 'my mountain' again without the encumbrances of ropes and poles.

COSTA RICA

Letter Four - December 2nd
    A View across Two Countries

Yeah!!   I made it to the top of Mount Cerro Enchandi – 3,162msl: two days to get up and ten hours down. That was one tough hike!

The lower reaches that I'd trod before (on the measuring exercise) had been trampled by horses, so it was like walking up a steep, newly ploughed field with the soft, peaty earth clinging to each boot.

Coming back down the next day was more fun as the path had turned into a quagmire after heavy rain. But that was a cinch compared to the last five hours down and through the bamboo. Imagine the three little pigs' house of sticks after the big bad wolf blew it down, then imagine the effort of climbing, in tennis shoes, a frozen water-fall which has had a recent fall of light snow, put the two together and you begin to get the picture.

Although the trail had been cleared by the locals, the very clearing had removed support for the plants so that the three to six metre high bamboos, some as thick as your wrist had, in places, collapsed drunkenly across the trail. Twice I lost the trail completely and had to crawl around in the midst of the tangle of stems to find a way through. Just wait until I tell Phil!

This time I'd taken my sleeping-system with the hammock.
The first night was OK. I slept fitfully in dry clothes wrapped in the poncho. But the second night at 2,880msl was something else. My poncho was soaked inside and out and so not very effective. I'd not taken my three-season sleeping bag as I was carrying a load of water and I took just my buffalo sleeping-sheet bag.

I'd made camp at 3.30 p.m. and shivered my way through the hours until 5 a.m., when I gave up and got up, noting that the temperature was 10° C. I left my camp and climbed to the tops unencumbered, to watch the gold and then silver dawning across the mountain tops.

    A beautiful, beautiful, rich morning.

From my bare-top mountain, I could see for miles and miles (saying 'I could see for kilometres and kilometres' just doesn't have the same ring to it, does it?) in every direction across the rumpled folds of valleys and mountains into Panama. In fact, I found the trig point and stood with one foot in Costa Rica and the other in Panama.

Part of Phil's grand plan is to bring up tourists to stand in two countries at the same time.

The vegetation up there was mostly of knee-high 'bushes' of bamboo, bilberry-like plants, club mosses, bracken, sphagnum and other unfamiliar flora. I wandered around for an hour or so and then started the seventeen kilometre hike back to my hammock bed.

Of note: at 1,990msl - Spider Monkeys with pale foxy-red bodies with darker limbs and long, long prehensile tails. They made a noise like the yap of a small dog with a sore throat.

At 2,600msl - White-faced monkeys tearing off bromeliads and moss from the canopy branches. Their sound was a short, single bark, probably a warning that a stranger was in their patch.

4th December 1990

Anne, I'm going to have to leave you for a while, but before I do so, I want to write for the record that my personal wall was breached. It came about this way: Clare had left and curious Phil was intrigued as to why I was travelling alone – Was I married? Did I have a family? I couldn't answer his questions. I choked-up, throat constricted, eyes filled and tears spilled. I just couldn't get the words out.

'Look, I'm sorry to upset you,' he said gently. 'It's not my business, but some things are better out than in. If you want to tell me later, that's OK, if you don't want to say anything at all, that's OK too.'

Embarrassed, I went to my room.

On a later day and with a glass or two of wine, I told him how my sense of self had shattered when I found out that Mike, my ex., had fallen deeply love with a sixteen-year-old Singaporean boy, lithe and beautiful and bronzed. (My ex. used to go to Singapore on business.) He was forty-years-old at the time. I was devastated. I felt totally led up the garden path and had married under false pretences – to a queer. (We're talking the mid-sixties when homosexual acts were against the law.)

For years I'd known something in our relationship wasn't right – why didn't he love me? He never once said 'I love you.' We didn't hold hands walking along, we never cuddled, we never French-kissed; I never felt we belonged together.

I felt so lonely so much of the time.

And when he found his teenage Singaporean lover on his trips to Singapore in the late sixties our relationship really slid downhill. I felt used and abused (mentally). I felt the last fifteen years had been a complete sham and cover-up.

Can't say any more now; my eyes are tearing again. Self-pity is all.

Tomorrow Phil will take me down the road to get the bus to San Vito; from there I can get a bus going south to Panama.

I'll continue my story when at my next place of rest.

Wishing you a joyous Christmas from the mountains of Costa Rica.

Bron

PART THREE
A year In The Panama Canal Zone
Working On Barro Colorado Island

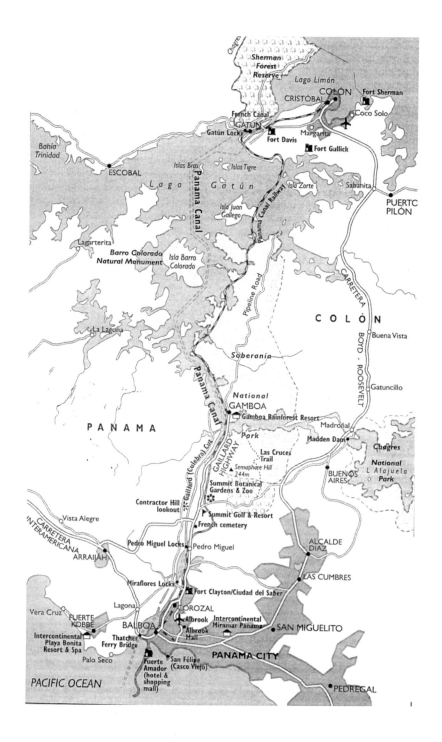

22. PANAMA
Arrival & Adventures on BCI

December 8th 1990

Dear Anne,

As you will see from the postage stamp, I've left Costa Rica and am on my adventures further south. I left Las Alturas at dawn last Wednesday (5th Dec), waving goodbye to 'my' mountains cast into gilded and shadowed relief by the rising sun.

I came to Panama 'on spec' looking for a job.

(The money here is called a Balboa - fortunately it is pegged equal to the American dollar - after the conquistador Vasco Nuñez de Balboa.)

(Please skip the next bit if you don't want to read a 'travelogue'. It's really for my sake, as I know that you are holding my memory 'n' information bank.)

[I changed buses at San Vito for the half-hour journey across the misty mountain slopes, blanketed by plantations of coffee, coffee and more coffee: it grows best at around 3,000msl. We must have been at 2,000msl before the bus began its slow, switchback descent. Fleecy clouds far below hovered intermittently above the landscape of rivers and farms.

I changed buses again at Ciudad Neily, eventually finding the next bus stop after a hike across the small town. Then waited an hour for the bus to Canoas – it arrived already very crowded. (Canoas is the border town between Costa Rica and Panama.) The open-sided bus (there is heavy-duty, green ground-sheet-like material rolled up at the 'windows' – a meagre concession as rain-protection for the passengers) was crowded because locals go to the border to shop at the many small supermarkets and innumerable street stalls selling mostly very cheap clothing and electrical goods brought across from Panama.

The border crossing was pretty painless, except that I had inadvertently walked past the baggage check and was absent mindedly looking around in the rain for my next bus, when a chap accosted me. I looked at him suspiciously. Waving his hands he said something about my luggage. I grinned and nodded and wandered on. He came after me. He was the Customs officer! No uniform, so how was I to know? He made me open everything, which took some time because of all the padlocks and the bits of string I'd used to tie-on the gear that wouldn't fit into my backpack. By time I'd opened up, he'd got fed up so just briefly poked through my stuff and then wandered off, leaving me to fasten it all up again.

On the other side of the border I got the mini-bus to David, a small town about halfway to Panama City, where I spent the night in a not-too-bad-doss-house.

I found the post office and posted all the letters I'd written while staying at Phil's.

The fourth bus was a Greyhound – strange, I thought they only lived in the U.S.A. – which I caught bright 'n' early for the seven hour ride to Panama City.]

To me, Panama City is like all the capitals from all the other Central American countries (including Belize and Mexico) rolled into one. Hell is milling throngs oozing off crowded pavements and dicing with death as the noisy, oily, careless traffic passes by regardless. I wished I were a tortoise, able to pull my head into my shell and pretend I wasn't there. It's a big culture shock after the solitude of the jungle mountain forests.

I've never liked a city on first arriving; although for most I've developed a reserved fondness after a few days. I don't think I'll ever like Panama City. It's too big and has too many security men with their carbines (rifles) standing in the shop doorways. They're no more than teenagers and I just hope that they're not too trigger-happy.

The old colonial part of the city is so run down; so full of uncollected garbage stinking in the heat, and cats – thin and slinking scared, and dogs with ribs for counting on, and street people.

A taxi driver at the bus station refused to take me to the address I asked for, others pretended not to know where it was or said, 'Too far, too far.' I knew it couldn't be that far (judging by the street map in my trusty South American Handbook) and so I thought, Up yours! and walked.

The first hostel I went to in the old town no longer existed, just a decaying empty building with its door missing and the shutters hanging askew.

I found a 'pension' (a B&B) in a reasonable street, but as it charged US$10 per night I could only afford one night. I dumped my backpack and spent the rest of the afternoon striding manfully around trying to get my mapless bearings.

On my way back, a small man (now why do I say small? – because all these Latinos are small compared to my height: oh, and they call me 'Señor' because I'm tall and wear a Stetson-type hat) of about my age, clutching a brown paper bag, opened the conversation with, 'Do you speak English?'. He'd seen me walking in the old town and proceeded to caution me of the dangers of walking about after dark – by then it was about 5 p.m. and already getting dusk in this almost-on-the-equator city. He turned out to be a local resident on an errand for his mother and proved most helpful in telling me where to get buses, where to find the Smithsonian Institute, where to go shopping and so on. His conversation was also much filled by stories of thieves, traffic killing pedestrians, buses cutting corners and knocking pedestrians off pavements. 'No-one cares, it's just another accident,' he states. After ten minutes of this I was quite twitchy.

Chores for tomorrow: find the Smithsonian Institute, find some money, find a city-map and find another bed.

At the Smithsonian, a very helpful Visitors' Office gave me a city map, put me on the trail to find the people I wanted to meet regarding a job and booked me into Barro Colorado Island Research Station; familiarly known as BCI and so called for the red of its clay soils, (barro is clay and colorado is coloured in Spanish). I jumped at the chance to get out of the city, but couldn't go until Monday when the STRI ferry would dock at Gamboa to pick up the island workers. I'd just have to risk that Dr. Robin Foster (the contact I was seeking) was still on the island and didn't come off on Monday: his work was nearly finished and he was due to return to the States.

Barro Colorado Island is a man-made island created in 1914 when Gatun Lake formed as the River Chagres flooded valleys, leaving the hill-tops as islands, during the building of Panama Canal. The 1,600 hectares of BCI was, in 1923, initially set aside by the United States government as a nature reserve and administered by the Panama Canal Company (U.S.).

In 1946 the administration was taken over by The Smithsonian Institute.

BCI has been a mecca for tropical research dedicated to rainforest ecosystems since 1929. Research blossomed during the 1930s when scientists visited from North America and conducted pioneering research on tropical fauna and flora.

Now BCI is recognised as the most comprehensively studied piece of land in the world.

Monday morning: I eventually found the American Express Bank, way, way across town and the only bank that would change my AMEX travellers' cheques. (I tried several.)

Next to find a bed for a couple of nights.

Peering at my photocopy map, I could see that it wasn't so very far to walk from the new town to the old town around the harbour with its many closed fish restaurants (closed because of a recent cholera outbreak). An hour and a half later I had found myself a bed at another address from the SA handbook. The area was run-down, but the landlady seemed nice. The room was adequate and only US$5.50. The landlady turned out to be a retired primary school teacher and we chatted about families and schools.

I'm finding it harder and harder to talk about my boys. It's so difficult to say that I don't know where they are or what they're doing. It just breaks my heart that they don't communicate. I do wonder what their father said to them to make them so. I well know from experience that he holds a grudge for years and is a spiteful, vindictive bitch. He would turn my boys against me just for revenge.

Today I caught the 6 a.m. bus to Gamboa, there to wait for the ferry to BCI.

Gamboa, a small development that grew around the canal-dredging activities, is a typical company town.

It was built in 1911 – at the point where the River Chagres enters the Lake – as housing for the Canal workers. It became the Dredging Division town of the Panama Canal Company in 1936 and reached a peak population of 3,853 in 1942. The population decreased during the subsequent years as the Americans moved to their new site nearer Panama City and when the railway closed in the late 1980s there was further population loss.

The only access to the town is by of a single-track, iron and wood bridge – and no traffic lights!

The other lone passenger on the ferry was a researcher on the Island and he told me about his work on plant growth in different conditions.

On arrival, he kindly showed me around this scattering of buildings set into the hillside, gave me coffee and tracked down the person I had come to see. Fortunately, Dr. Robin B. Foster was still on the Island and I was able to explain to him my situation and how I came to be there. He showed me his project (counting trees in a fifty hectare plot) and said that he could certainly use another pair of hands, but there was the money side to be considered. After lunch he left the island and I spent several hours walking over the project area in the centre of the island.

The laboratory side of the island had been cleared by people before and during the canal development and so is now secondary forest of forty to one hundred years old.

The far side of the island is primary forest, on land rising to about 170m above sea level, and is a very different-looking forest compared to the mountain rain-and-cloud forest I've recently been in, in Costa Rica. Generally, the trees are much smaller, although there are a few giants around shadowing the forest floor so that one can actually see through the under-storey for several metres.

I saw: agouti *Dasyprocta punctate,* a short-tailed, plant-eating rodent. It lives on the floor of rain-forests in South America and looks like a long-legged guinea pig about the size of a rabbit;

coati families (pronounced co-aah-tee) – looking like raccoons with long black and white banded tails waving in the air. The females live in troops with their young of various ages, but the males are solitary;

black howler and white-faced monkeys;

deer – which snorted and barked alarm at me;

three different-looking tiny brown frogs not much bigger than your thumb nail;

a *Tinamou* – a ground-living bird looking like an over-sized grouse with a long neck and very small head. It was using its down-curved bill to sift through the leaf litter for food. It lives only in South and Central America;

and I saw a tiny blackish snake.

(I've spent time in the library to add the notes for your edification.)

On Sunday it poured all day so I spent the time writing up my diary notes, exploring the herbarium (which has specimens dating back to the 1940s), learning the rudiments of a Macintosh computer and checking other people's field-work data.

Now here I am, lucky enough to get taken on as a volunteer worker because Dr. Robin needs all hands to finish the 1990 census and that involves re-measuring and re-checking the 300,000 trees; 36,000 trees left to do. Fifteen people have already laboured for eleven months and I am able to join in the final stages.

And so it came to pass that I'll spend time on BCI.

I'll leave you for now, while I go to work in this exciting new environment. So far, it beats teaching any day.

Please pass on my letters to those who might like to read them and thank you again for storing them.

I'm sure that one day I'll be around to re-read these letters and say, 'Gosh, did I really do that?'

Wishing you patience in the run-up to Christmas and enjoy your holidays.

With love.

Your jungle friend Bron looking for her Tarzan.

Panama City Bus

23. PANAMA
A Night Walk on BCI

December 1990

Dear Anne,

I've just begun my new job as research assistant, general dogsbody more like, doing the mind-numbingly tedious stuff of collecting data for the researchers.

The island is covered with tropical lowland forest over most of its 3,865 acres, with fifty kilometres of well-worn trails, named with small signboards at their beginnings. The land is fairly flat; the highest point being only twenty-seven metres above Gatun Lake level.

I'd studied the crude trail-map on the board outside the dining room and, having half-an-hour to spare before dinner, decided to go on an exploratory walk: a short walk that turned into an overnighter. And now safely back in my room I can re-live my night.

I wandered along slowly, enjoying the unfamiliar sounds of the two-centimetre sized tree-frogs piping their calls, the saw-buzzing of the cicadas whose ear-splitting din rose to a crescendo to stop, suddenly, before starting up again all in unison and the unknown, strange-sounding bird calls. The vegetation is very large and lush and all the leaves look similar: I couldn't see more than a few metres to either side of the trail.

I strolled on and on and on thinking, Oh, I'll just see what's around this corner. I'm sure that if I continue along the trail, it'll join up with the Sebo Trail and that'll loop back to the dining room.

I felt a little anxious, even knowing that there are no dangerous animals on the island; just wild boar and snakes and biting spiders with their oh-so-toxic venoms and the army-ants on the march.

Soon I became aware that the light was fading. I'd forgotten that darkness falls very rapidly in the tropics – by about 6p.m. it's quite dark. I hadn't taken a torch or water or anything. After all, I was only going to be out for no more than half-an-hour. I'd better get back, I thought. 'And get a move on!' I admonished myself.

The trail unwound forwards, but to my hurrying, silent foot-steps it seemed unending.

Hmm . . . where is the trail junction? I puzzled. Suddenly, I spotted a small track leaving the main trail in what I felt to be the right direction back towards the buildings. I did vaguely remember it as a short-cut back to base.

And so I ran, trying to beat the fall of total dark. I hurried onto the track and as quickly as I could pushed through the undergrowth, jumped a small rivulet and got muchly scratched – unsuccessfully avoiding the spiny and thorny plants – and squelched through the boggy, mossy patches. But soon, very soon, too soon, the daylight was gone. How coalmine-dark it was under the dense canopy! No moonlight, no starlight penetrated the overhead foliage.

I became afraid and turned to follow the footpath back through the forest to the main trail.

I couldn't see it!

My thoughts in a whirl, I didn't know in which direction to go. Now what? It couldn't yet be 6.30p.m., I calculated. No-one will miss me yet. Even if I don't appear at dinner, no-one will bother that the new girl hasn't shown up.

I stood still while the mole-velvet dark wrapped around me. I was able to go neither forward nor sideways nor to backtrack. I felt very stupid and sorry for myself.

And then it began to rain.

Lightning, for the blink of an eye, lit the trunks of the soaring trees and the giant ferns and the fallen logs all about me. Thunder roared through the forest making my heart pound. I stood straight under the broad but inadequate leaf that I was holding as an umbrella. The water ran down its stem and streamed off the leaf-blade edges. Within minutes I was soaked.

Without a watch, time was immeasurable, unending.

I wanted to sit, but daren't. I thought of the red fire-ants and the black marching-ants, the golden-ants and the termites; so many species.

I questioned myself, 'What about the snakes that go hunting in the night? If I move I might tread on one'.

I crouched for a change of position, but my leg muscles cramped and in the end I sat on the peaty, sodden soil, fearing the unknown, still holding my inadequate leaf over my head.

'Oh crikey, what's that?'

I'd noticed something long, thin, shining luminous-green. I was sure it wasn't there a few minutes ago. Was it close to me or at a safe distance? I couldn't tell it was so dark. It never moved. I know about bio-luminescence in fireflies and glow-worms, but what is this that doesn't move?

After an age I felt emboldened enough to stretch out my fingers and tentatively touch . . . a stick. How weird was that?

(I later learnt about luminous fungi that grow on rotting wood.)

Lulled by the pounding rain, I eventually dozed, drifting in and out of dreams as the storm passed and the rain eased. When I surfaced again from the land of nod, I realised that tree shapes were discernible in the pre-dawn light.

'Patience,' I told myself sternly, 'wait a little longer and then you'll be better able to pass through this jungle to where a proper path might be.'

Which I did.

At last I set off, hoping that down was the way to get off the plateau and meet with a proper peripheral trail.

'Yippee, at last, finally, there is the trail,' I shouted gleefully, punching the air in triumph.

I jumped from the bank onto the wide track, heaved a big sigh of relief and set off at a jog – soaking wet, bleeding from the many scratches and very muddy after all the innumerable slides and falls – towards breakfast.

I got cleaned up and went to eat.

It was still early.
No-one had missed me.

You know Anne, I do sometimes wish that I wasn't quite such an independent person and then perhaps I wouldn't get myself into such pickles.

But I can't know how differently I might have turned out if Mum hadn't died when I was only twelve.

Or maybe this 'go-it-alone' is in the genes I inherited from Dad. He was always going off camping and cycling for days on end before he met Mum.

So . . . wiser after the event, as usual, I'll get to know this island and get it mapped in my head before setting off alone again.

What am I? . . Just your wandering friend *Bron*

24. PANAMA
My First Job as a Field Assistant

December 16th 1990

Dear Pal,

My dorm – top right

I see from the calendar that my year is starting with a new job and yours is finishing with the festivities of Christmas. Shall you sing the Nine Lessons and Carols at school or do you all still go to the local village church?

I've been here a week now and am slowly being accepted, although I feel a bit alienated amongst all the Ph.Ds. and have no suitable response to, 'What's your line of research?'

Some folk have been here for months or indeed years and some come and go after a few weeks. The researchers are mostly aged between twenty-three and thirty-five years old. Most of them are doing research for a doctorate or post-doctorate. Most come from universities in the U.S.A., but there are those from further afield too. They look at plants, frogs, insects, or whatever question merits a research grant.

Some of the subjects seem to me to have little relevance to the grand scheme of life. I'm assured that knowledge for its own sake will open new doors for someone somewhere on the planet.

My food binge is slowly abating as my taste buds become again familiarised to Kellogs Raisin Bran and marmalade and lettuce and peanut butter and so many of the goodies of a westernised diet. (When I first arrived I just couldn't stop eating and really binged on so much good food. It was such a change after months of eating rice and beans or spaghetti and something.)

The work-site is split into two. The new complex, very recently opened, comprises new offices, conference halls and a dining complex, with new dormitories and lounge sited below the dining hall and with views across the Lake.

I'm up the hill in the old complex built of wood in 1929. Here are all the old laboratories and the tiny old lounge with its sagging sofa and the stuffing coming out of its cushions. Each morning I trot down one hundred and twenty-one steps, across a plank bridge over a stream, (where I saw sitting on the hand-rail a penny-sized, blue frog with red trousers) and up forty steps to the dining room, have breakfast and then trot - not so rapidly - back up to the old labs.

I've spent two bewildering days on the Forest Dynamics Project (FDP) plot. It's half an hour walk through the jungle and I arrive at the site dripping sweat and the hot, dry-season is only just starting! It's very, very humid. I'm told that although it gets hotter, winds spring up and so the climate isn't so uncomfortable. My poor body doesn't know what's happening. One day I've just got acclimatised to 2,000msl mountains and the next I'm back at sea level and much nearer the equator.

The Forest Dynamics Project began in 1981 when a fifty-hectare plot was set up to study the change in plant ecology over time. The first census was completed in 1982. The plot is being re-censused every five years. It will provide unparalleled data on species' distributions and changes in forest composition. Computerization of the data is used to facilitate theoretical models about forest ecology. A parallel study, set up in the Pasoh Forest Reserve in 1987 in Malaysia, is providing a comparison.

And what are we actually doing?

I'll tell you.

The total plot is a fifty-metre square which has been divided into twenty-five metre squares, which are sub-divided into five-metre squares, each corner being marked by a metal pole. Within the small squares each woody stem of more than 1cm diameter at 1.3m height above ground, has been identified, mapped, numbered, tagged and measured. There are already about 240,000+ stems recorded, with more being added as seedlings have grown and now fall within the criteria.

Trees with great buttress roots are the most difficult to measure. The lads carry extending ladders to the site and climb up five to seven metres to get to a point more or less above where the buttresses start to fly out and measure there the trunk diameter.

Buttress roots: the name is taken from church architecture.

The Team have to get the tape-measure
above the buttresses to measure the
Trunk diameter

I've also been trying to learn some of the species' names. There are three hundred and eight different tree species on the plot (more species in 50m^2 than in the whole of Europe!). The double Latin names are a mouthful. I take a few samples to my bedroom and lay them out with their name tags. Instead of counting sheep to sleep, I recite Latin names.

I'll give you an idea of what I do for my day's routine and you can compare it to a day in school.

It's quite a palaver getting ready for a day's work.

Before we set off into the forest we have to protect ourselves against the ticks and chiggers (see notes below). I soon evolved my technique which, at last, seems to exclude most of the little suckers.

First, on go cotton socks and a liberal dusting of sulphur powder around the ankles. More powder is liberally shaken into my knickers, although I'm sure that most of that gets sweated off and (other than giving me a strange sulphurous odour) serves little purpose.

Next, on with the long-sleeved shirt and army pants – made of a dense jungle material which does seem to baffle the penetrating perpetrators of human flesh.

Then, on with another pair of fine-weave socks to cover trouser bottoms and out with the sticky-tape (it's like four-centimetre wide sticky parcel tape) and wind it from ankle to mid-calf, with either a twist somewhere mid-way to expose the sticky side or with the addition of a separate strip of tape folded so that the sticky side is out. (With the proliferation of ticks in the dry season, the tape is nearly black with them at the end of the day.)

(This defence might foil the ticks bent on their journey from leaf-litter to crotch, but of course, misses all those that get brushed off the vegetation.)

I add sweat-bands, well doused in sulphur powder over my shirt cuffs and spray with insect repellent, on with the boots, pick up my small back-pack containing lunch, camera, insect spray, large plastic sheet to sit on, compass (so easy to get disorientated amongst the trees and sky not visible), hand-fork (for digging out lost flags and tags), new tag-tape and labels, new flags and water; must never forget the water or I'll be fainting from dehydration by the end of the day.

N.B. Ticks: (Family: Ixidae, Order: Acarina, Sub-order: Ixodides; I do so love these Latin names. I feel I should be able to set them to music – if only!). I guess most people know what a tick is and if they keep pets have probably seen one, at some time or other, as a little blob of chewing gum lookalike stuck to the animal's fur.

Ticks feed by first sawing a hole in one's flesh with their crab-like pincers (chelicerae) into which they then insert a barbed tongue-like thing called a hypostome, which acts like a drinking straw through which blood is pulsed up. In some species the whole structure is cemented into place, so the policy is to get 'em before they bed in. Sometimes the bite is felt, but usually not.

Blood meals are needed before the female lays her eggs on or near the ground and also before the larvae metamorphose into nymphs or adults. The six-legged larvae are called seed-ticks. They look like tiny poppy seeds or ground pepper grains, quite hard to see. I've dislodged, intentionally, a tick-ball from a leaf to be awed at the speed with which these mini-mites can cover the ground or host. Some researcher, in the interest of science, timed them – fifteen minutes from ground to crotch!

N.B. Chiggers on the other hand are impossible to spot. They are the six-legged larvae, 0.2mm, of the *Trombiculidae;* the young of the pillar-box red mites that live in the leaf litter – you may have seen their larger cousins in your greenhouse.

They scurry up one's body and race for the hair follicles or pores or soft wrinkles (under the bra for example) where they bite the skin, pour in their saliva and suck up digested cells. They feed there for two to three days – if allowed to. One's body reacts to form hardened skin cells which line the hole and form a stylostome. Like a tick, the chigger forms a straw-like structure through which it sucks up its dinner. It's the hard stylostome and the feeding enzymes that cause the severe itching which might go on for several days.

I react by producing small pink swellings which itch like crazy and form a lymph-filled blister. I've found some cream to apply which seems to be fairly effective.

At first all I saw of the forest was green leaves, all remarkably similar.

Now I'm beginning to see the faces amongst the crowd, so to speak. The trick is to spot the identifying characteristics, such as a particular pattern of veins, or hairs in a certain place, or a singular bit sticking out. This is all very well for the saplings growing within hand reach, but their grown-up siblings are tall trunks and one has to peer through binoculars at the leaves which may be thirty metres or more above one's head. The branches and vines are such a tangle up there; it's quite difficult to see which leaves belong to which trunk.

Practise will improve my ID skills.

Our job now is to re-measure each tree, replace old tags – some trees have a relationship with ants which delight in cutting off the tags – and record new stems.

I do the recording and those who know do the identifying. The Panamanian lad whose 'assistant' I am has already spent eleven months here so he recognises at a glance all the species. We have a few mistakes when I mishear his pronunciation of the numbers.

He's very patient with me and good at teaching me the identifying characteristics of these oh-so-similar leaves. We work for about four hours and then go back down the hill to our rooms to shower off the ticks and mites.

The rest of the day I spend in the lab cross-checking records, making new number-tags or trying to learn some trees' identifying features and their names.

As Robin's FDP Census is due to finish in the next week or two, he has very kindly and generously said that he'll pay, from his own pocket, my board and bed until January 1st. I trust that by then something else will have turned up.

Meanwhile, I'm reading loads of articles published on findings from the 1985 census: things like 'Sapling Response to Gaps', 'Diversity of the Canopy Trees in a Neotropical Forest', 'Short term Population Dynamics of Trees and Shrubs' and so on. I find it all such interesting stuff that I suggested to Robin that it would translate into a fun cartoon to show the dynamics of a forest over hundreds of years.

I think your evenings will still be busy with marking and preparing lessons.

I'll think of you as I attend our evening presentations by the researchers of their work, or a discussion of some recently published article, or we watch a video, or I could go for a walk around the camp, or swim in the moonlit Lake Gatun.

It's a very new style of life and I'm meeting some most interesting people who talk about visiting Asia or India or Africa as if it were a trip down the road to the next village.

Stay busy, stay happy.

Wishing you a joyous Christmas with your family.
Looking forward to your next news.
Bron

Spines on Black Palm

Spines on Hura Trunk

25. PANAMA
Marion & Nora

February 7th 1991

Hi there Dear Anne,

I hope you had a fun Christmas and New Year and were able to find some quiet time to recuperate from the frenzied end-of-term activities.

I suppose that by now you are well into a new round of exam entry activities. Are you still running to stand still, being housemistress as well? Don't do too much; leave time for yourself. Life's too short to give all your time to things you really don't want to do.

It was good to see Marion M. when she came for a visit in December, taking time out from her school in Cali, Colombia. I hardly recognised her; she'd lost so much weight. She's still the same in character though and created quite an impression on BCI with her extrovert sense of humour.

She's got herself a good job and has been offered Head of Science at her school. I envy her her money, but not the work.

I took a few days' break from my work and we went to visit Taboga Island, old Panama City, the Botanic Gardens and watched the ships passing through Miraflores Locks. On the days in between, while I worked, she explored BCI.

Passing through the locks

201

Marion brought me up to date with the gossip of Piper's Corner School after I left and before she left (she claims it was my example that motivated her to leave the UK) and what's happened since. She'd had news via Audrey's letters. I am so glad to be out of all the school pettiness.

She wrote to say the new Chemistry teacher (at the Cali school) didn't turn up at the start of the autumn term so she had to run all those classes as well as her own; and do all the grades and reports for both sets of classes.

Took her two weeks! Sound familiar?

I've been very busy during the last two months. Firstly working on Robin's Forest Dynamic Project, which has now finished, and then for Nora.

Nora works for the U.S. Forestry Department and is based in Hawaii. Two years ago she set up a project here to monitor the growth of transplanted seedlings of five tropical tree species. Her aim is to discover which species might be the most suitable to use for reforestation.

On Gigante – a peninsula of the mainland across from the southern side of BCI – she has twenty sites laid out in clearings; ten natural ones made by the high winds of nature blowing down big, and I mean big, trees maybe fifty metres high, and ten sites in clearings that she laboriously created (with man-help of course) by felling and removing the trees. Within the clearings, and extending into the forest on all sides, she planted three thousand tree seedlings of the five selected species at three-metre intervals on a grid system. Each plant was marked by a stout, forty-centimetre high wire rod topped by a three-centimetre square of red plastic to make a flag. Around each flag was tied a small, metal, numbered tag.

That was two years ago and now Nora's back to find and re-measure her seedlings.

And that's where I come in, to help Maria Elena the Panamanian worker, to locate the flags, find the seedlings and re-measure them. It's really a hunt-the-flag exercise as most of the marker flags have become buried under leaf-litter, tree-falls, the rapid growth of the under-growth, or been eaten by ants or whatever else might like to remove or disguise a red forestry flag.

The following is a typical day's work.

The day's activities soon slipped into the ease of routine; starting with the after-breakfast ritual of girding my body against the pervasive onslaught of ticks and chiggers. (By now I am well practised in putting on the tick-defence-armour.) Suitably garbed and guarded, I trot down the one hundred and forty-six steps to the dock where Nora is already loading the three, six-gallon gas-tanks into the dinghy (a flat-bottomed Boston Whaler about two metres long and powered by a 30hp motor) which we use to take us the twenty to thirty minute ride from BCI to Gigante.

We wait for the arrival of the ferry bringing the Panamanian workers across the lake from Gamboa. Marie Elena, a buxom dark-skinned mestiza (of mixed Spanish and white blood) of cheery, chatty disposition, disembarked and joins us. (She has worked before with Nora.)

The lake waters are usually fairly calm for our morning journey to Nora's site, although the bow-wave-swells fanning out from the prow of a huge cargo transporter ponderously moving along the Canal from Atlantic to Pacific, or vice versa, can cause exhilarating moments. If one is passing, Nora slows and turns our boat to meet the oncoming waves. Once, the waves were travelling so rapidly and so close together that our prow dipped and was unable to rise fast enough before the next wave broke over us and dumped three-centimetres of water into the bottom of our boat. We bailed out using litre bottles with the top cut away.

A passing transporter

Bumping along at twenty-five knots throws up a fine spray from our prow. The spray catches the morning sunlight and turns into an accompanying rainbow.

We turn away from the main Canal and away from the wash of the big cargo transporters into a channel with protruding posts marking the navigable route. One morning, on turning the corner into the channel between the island of BCI and the mainland peninsula, the water appeared as if frozen: a dead flat, opaque expanse mirroring clouds and trees. Magic!

Oh, how lucky I am to be no longer in a nine to five office job!

Valleys were flooded when the Canal was built so we are actually moving between hill-tops – a strange thought. Occasional gaunt, silvered trunks near the water's edge stretch out denuded, lifeless limbs. Their contemporaries in deeper water extend a topmost branch above the lake surface providing a site for the growth of water plants and the beginning of new islands.

Cormorants (and occasionally gulls) sit on the marker-posts at regular ten-metre intervals, doing apparently nothing. Heads flipping from side to side as they agitatedly watch our approaching boat. If we pass too near they launch themselves awkwardly off their posts, clumsily dipping down to paddle the water and creating twin spreading pools of ripples before they gain enough speed to wing away. Over several mornings the numbers of cormorants increased until not a post was without its sentry, and those birds without a post were swimming as a flotilla of submarines.

Then one day they were all gone.

We tie up the boat at the Gigante landing-stage and make our way along the broad trail to the plot of the day. Two years of leaf-fall, rapid growth of vines and under-storey plants and new tree-falls bringing down a mess of canopy, all combine to make the task difficult and in places impossible.

In the tropics just about every tree and shrub has its attendant ants, which shower onto us as we push through the vegetation. Vines, the size of string or thin rope, wrap around one's feet and impede progress; seemingly solid trunks crumble at a touch as we scramble over them, their insides macerated by termites.

We doggedly move up and down the plot-lines, tracking flags and plants, many of which have died. Some tags are untraceable, some eaten into doilies by the ants, or made invisible with moss and lichen. We tidy and replace and rejoice when a living seedling is found – some seedlings had grown a lot, others hardly at all, others had disappeared completely.

When all the data is collated, Nora will be able to know which plants are good for reforestation – Panama has only five per cent of its original forest cover remaining.

There is no breeze in the forest. If one stands still in the patches of sunlight, sweat instantly runs in rivulets down one's chest and back, drips from one's nose and runs into one's eyes. (Marie Elena seems hardly to sweat at all and her skin is cool to touch. I wonder if her Negro genes give her that advantage.)

Each day brings a new gem: a brilliantly coloured butterfly; an insect on bark masquerading as a piece of lichen; a strangely-shaped beetle; a pale fawn, bootlace-snake with a lizard in its mouth; a troop of spider or white-faced monkeys; a mosquito with iridescent blue feet; an intricate spider's web with gaudy red spiders hanging therein; a big, fat toad all puffed up in indignation; a tiny, leaf-shaped, green-brown frog; a large white-with-purple-scribble vine flower looking like Laura Ashley velvet.

We watched a yellow manakin, a small black bird about the size of a house sparrow and wearing a lemon-yellow cap, displaying on its lek. It made a sound like two stones being banged together as it hopped from perch to perch or jumped across its courting ground – a patch of earth, about thirty centimetres across, that the bird had cleared. Holding onto its perch, it leant forwards and made a noise like a stick dragged rapidly along metal railings. Both noises are made by its wing feathers; surprisingly loud for such a small bird.

It's a biologist's paradise.

I am so very lucky.

At last it is time to pack up and get Marie Elena back to catch the returning ferry.

We walk smartly through the incessant wheeee, wheeeeeeeeeee, wheee, pause and repeat, of the cicadas' high-pitched, chain-saw-buzz sort of noise that rises and falls in waves of crescendo and diminuendo as the thousands of insects all sound together and pause together.

The howler monkeys begin their evening chorus. It's the males that call, sounding like some giant groaning and ending with a plaintive, 'Oooooh, uh'.

Green parrot flocks fly to their night roosts, busily telling each other in high-pitched Mr. Punch squeaky voices, 'Let's do it, let's do it', or, 'Can't do it, can't do it'.

The afternoon winds have whipped the lake into white-crested waves. The return journey brought to mind riding a bicycle with a flat tyre over cobblestones. I felt a mixture of, Isn't this fun! and, Stop, I want to get off! The bow of the boat smacks down hard and soaks us in spray, but Nora keeps the throttle fully open and we bounce from wave to wave grimly hanging on.

Yesterday's bum bruises will be worse than ever. I tell myself to remember that this has got to be better than commuting to London and of course it is. Not every day is so rough.

Back in my room, I divest myself of my field clobber and hang everything outside on the balcony rail. Then, sticky tape in hand, several minutes are spent searching my naked body for and mopping up any ticks that had got into those tight, cosy places they like so much, such as armpit or groin. Next, into the shower as hot as I can bear it and a good rub all over with a rough sponge.

In spite of all that, clean ticks must now be removed, necessitating the use of a mirror to search those places the eye can't see – you'd be surprised where the little suckers can get to. It's easy to grab them between my nails to crush them with a satisfying sqidge.

Feeling clean at last, I go down to the dining room for a good meal and lots and lots of drink – water and squash.

The month spent with Nora was very hard work. We worked weekends too, because Nora had to finish before the end of February when she returns to Hawaii.

We'd mapped the plots, marking the location of each plant onto graph paper, and drawn in streams, paths, fallen trees, gradients and clearings. From each plot we'd extracted eight soil samples using Marie Elena's superior strength to push the two-centimetre diameter soil auger thirty-centimetres into the rapidly drying red clay soil. She actually twisted the thick steel tube twice; we had to get it straightened in the workshops. During the evenings in the labs, the soil has to be weighed and put into a drying oven and the previous day's dried samples re-weighed; so that Nora can get an estimate of the soil-water content to see if that has any effect on the death of her plants.

It is without regret that I've returned to the easier life of another stint on Robin's Forest Dynamics Project; I'm just wandering around replacing the marker flags. But, however sweaty, dirty and bitten I get, it's always better than teaching at Pipers.

Chugging to work in a dinghy in the silvery, early morning light is magic. By the way, I now have a Panama Canal Commission Motorboat (up to 8m) Operator's Licence (what a mouthful!) to add to my collection. (a PCCMOL)

It was a bit like taking a driving test without the driving. I had to learn all the different light and sound systems of the various types of vessels plying the canal: while under-way, at anchor, aground, passing in fog and so on. It was all very confusing until I'd drawn myself lots of little pictures of boats.

Nora showed me how to do the actual driving, which was very easy really, in our little Boston Whaler. It was twenty minutes to get to her project site on Gigante, but I didn't drive then and now I don't need to. I don't suppose that I'll drive a boat very often as the petrol is about $6 (£3) a gallon.

While waiting for another job to materialise on BCI, I went back to San José (Costa Rica) to get my dive gear from where I'd stored it in the youth hostel and check if any mail had arrived at the city *poste restante*. (Zilch)

Ten days later, when I returned to BCI, I found a note saying that Dr. Lasker could use me on his project; working on the coral reefs around the San Blas Islands.

Sounds exciting and different.

How fortuitous that I now have my dive gear with me.

To be a STRI diver I had to take a STRI diver physical at the American hospital in the city; blood, urine, ECG, hearing, vision, everything you can think of, to test my state of fitness for diving. In typical American fashion lots of paperwork was involved.

The word has spread that I am interested in diving and the other night, at dinner, one of the game wardens (José) came to chat about the night-diving course he's running with SCUBA Panama. After some consultation, I'm pleased to hear that I can join them. I'm looking forward to my first dive in six months. We go next weekend.

Living on an island – sounds like a cue for a song – one occasionally has to go to the city to buy personal wants, or just for a change of scene.

I'm writing this letter on the old STRI ferry which plies between BCI and Gamboa; the dock on the mainland on the other side of the Canal. The journey takes about an hour, twice as long as the newer launch, which is out of the water for its service.

We left the island at 6 a.m. to fetch the morning workers, early enough to watch the dawn pinkly staining the sky and canal waters.

The ferry returns at 5.30 p.m. so one has to plan one's day carefully to catch the bus in the City to get back to the ferry on time.

Now my good friend, I'm going to impose upon your good nature and ask a big favour of you, to do at your convenience (no pun intended).

I have today posted off a large, long, oblong box to son Simon, care of your good self. It's my youngest's 21st birthday in April and I didn't know what to get him until I saw the hammocks in Costa Rica – that should do nicely, I thought. So I lugged one back on the buses to Panama and all the way around Panama City to find the only post-office that deals with 'large' parcels. They wanted $40 air rate so I had to say, 'Phew! No. What's the sea rate?' It's almost half the air price, so it's coming by sea and will take six to eight weeks.

I'm sending it via you because I'd love you to use your ample powers of persuasion to extract from him his current address – which you can then send to me. Even the correct D&B address will do, if that's where he's still working. I've written and written and written during the past year and have had no reply, so I don't know if I'm farting into the wind so to speak.

Mark is just as bad. It was only through a letter from step-mum that I learnt that Mark is now engaged. I suppose I ought to just stop minding and feeling so hurt each time I collect my mail and there's nothing from either of them – not even a Christmas card. It saddens me so. I'll soon have to stop writing anyway: I just don't know how to contact them and I can't keep on asking you to do things.

I'm enclosing a letter to Simon which perhaps you'd take to him together with his Birthday parcel which should arrive sometime in April.

Well, I'm sure I've bored you enough with this long saga, so will sign off now.

I wish you well and happy in your job.

Bron

February 12th 1991

Oh Anne,

I was so thrilled to find your letter in the mailbox this morning. I hugged it up into the forest where I could find a quiet spot to savour the reading of it.

I'm so glad that Fro, your beautiful horse, has recovered so well. What a sad, worrying time that must have been for you. Didn't you say that he might have suffered some liver damage after his fall?

My ankle is pretty good now – thanks for asking – although it still aches after stumbling around the forest for several hours. I guess the ligaments are still tight, but at least the foot doesn't swell now.

A friend (charged with dealing with my monetary affairs and forwarding mail) sits on my mail, sent via him, and some letters (when I do eventually get them) are six months old. But news, no matter how old, is important to me. And I do still like news from Pipers. Please feel free to spill your heart out, you're my only source of gossip from there. Please remember me to Jenny and June and send them my commiserations or should I say jubilations. What will they do now they've retired?

My Spanish doesn't improve much (though I was secretly pleased that it's better than Marion's). When she was here we didn't speak Spanish, but as she has to use the language in her working environment I'm sure that she'll quickly become very fluent; she has a fair aptitude for languages. I've decided that my brain is too stiff and given up worrying about ever being able to converse properly.

I'm pleased to hear that you're out riding both horse and bike. Consider the bike yours. I don't suppose that I'll ever need it again.

Talking of riding, not so long ago I'd taken a few days off from BCI to go into the interior with a chap (also from BCI) who's collecting tree leaf samples, same tree species, different sites, to compare them with his trees on BCI.

We went to a mountainous area in the north of Panama – it took more than three hours in the jeep to reach the foothills.

When getting to the actual site in El Vallé, in the North of Panama, I spent six hours in the saddle of a very stubborn pony.

The saddles were huge contraptions compared with our light English saddles. They had tough leather strappings (no softening saddle-soap here) and a pommel big enough to rope a cow to. The stirrups were like half a bowl turned on its side into which one thrust one's toes.

I reckon my leg grip was all wrong as the insides of my thighs had swelled up mightily by the next day and I felt as if I was walking holding a rolled-up towel wedged in my crotch – very undignified!

So you're still going out with David, uh huh, nudge nudge, wink wink. An adage my Grandma used to say and I've found to be very true – if in doubt, don't – and you seem to be in doubt, so don't. You'll know when it's right.

And he has two kids of six and nine! Starting over with someone else's kids when you've attained the age of freedom – no way! Go out with the guy by all means, but unless you can't live without him, don't lay yourself down (oh, is that a Freudian slip or what?) to be his house-keeper-cum-child-minder.

Perhaps you might try living with him. That might give you a better feel to know what you want.

And if you take on kids of that age you're looking at ten to fifteen years of coping with teenagers again. That'll make you nearly sixty with teenagers in the house! Yipes! I know it's very difficult being alone, but problems do disappear as one becomes more self-reliant and self-confident.

Enough advice from me – telling grandmamma what to do! Being surrounded by so many self-competent individuals, I'm having to revamp many of my notions of how people interact.

February 13th

I've just been talking to José about the SCUBA trip this weekend.

I have to go and meet the instructor on Friday evening, to be vetted I guess, and to pay.

(I earned $200 working for Nora and I got $200 from Jack for counting fallen nuts in twelve by twelve metre plots under five different trees, at three day intervals, for two months.

Half of the money went on the Costa Rica trip and the rest will be swallowed up by SCUBA membership and outings' costs.)

Enjoy half-term dear friend.
Thinking of you with love.
Bron

26. PANAMA
Golden Visions Along the Canal

March 4th 1991

Hi Anne,

How's the weather been in your neck of the woods? Variable I bet. Always plenty to talk about with the weather in the UK!

In Panama there is the wet and there is the dry. The dry lasts about three months from December to February and the rest of the year is wet.

In February there were two weeks of dry and then several days with quite a lot of wet.

A week or so after the rain several species of tree burst into bloom. One day nothing, the next a riot of daffodil yellow or scarlet or summer-sky blues, then three or four days later nothing on the trees, but the ground underneath is a mass of their fallen petals; splashes of bright colour among the browns and greens of the forest floor.

Robin doesn't think that anyone is researching into why some trees flower at the start of the dry season and others at the start of the wet – yet!

The *Tabebouias* (don't have an English name) are very tall emergent trees lauding their crowns of gold over the canopy like so many rising balloons. They drop all their leaves at the start of the dry season and so the massed display of their flowers is quite unimpeded and startling against the greens of the forest canopy.

I went on the ferry to Gamboa, just to see the *Tabebouias'* display along the canal. The petals fall to carpet the ground and I was reminded of a field of buttercups when walking through them: a touch of beauty, but for me not as soul-stirring as an English beech wood wearing its new, spring, lime-green over a carpet of bluebells.

It's feels odd reading your tales of snow and frost while I sit in this hot humidity. I think of the things that were special to me while walking in England – trees sparking with their coating of hoar frost, the deep shush of walking on a pristine blanket of snow. I do miss the English spring. The tropics have their moments of glory, but one really needs to be in a helicopter to fully appreciate the trees in flower.

Good news. Hooray! I am now allowed to drive the STRI jeep. I had to get a Panama licence in addition to my UK one.

To get the licence took a whole morning to-ing and fro-ing around the various hospital departments: for a hypoglycaemic (low blood sugar) test – so no breakfast that morning - proof of my blood group, and $30 lighter in pocket.

It's good to drive again after eighteen months of relying on shank's pony and the packed buses never on schedule. It took me a while to remember to release the hand-brake; too busy concentrating on all the controls being on the wrong side in the car and driving on the wrong side of the road.

So what with my Panama Driver's Licence, my Motorboat Driver's Licence, my STRI Identity Card and an American Driver's Authorization card, my wallet is quite bulging with plastic.

I'm still ploughing through the red-tape to be a STRI-diver: $91 for a hospital medical that took three visits into the City and lots of tests from which my blood showed anaemia, high cholesterol and low protein (the doc asked me if I lived on BCI!!) AND my heart had a systolic murmur when I did heavy exercise, huh!!?? That's news to me.

Otherwise A1 OK.

I had to have my scuba regulator serviced, another $24, and CPR certification. So all in all quite an expensive week.

Last Saturday Steve Miller, the STRI diving officer, ran a class for CPR; although I've read all the books, I've never before practised on a dummy. I hadn't realised how fast and hard one has to pump the chest and breathe into the mouth. I was too slow and had to do it again.

So that's that. Well and truly certified. But I still have to wait for the OK from Washington D.C. and go for a check-out dive with Steve.

Meanwhile I've been diving with a club called *SCUBA Panama*.

I drove the jeep to the Caribbean coast, to a diving place near Portobelo. The water was a bit murky, but I was still able to see lots of corals, although few fish. I've been spoilt by the crystal-clear waters and the excellent diving conditions off the shores of Roatán, Honduras.

On one Honduran dive we went down the anchor line for thirty-seven metres – a strange experience, in deep, dark water, with nothing to refer to except the folk on the line. We just went down and down and then came straight back up, stopping for decompression (which means we have to hang onto the line and remain stationary for a determined amount of time to allow our blood pressure to equalise with the lessened water pressure) on the way.

I would've liked to have spent a few minutes on the silty bottom to get orientated and register sensations.

Some of the other dives in Honduras were at night. The corals were much more colourful by torchlight and one sees different things, such as the hunters who came out from their hidey-holes. I'm looking forward very much to being a STRI diver on San Blas.

It's bucketing down at the moment (I'm watching from my room); a real tropical thunderstorm. Dry season? Huh! I got drenched coming back from the forest. Creeks that were bone dry a few hours ago were soon rushing torrents.

I'm enjoying myself here. I was only thinking today that I don't have to stay here. At a moment's notice I could pack my backpack and take off. But I've rather got to like this cushy life; good food, no food preparation or washing up, good company (even though the folks come and go so it's hard to make a friend), a room to myself, hot water and free laundry facilities.

I'm conscious of the fact that I'm living out of Robin's pocket. The project funds have dried up. I get the feeling that he's hunting for useful things for me to do, but is too kind to tell me to scarper. I've put an advert in the STRI newsletter to ask if another researcher needs a field assistant.

Sometimes researchers would rather collate and interpret data than spend the hours, nay, days after days, collecting it. That's where I come in – if they have grant money to spare.

I enclose some *Tabebouia* flowers for you.
Hope they stay yellow for your Easter.
With love
Bron

27. PANAMA
Job Change

March 17th 1991

My Dear Friend,
Thank you for your most welcome letter, read and re-read several times. I've been missing your company.

Are there *still* girls at Pipers who remember me?! It seems such a long time since I left. I thought I'd passed into history.

Perhaps, by now, you will have read my more detailed account of a typical working day on the island and not envy me too much. The recent rain has brought out a flush of chiggers, which I can't stop from making a home in my person, so I scratch, scratch, scratch, scratch.

I pushed through the undergrowth this morning, working my way up and down the Forest Plot lines, tying my strips of Day-Glo red ribbon on overhanging branches or nearby tree trunks, at each twenty metre interval, stopping periodically to mop up ticks with sticky-tape and sweating enough to soak my clothes. There is no breeze at all in the under-storey.

I was imagining crisp, cool air and mountains. I think I'm beginning to not like this humid heat with the temperature always hovering around 30°C (85°F) and the flattish landscape.

Your talk of snow seems another world – like mine must to you. I still have to pinch myself and ask, 'Am I really working in a tropical jungle?'

I had a few days of uncertainty last week before the penny finally dropped – Robin is leaving the island for nearly six months and the FDP has really finished for the next five years. I'm out of a job!

I'm not mentally ready!

I don't want to leave – off to face the unknown again.

I've started asking around again; perhaps someone else needs an assistant (meanwhile I am starting to think of moving on).

Ah ha! I've been offered more work through April and May, on the same terms with just my bed and board paid for.

March 25th 1991

My new boss has spent a life-time studying the conduction of water through plants and is a world authority on the subject. Although a lot is known about the hydrodynamics of trunks, branches and leaves, next to nothing is known about how water moves through roots, and so this will be the thrust of his latest research.

My job will be to count the pipes (xylem vessels) in the plumbing system of plants, just two species actually, and to excavate the root systems of said trees and so work out their entire architecture.

My boss and I went to find a possible specimen and we found a balsawood tree; about ten metres tall, perhaps five years old and surrounded by grass. It stood as a lonely tree, at one end of a small, flat-topped island maybe fifty metres by thirty metres and ten minutes boat ride from base.

When I first heard about Panama grass I had imagined something like English meadow grass.   Not at all.

This "grass" is three to four metres high, with razor-sharp leaves covered with fine hairs that stick in you, like fibre-glass, and with bamboo-like stems up to three centimetres in diameter. My boss said that he would get the workers to clear a sixteen metre diameter circle around the tree for me to work in.

By the way, Panama "grass" *Phragmites australis* is thought to have been brought to Panama as seed carried inadvertently by ships coming from Asia. It has spread rapidly and smothers water courses and ponds. It is a common reed which can spread five metres per year by horizontal runners. The erect stems grow two to six metres in height.

Well, I won't ramble on any more just now, except to say – 'Anne go for it, "Judge in Service", and get judging them 'osses.'

Your tick-picking pal.

Bron

Me walking through the "grass" to work

A Jesus Lizard

28. PANAMA
An Island Crash

April 6th 1991

Here I am again Dear Anne,

You must be in, or about to begin, the Easter holidays. I hope that you're indulging yourself in some light pleasures and will do something that'll be a first for you. You'll be riding Frodo, I'm sure: will there be any judging sessions this vacation?

My new first was diving in the lake while waiting for the BCI workers to clear a clearing around my balsawood tree whose roots I am to unearth. I went diving with another BCI worker, José – he's one of the park wardens who are employed here to stop the poaching of our animals for food or the exotic pet trade.

Diving in fresh-water is quite different from the sea-water that I've been used to and we had to re-adjust my weights downwards to the correct buoyancy. To get the buoyancy right I had to put on all my gear but leaving the buoyancy jacket deflated. I got into the water, José handed me lead-weights to put into the jacket pockets until I could hang suspended in the water with just my nose above water-level.

That sorted, I hung onto to the boat and waited whilst José put the selected weights into the weight belt which I then fastened around my waist.

While finning around in the murky water of a channel between islands, we found a sunken boat, upside-down in ten metres of water and nestling at the base of a huge buttressed tree.

It was weird down there. Half-dark in the brownish-green gloom from out of which loomed skeletal trunks of all sizes and covered with a thick, mossy layer of some brownish alga that came off in clumps when touched and floated away in the sluggish currents.

One side of the boat, a small motor launch that José reckoned had been down there for about twelve years, was deeply embedded in the fine, silty ooze. Feeling around stirred up the mud causing total blackout. Good job we were using a buddy-line which loosely tied us together and to our surface boat.

José wanted to try to salvage the boat.

Uh-huh, mañana, mañana, and we know tomorrow never comes. It would take several dives and a heap of work. Even getting air-tanks takes a lot of organisation as we have to co-ordinate STRI jeep availability with the ferry schedule and with the dive-shop being open. (We must get and return the tanks from the STRI dive shop in Panama City, where they are serviced and re-filled.)

So that was an interesting break and now it's back to work.

My new job is like an archaeological dig. I'm to trace the path of roots, centimetre by centimetre, millimetre by millimetre, from my balsawood tree trunk to its finest root tips. After all is mapped and measured and numbered, I shall cut representative samples from the roots and take them back to the lab to run the water-conductivity test – just as I was doing with the *Tabebouia* branches.

To follow all of the root ramifications is quite a challenge of perseverance. Bit like gardening really, hard on the knees and tough on the hands as I try to carefully prize loose (with my dentist's pick and toothbrushes and paintbrushes) the baked-hard clayey soil and the stones. Fortunately, the roots run more or less horizontally and I can crouch on my stool or kneel on a mat.

Each day I spend some six or seven hours mapping and measuring and labelling as I go along, taking a break in the shade or going back to base for a rest and escape from the mid-day heat.

As I work, sweat continually runs down and soaks the waistband of my shorts. After a few days I started to develop salt sores around my waist: now I work naked.

I am surrounded by a five metre high wall of Panama grass – no boat passing along the Canal would see me. If I had a visitor I would hear their arrival as they pushed through the reeds, so I'd have plenty of time to throw on T-shirt and shorts.

Until the day of the crash.

The work is very meditative. I think of nothing but the tool in my hand and the root to be followed or the stone to be moved. I am watched by my new friend Basil; a Jesus Lizard *Basiliscus basiliscus* so called because it can run fast across water on its back legs, holding its front legs out to the sides and its tail curved up into the air. It's about thirty centimetres long and sits on a stone nearby, eyeing my movements.

One day I was engrossed in my work when I heard the strangest of noises – a huge sound, like a behemoth grinding rock in a gigantic rock-grinder, then fishing for more by throwing and dragging a chain to gather the rocks.

Puzzled, I pushed through the reeds to the Canal edge and saw one of those two hundred and fifty metre long, enormous, cargo transporters piled high with containers like so many coloured Lego blocks, veering out of the shipping lane: its prow swung in my direction. I said to myself, 'Oh, no! It's going to crash into my island. It'll push its nose right into my clearing. Uh-huh. No, it's not. It'll go between my island the next one thirty metres away. No, no, that's not it either'.

To see better, I hurried back to my clearing and climbed my tree, just in time to see the prow of the vessel crash into next-door Orchid Island. Men swarmed to the front and I heard the yells of amazement as they found the jungle literally within reach. There was a lot of gesticulating and shouting. I sat on my branch fascinated, until I realised that if I could see them so clearly they could see me! I scrambled down and got dressed.

As it was lunch time, I went back to base. Everyone was already in the restaurant and I animatedly reported the crash. The BCI manager got up, leaving his half-eaten lunch, to go and phone the powers that be in the Panama Canal Commission.

It took three days for several tugs to pull the cargo transporter back into the Canal shipping lane.

(I heard later that the anchor had gone AWOL and had acted as a pivot at the stern.)

As my work progressed downwards, the stones got bigger and became boulders. The root I was following sneakily disappeared under a boulder which defeated my strength to shift. (I've marked the position on the map; perhaps someone stronger will do more work when I'm gone.)

The long hours of chipping and brushing away the rock-hard, clayey, stony soil were made only marginally easier by the start of the rainy season: I'd been using a pickaxe and shovel to shift a cubic metre of soil 'n' rocks only to expose a few more centimetres of root.

At the end of my time working there, I had managed to more or less clear only two superficial roots with all their ramifications.

And so ends job number four and I move to job number five.

I haven't dived, or dove as the Americans say, for the last three weeks and am looking forward, with some trepidation, to my check-out STRI dive tomorrow. I've dived in the Pacific with the club a couple of times; this test-dive will be in the Atlantic.

When I was at the Balboa Dive Club meeting last week I met a woman called Anita, a big, jolly, American lady, with whom I'll go diving at the end of the month. She offered me a bed that night: it's impossible for me to get back to BCI until the workers' boat in the morning.

What else is new; ah yes, we recently had a chap from Rothampstead here to give a talk. It was so nice to hear an English accent again after all the various American drawls.

In fact Nora, rather unkindly and tactlessly I thought, told me that she couldn't stand my clipped English accent. I didn't retaliate.

I'd heard that the U.S.A. is heading for recession/depression, but didn't realise that the UK was so bad. I hope Simon is still holding his job and what on earth will Mark do? I think he finishes University this summer. I hope I'll get to hear one day.

And next it's off to San Blas to catch gorgonian coral eggs. I'll explain that cryptic remark later.

Wishing you a Chocolately Easter – I know how you love chocolate. I scarcely know it's Easter here, not a bunny nor chocolate egg in sight.

The year seems to roll around with little demarcation. One month is very like another hot, muggy month so that my time seems to be broken up into chunks remembered by what job I was doing.

With love from your root-brushing, muscle-bound friend, *Bron*

the water bottle and plastic tubes to keep the strings horizontal

measuring the horizontal under the boss's scrutiny

29. PANAMA
A Consequence of Low Lake Level

May 8th 1991

Dear Anne,

Now that my favourite months of April and May in England are nearly over, I wonder if you'll get a flaming June? Here the rainy season started this week - yes, just like that.

After weeks of baking sun we had two days of thunderstorms. I was totally astonished by how much water fell in such a short while.

The level of Lake Gatun had fallen by about two metres, exposing many of the tops of the drowned trees so that it was quite hazardous driving the small boats. We're supposed to stick within the marked channels, but one section is particularly badly marked by the posts and I rammed the Boston Whaler into a trunk thinly disguised as water and bent the engine housing.

Ooops!

Within two days most of the stumps had submerged again – the lake level had risen by over half-a-metre, and it's a very big lake!

And most of the deciduous trees are putting out their fresh green leaves, reminding me of an English spring.

Aaaaah, the nostalgia.

Sometimes I take the group of Saturday visitors along the nature trails. I have to warn them of the need to drink plenty; most folk don't drink enough, not believing they need to take in lots of fluids in this humid heat and so they get dehydration-headaches. If that happens I have to run and find the aspirin.

This week I met a chap working with conservation in Belize. He said he'd be very pleased to see me there.

So there is work around, once one has started making contacts, or I could take up Nora's offer to go and work on Hawaii – oh, decisions, decisions!

Strange, or not, how fate plays such a role in our lives.

I was messing around in the City today when I was spotted by Josh. (He's the guy who was on the SCUBA expedition trip and spent time carrying me pick-a-back when I had my leg in plaster.) He had left us when the trip folded in Costa Rica and now was staying in Panama City doing odd jobs to earn bread-and-butter money.

I had a spot of very welcome and much needed rumpy-pumpy that night. Well, well. Small world ain't it?

I hope you had time at Easter to re-charge your inner batteries before the onslaught of the worst school term of the year and I'm glad to hear that your son is doing OK at Exeter University.

I'll be sending you some more photos and mementoes with my next letter. Can you please add them to my storage box?

So long for a while.
Take care my friend,
With fond love as ever.
Bron

30. PANAMA
Gorgonians & Molas

August 12th 1991

My often-in-my-thoughts friend Anne,

How the months rush by – big apologies for the long delay in replying.

At the end of May I started my new job at San Blas; a group of islands belonging to the Kuna Indians. The islands form an archipelago stretching some four hundred kilometres along the Panama Pacific Coast. They are small, flat, coral islands just offshore so the Kuna men needs-must farm the mainland coastal strip; they usually spend several days there before returning to their families.

The STRI San Blas field-station is on a tiny island measuring all of fifteen by fifty metres. On it are just a few huts constructed from wood and with corrugated-iron roofs – very noisy in the rain – built on stilts that rise from the shallow Caribbean Sea slightly to the north of Panama Canal.

STRI Field Station

It's very quiet. I fall asleep lulled by the splish, splosh, splash of wavelets under the floor boards and the generator drone from the hotel on the island a hundred metres away.

The field station is within spitting distance (metaphorically speaking) of two Kuna islands covered with Kuna houses built of bamboo and thatch; the reeds being brought across from the mainland.

I'm being a tropical-marine-biologist and it's GREAT.

A Kuna Island in the San Blas archipelago

Nala Nega houses on a San Blas Island

I'm an underwater assistant, sitting on the ocean floor in my SCUBA dive gear, one to seven metres below the surface and swaying gently back and forth in the warm wave surge.

I watch colourful reef fishes and corals as I hand out tags or collect and bag the specimens handed to me by the researcher, Professor Howie Lasker from Buffalo University, U.S.A.

One of his projects is to study the reproduction of a couple of gorgonian coral species *Plexaura flexuosa* and *Pseudoplexaura*. These are soft corals that look so very like miniature weeping willow trees. Howie has discovered that the corals spawn for two nights only; after the full moon in the months of May, June and July, between the hours of 6:30 p.m. and 7:30 p.m.

The team loads collecting equipment and dive gear into the two motorboats and the six of us set off for the reef. As it's already getting dark, the moving boats kick up a green phosphorescent bow spray and trail a tail of phosphorescence at the stern.

Once in the water we can see the myriads of coral eggs shining white in the torchlight as they rise like minuscule balloons from the birthing female corals. We suck eggs into ten-millilitre syringes (without needles) and expel them into plastic bags fastened at our waists. Every so often a collector has to rise to the boat to deliver the bags and collect more. And so it goes on until 7:30 p.m. when it's all over for another night.

(The sperm of the male gorgonians rises like drifting smoke to mix with the eggs and fertilise them so that the boss can grow them on in the lab to develop into baby corals. These will then be seeded back onto the reef and he can continue to monitor their growth over the years.)

As I was swimming around with the flashlight (torch) I saw my first open basket-starfish (they curl into a tight ball in the day). Bigger than a football, its delicate tracery reminded me of an elaborate doily.

A small, reef shark nosed around the fins of Kio as he knelt on the sand to collect eggs.

When we get back to the lab the eggs in the bags are counted as they are transferred to the aquarium tanks, where the fertilised eggs will settle and grow. It takes hours. One night I counted over fourteen thousand eggs and there are four of us workers counting eggs in the semi-dark!

The frenetic frenzy ceased after six days and then it was back to the gentler pace of species monitoring: mapping, measuring and counting selected species so that any reef changes over the years will be spotted.

(I found my first seahorses; they are so small, about six centimetres in length, and so cute.)

In free-time we go for fun dives or just laze about. It's as good as going on a tropical island holiday.

I think maybe I'd like to be a marine researcher, but like all jobs the glamour wears off. Research is a matter of weeks, nay months or years, collecting enough numbers to crunch through the computer. One chap researching here has every day (almost) for the last two years gone to the same bit of reef to watch the movements of one little fish dash in and out of its holes as it busily and bossily guards its territory.

But how else should we learn about the behaviours of our fauna?

Staying here is a real change after the luxury of BCI. I work for three weeks (and get paid a bit for it!) on the island, then one week off and back to Panama City to recover and do shopping – we do our own cooking and so must buy supplies for three weeks.

This job will occupy me until mid-August and then I'll probably return to BCI until December. I've been offered work, but am awaiting official clearance.

As you can see, I'm gaining much in experience if not in expertise: I hope some knowledge may stick in this ageing brain.

I'm very content; so nice to relinquish all the hassles of the rat-race and have no worries about bills to pay or house to maintain.

If only I had some news from my boys my cup would overflow. But what's a mother anyway? We bring kids into this world and then desert them or they desert us.

Thank you for getting Simon's gift to him. I hope he can sway peacefully in his deluxe hammock in some calm place.

Thank you too for finding out about renewing my travel insurance. In Panama they looked at me askance, 'Travel insurance? Never heard of it', they affirmed. After lots of dead ends I did find one company who sold travel medical insurance only; at three U.S. dollars per day for a maximum of three weeks, plus costs to set up. Well, that's no good for me. My medical costs so far have been below, or just about, the excess I would have had to pay on any claim.

I shan't bother with travel insurance.

N.B. The Kuna Indians arrived in Panama from northern Colombia; fleeing first the Inca expansion and then the Conquistadores. They settled on the Atlantic coast of what is now Panama, but as the Conquistadores encroached on their lands they were forced to flee to the San Blas Islands where they have lived ever since. They farm the coastal lands and are totally self-sufficient and with their own laws and hierarchy.

They have Mayan look-alike faces and wear very distinctive hand-made clothes.

The panel stitched onto the bodice of a blouse worn by the ladies is called a mola. Molas are the primary expression of visual art in Kuna society, representing in abstract, stylised ways dreams and magic, birds and flowers or other objects around the people.

The Kuna lady makes her mola in a type of reverse appliqué, to create a focal point on her own blouse; expressing herself and demonstrating her talent in sculpture through motif: geometric, non-representational designs are the most traditional.

She cuts two, three or even four or more rectangles of cloth to form the mola panel. The several layers of different coloured cloths are stitched together and then the designs are carefully cut out and down through the layers, so exposing the different colours and forming primitive and ingenious designs. Tiny, tiny stitches secure the cut edges. She creates a different mola panel for the back of the bodice. Voluminous sleeves of man-made fabrics, with cuffs which she embroiders, are attached to the finished mola bodice.

A skirt in a different material, often clashing in design and colours with the mola, completes the dress. Colourful woven strips around the lower leg complete her decorations.

Towards the end of our stay on San Blas we were taken by cayuco (dugout canoe) to some more-distant islands (where the ladies are reputed to produce work of outstanding quality) on a mola shopping trip.

Unfortunately a few days earlier an enterprising American had visited and bought up trunk-loads of molas to sell at greatly inflated prices in the States.

Since the civilised world arrived at their islands, the ladies want our fashion magazines, or indeed any magazines, from which they copy and design motifs for their molas to suit Western taste; and the standard of work is far inferior too.

Inferior quality molas by their hundreds are taken to the City and sold to tourists who buy them to make into cushion covers or mount as pictures.

To make extra money, lobsters are caught by the men and taken to the city restaurants.

On our last day, we went across to the hotel island and were presented with three lobsters fresh from the sea.
Succulently delicious!

Buying best molas at source (above) and cheaper molas in the city of Panama (below)

Mola Market on Panama City Street

The Kuna are nice people, very friendly and helpful to the strangers visiting their islands.

One hopes they stay that way. But we know they won't as commercialism invades.

I think I must count the gorgonian experience as my best-ever job to date. It'll take a lot to beat it.

But egg-laying is done for another year and I must return to BCI.

Until the next time, hugs from *Bron*

31. PANAMA
Yachties & Canal Crewing

August 20th 1991

Dear Co-respondent and Faithful Friend,

To take a break from diving I went for a sail up the coast and through the Canal.

'Yachties' going up or down the eastern coast of North America, or even around the World, occasionally park off our San Blas island and so I met Whitey (John White from Perth, Australia) and his fiancée Maxine, more affectionately known as Blue (from San Francisco).

One morning we woke and saw a yacht parked not far from the lab. I swam over and so became friends with the couple on board.

Whitey is a blue-eyed, always smiling, always talking, fun-loving Aussie who had spent some ten years working in San Francisco where he'd built up a security devices business (you'll appreciate the irony of this later in my letter) which he'd subsequently sold and together with all his savings purchased a yacht. The yacht (named *Harmony*) was totally destroyed in hurricane Hugo, with winds gusting at 240kmph, when it hit the Virgin Isles in September 1989.

Maxine had met Whitey in San Francisco and had thrown in her lot with him to sail the oceans wide in their second yacht (*Harmony Two*), second-hand and smaller at thirteen metres. They were now indirectly on their back to the Virgin Isles to be married on February 14th of next year.

(I'm invited. Wonder if I'll go?)

On my last week's break between diving stints, Whitey invited me to sail with them on their journey from San Blas to Colón (at the Atlantic end of the Canal). And so we sailed; if puttering along on a motor with the sails stowed can be called sailing. *Harmony Two* carried a single mast and had her fore and aft cabins stuffed with all they possessed in the world.

The first six-hour leg of the journey was to an overnight stop at Isla Grande, about forty-four sea miles away. The sea swells were enough to make Blue – a hardened sailor – sea-sick and she spent most of the journey on her bunk, but she did rouse herself to come on deck to watch the eclipse through the smoked lenses of the ship's sextant.

The moon crept over the sun and covered about seven-eighths of it. (We would've had to have been on the other side of Panama to have seen the total eclipse.) The whole sequence took about half-an-hour, during which time dusk bathed the sea-scape. We didn't see any of the dramatic events that others subsequently reported, like reversal of wave direction or birds flying to roost. Whitey did spot a bloated piglet floating past, undulating in the swells – was that a portent? Should one connect it with his losing his dinghy and fifteen-horse-power outboard in Colón?

We parked *Harmony Two* in the quiet bay of a small island next to Isla Grande and passed a peaceful night. The next morning we puttered over to the bigger island in their inflatable (*Sequel*) for a beer before setting sail for our next port of call – Portobelo.

Portobelo is a deep natural harbour 'discovered' by Christopher Columbus in 1502. He gave the harbour its name, meaning beautiful port. Later – on March 20th 1597 – King Philip II of Spain ordered Don Francisco Valverde (a Spanish explorer) to found the town.

As the port was then primarily used for exporting the silver coming from mines in Bolivia and the looted treasures of the Incas, the Spanish built a huge storage warehouse and four defensive fortifications around the port and re-named it San Felipe de Portobelo.

Arriving after a few hours of easy sailing on the gentle sea, we joined the other yachties in Portobelo harbour for the never-ending cocktails on each other's boats. Like any long-term travellers, the yachting fraternity keep bumping into each other and have to meet to update the gossip. They rarely seem to go inland from all the ports they visit; 'Too afraid to leave our boats', I was told, 'We might return and find the yacht gone or at least the dinghy and outboard motor gone.'

It seems a shame to travel the coasts of all these different countries and know nothing of their hinterlands and see little more than the waves and shores. I should find that very boring. After all, the port people are not very representative of the country.

We went line-trawling for fish up the river flowing into Portobelo harbour. Blue caught a snook which we barbecued for supper. I didn't much care for its muddy-water taste. Far better flavoured were the stoplight parrot fish that Whitey had harpooned while Blue and I snorkelled the shore rocks. I enjoyed the meal, but couldn't help feeling a mite sad to eat one of the beautifully coloured reef fish I'd watched nibbling the corals with their hard beak mouths.

I thought some of the other yachties very interesting. One couple was sailing the world with a toddler and baby and cat and dog on board. Others had given up the land-lubber life and lived on their yachts, moving on when the whim moved them.

Portobelo harbour with the church behind *Harmony Two*

Portobelo has a Black Christ, *El Cristo Negro*.

We all went to the Sunday service to see it, but as the service was all in Spanish we found it very difficult to follow.

The Black Christ is one of very few in the world. It miraculously arrived in the port on October 21st 1658: the story goes that some Portobeleños were fishing in the harbour and saw a big, life-sized bundle floating in the sea. They recovered it and carried it to the town. You can imagine their surprise when they opened the bundle and saw an image of Jesus of Nazareth carrying a cross. The carved wood log was all blackened, either from the effects of the sea or it was carved from a wood that was very dark.

The people put the black Christ in the church and prayed to the effigy to liberate them from an epidemic (possibly the plague) that was raging in the region at that time. The sickness disappeared immediately and there were no other sufferers.

Since that auspicious day the Church Fathers have always celebrated October 21st between the hours of 8 p.m. and midnight, processing the image round the town. Each year more and more people have come to Portobelo: news of the miracle powers had spread throughout Panama, through all America and round the world.

Thousands and thousands of pilgrims come to the Black Christ to thank him for favours received.

We left the church after enjoying some of the robust, unaccompanied singing and headed for Divers' Haven, a dive centre with sleeping cabins, dive shop and surprise, surprise, a bar. Over drinks we chatted with four Americans who had come here to dive for Spanish treasure. By all accounts, Inca treasure was brought overland on pack animals (traversing the Panama Isthmus) from the Pacific to the Atlantic to Portobelo, where the waiting Spanish galleons were filled to the gunnels with the purloined Inca treasure and taken to Spain. There it was melted down. What a great loss for posterity.

Occasionally a Spanish galleon would set sail, but before it could clear the narrow harbour entrance, a tropical storm would spring up and sink the ship: no weather forecasts in those days.

They say there is still tons of treasure waiting to be recovered, although after all these centuries I would think it well covered by the drifting sands and mud.

Monday dawned bright and clear and by lunch-time we were sailing into Colón. Whitey insisted that we park in the marina, even though it was expensive.

Harmony Two was dwarfed when we moored next to the forty metre *Vadura*; a beautiful two-masted vessel built in 1928 in Scotland. She was all gleaming wood and brass – a beauty being taken to San Diego by four lads and the captain and his wife to join the next Round the World Yacht Race.

Whitey hooked up *Harmony Two* to the dock hosepipe and filled *Harmony's* tanks with three hundred and thirty gallons of fresh water and then we went shopping.

Colón is a horrid, dirty, dangerous place. I was glad to be walking the streets with my friends as we bought supplies. When we returned to the marina, shock horror, the outboard and dinghy were gone! (I heard later that the damaged inflatable dinghy was found abandoned up the coast, but the outboard motor was never discovered. Lesson: get the dinghy on board when not in use.)

At Colón I changed yachts. I wanted to transit the Canal and see my island (BCI) from the water. That meant hanging around in the marina to hitch a ride. Not exactly a freebee as the captain would take on hands at Colón to help manhandle the ropes when the boat entered the three double locks at each end of Lake Gatun. (Boats were raised sixty-eight metres at the Atlantic end and then lowered sixty-eight metres at the Pacific end.)

The Panama Canal was started in 1880 by the French who abandoned the work in 1890 leaving twenty-two thousand dead, primarily of malaria and yellow fever. The French had tried to construct a sea-level canal, but the Americans realised that that just wasn't going to be possible given the periodic flooding of the river Chagres and the nature of the land.

A second effort was started by the United States in 1904. They bought the French rights for forty million dollars and signed a treaty with Panama which granted the U.S. control of the Panama Canal Zone. (I wonder if Panama will ever regain control of the canal area.)

The Americans built a dam thirty-five metres high (the biggest in the world at that time) at the Atlantic end of the valley and a similar dam at the Pacific end.

The dammed river formed the Gatun Lake, twenty-six metres above sea level.

The canal was opened in 1914.

After a few dodgy interviews with boat-captains-looking-for-crew (I certainly wasn't going to warm *his* bunk) I found Francoise, a French doctor, who with his sons of six and nine years were on their way from Martinique to the Marquesas – plumb in the middle of the Pacific.

The all-steel yacht, *Tiki,* was twenty-one metres and fitted out with all the up-to-date modern conveniences imaginable. It felt very spacious.

(Maybe I *could* travel on a yacht and not die of claustrophobia.)

The doctor had taken two years of weekends to design and build the boat himself; in his back garden of all places. Impressive!

I expect you'll be back to school by the time you get this letter.

Please write me your news of the summer and your plans for half-term.

Love and hugs from your rope-throwing, diving-buddy, *Bron*

32. PANAMA
Odd Jobs with Sex-changing Fish & Measuring Water Flow

October 25th 1991

My dear friend,

Your letter of July 23rd was waiting for me when I returned to BCI and I've just received your letter of October 10th. Thank you very much for those very welcome voices from the past.

I had thought my diving days were done – but not quite yet.

I'd not long returned to BCI when Pete, from STRI marine division, phoned to ask me back to San Blas to help him finish up his research work. He didn't have to ask twice. I jumped at the chance to spend another glorious week diving the reefs (that brought me up to a total of a hundred and four dives and about one hundred and twenty hours underwater – not bad for a beginner).

Pete had spent two years watching the behaviour of a small hermaphrodite fish (a guppy, about two centimetres long) that starts off as a female but changes to a male as it grows bigger. The males are territorial and have a small harem of females. Some middle-sized fish don't know whether to be male or female and act as both to get the best of both worlds.

Pete now has to catch all the fish in his study area to sex and measure them.

The fish live in holes amongst the reef rubble, which is just lumps of many-sized pieces of dead coral littering the shallow waters, so shallow that in places one could stand up and have one's head and chest out of the sea.

The only way that I could catch the guppies was to squirt knockout stuff into their holes, then chase them out of their territory so that they got confused and didn't know where to find their own hidey-holes. So they hid under anything. Quickly and carefully and secretly I popped my hand-net over the shelter to hopefully catch one and get it into my container.

On my second day I thought I'd done rather well to catch fifteen, only to learn that Pete had caught sixty-seven. I didn't even see sixty-seven! Mind you, he has his lungs so well trained that he can stay underwater for about four hours, whereas we assistants last about two and have to wait ages in the dingy for him to surface. Then he just stands up and walks to the boat!

Since I've been back on BCI I've been busy in the lab measuring water-flow through pieces of twigs and branches of *Pseudobombax*. (below)

Returning with *Psuedobombax* branches

I go out at 6 a.m. (in the Boston Whaler) to pick up my tree climber from the mainland and then take him to a nearby island where my trees are. He shins up ten metres or so to hack off a branch which I quickly stand in my bucket of water – so that the transpiring leaves don't pull air into the xylem vessels – and lug the lot back to the boat while he climbs down. We take the branches in their buckets to the lab and then I return him to the mainland.

Back again at the lab I take about six hours to prepare my bits of wood and run the system. A long day that I only do three or four times a week.

I set up my twigs in their water-flow system; a very fiddly job stopping all the leaks and my fingers get really wrinkly as it all has to be done underwater in the large sink – to stop air getting into the xylem vessels.

After getting readings of temperature, water levels and so on, I filled in the initial data on my program, switched on the flow-system and pressed "O" to go, but it didn't. The computer showed 'run-time error'. I tried all the tricks that I'd been shown and still nowt. Perhaps it's the lightening affecting the computer as we're in the middle of a thunderstorm.

But this system has a fail-safe device and should operate!

Huh, there are times when I wish I wasn't so computer illiterate and do you know that the Americans don't write the date as we do? They put month, day, year instead of day, month, year. That caused me a few problems with communication until I learned to write the month in letters.

Oh well, I'll give it a rest and finish my letter as I can't find any of the computer whizz kids. (There's a good crowd here at the moment, mostly in their late twenties and early thirties, nearly all doing Post PhD Research; dinner conversations can get very lively.)

Another job I have to do to keep me occupied so I don't get bored with all this free-time (ha, ha) is to monitor the leaf-fall of my *Pseudobombax* trees. This entails going by boat to another island and setting out twenty $2m^2$ quadrates in places where I have cleared all the leaf-litter debris.

I collected a lot of chigger bites on this exercise and am scratching all over.

Next, I shall make weekly counts of all the *Pseudobombax* leaves that fall into my squares.

On Tuesdays I usually go into the city to hear the lunch-time seminars at STRI HQ and take the opportunity to do any shopping.

At last my visits to the dentist have ceased. I've lost count of the number of times that I've had that soft putty-stuff pushed into my mouth to take impressions. Finally they got it right and now I'm the proud possessor of full plates, top and bottom, and I'm learning to talk again with my mouth stuffed with the very strange sensations of a dental prosthesis.

I'm glad that you're keeping up the riding.
Are you still teaching the handicapped girl?
And I forgot to ask you about Fro, is he recovered fully?
My thoughts go with you dear friend.
Bron

33. PANAMA
Last Days in Panama

January 22nd 1991

Dear Anne,

December and January have seen a big change-over in the researchers on BCI. But more importantly there is no more work for me. The Prof who gave me the roots' excavation job wanted me to go to the States with him. He reckoned he could find me something to do there. But no. That wouldn't work. He's too controlling and wants a full-time companion. (His wife works and spends most of her time overseas and there is talk of divorce.) But how could I get involved with a man again and suffer more shattering emotional pain? I'm still healing. My scars are tender. I've lost both parents and my dogs and a husband who towards the end was no husband at all. I just won't risk putting myself through all that pain again.

It's been a mixed month of some work, no work, maybe some work but don't hold your breath, which leaves me feeling adrift and purposeless.

For the first time since I left England I question my motives – is it really that important to get to Australia to see Aunty and Uncle? I miss my mates and so want to see my sons. They never write and as far as I know have never tried to make contact; Aunty knows where I am, step-mother has my address. I can only think it must be the stuff their father has said against me that they now don't want to know me.

My head is still a mess.

I wish my boys would come to South America, but I suppose they don't have the money and neither do I.

How can I go back now? No job to pay the mortgage and my house rented; the rent just covers the mortgage and the fees of the letting agent. I suppose could sell it, but I just don't feel strong enough to deal with all the hassle of that.

And I'm not ready to face the memories of the mental pain that so very nearly drove me to suicide. I know I never told you about that. And I've never told anyone else either: I'd been collecting pills for months; Aspirin and Anodin. I got so close to swallowing the lot.

One morning Mark and his father had walked out of the house without so much as a goodbye. I heard the front door slam and from my front-bedroom window saw the two of them walking across the front garden. I climbed up on the window sill, stuck my head through the transom window and screamed silently goodbye, goodbye, goodbye, goodbye.

Tears streaming, I looked at the pile of pills in one hand and the bottle of water in the other. It was only the thought of leaving my boys, now thirteen and fifteen, in the care of their effeminate, homosexual father (would he bring over his young Singaporean lover, who must be about eighteen by now and what might be the effect of that?) that stopped me.

I dried my tears, unlocked the bedroom door and got on with the day.

I find the language barrier daunting – no not daunting, more the feeling of being excluded, always on the periphery, missing the subtleties of conversation, unable to say what I want to say and so sitting at the edge, retiring from the struggle to communicate.

I know I'll never be able to do more than get by. I have no aptitude or adaptitude for languages.

Oh shucks, why am I being so pessimistic, must be the phase of the moon.

After spending days of agonising what to do, it was becoming obvious that nothing was about to happen that would push me off my fence.

A decision had to be made.

I would have to continue on and on and on until I felt I could/should return to England.

My final few hours in Panama were spent watching the sun go down over the canal whose waters were the colour of the rosé wine we were sipping.

I had gone with Anita to visit her friends and was listening to the teachers talk shop, as we do. Anita's school has had some DOD (Department of Defence) dignitary down from the States to show them the new, progressive way of teaching in junior high-school.

After the sun-dip do, we all went to a restaurant in the posh part of Panama City.

I'd spent most of the day re-packing my backpack and so was able to snatch a few hours sleep at Anita's before getting up at 4 a.m. to catch the very small plane that was to start me on the next phase of my life.

The plane landed at Puerto Olbadía, a tiny port at the bottom of the San Blas archipelago. In the airport (near the Colombian border) the office of Transpasa was no more than a shed in a field and nowhere to get coffee.

I met there three other gringos, Julia (U.S.A.) and Mike and Esa (lads from Finland) who were also heading for Colombia.

Flying across Panama I was saddened to see the land devastation. Only 5% of forest remains in Panama. The land was cleared for farming, but the tropical rains washed away the soils and the sun baked that remaining, so no crops grew and the land turned into an unproductive barren waste.

As we disembarked a customs official was waiting to collect our passports – I don't expect that he gets many visitors.

Puerto Olbadía is just a very small village of plank and thatch houses. We leant against a wall or crouched on the beach rocks chatting idly and waiting for the return of our stamped passports. (We have to be stamped into and out of countries.)

The customs man put paid to any idea of walking the hills to Colombia. Too many people (two Germans, three Colombians and two from the States, so he said) had been murdered during the last months for the contents of their backpacks. The customs man said they thought they knew who was the perpetrator, but not a shred of evidence – the hill villagers band together and play dumb.

The currencies I've muddled along with since leaving the States:
1. Mexican - peso   2. Belize - dollar   3. Guatemala - quetzal
4. Honduras - lempira   5. Nicaragua - cordoba
6. Panama - balboa

And now to discover what monies, Colombia, Ecuador, Peru, etc. etc. use.

I'll just keep travelling.

Might find a place which calls me to stay .....

To quote Jimmy Dean:
'I can‍'t change the direction of the wind, but
I can adjust my sails to reach my destination.'

Might find me someone/something very special I can't live without.
Time will tell.

With love and fond memories of our times together,
Your wandering friend
Bron